Women: The Last Colony

Maria Mies, Veronika Bennholdt-Thomsen
and Claudia von Werlhof

Zed Books Ltd
London and New Jersey

Women: The Last Colony was first published in English by
Zed Books Ltd, 57 Caledonian Road, London N1 9BU, UK, and
165 First Avenue, Atlantic Highlands, New Jersey 07716, USA,
in 1988.

Chapters 4, 6, 7, 8 translated from German by Peter Burgess.
Cover designed by Andrew Corbett.
Typeset by EMS Photosetters, Thorpe Bay, Essex.
Printed and bound in the United Kingdom.

Second impression, 1991.

British Library Cataloguing in Publication Data

Mies, Maria
    Women: the last colony.
    1. Developing countries. Women. Social conditions.
    I. Title.   II. Bennholdt-Thomsen, Veronika.
    III. Werlhof, Claudia von
    305.4′2′091724

    ISBN 0-86232-455-6
    ISBN 0-86232-456-4 pbk

Library of Congress Cataloging-in-Publication Data

Mies, Maria
    Women: the last colony / Maria Mies, Veronika Bennholdt-Thomsen,
    and Claudia von Werlhof.
        p.   cm.
    ISBN 0-86232-455-6. ISBN 0-86232-456-4 (pbk.)
    1. Women—Developing countries—Social conditions.   2. Rural
    women—Developing countries—Social conditions.   3. Sexual division
    of labor—Developing countries.   4. Capitalism—Developing
    countries.   I. Bennholdt-Thomsen, Veronika.   II. Werlhof, Claudia
    von, 1943- .   III. Title.
    HQ1870.9.M54   1988
    305.4′2′091724—dc19

Contents

Introduction

The men who rule the world have reached the end of their road. They have no answers to the crucial questions of our age. Automation and new technology – their response to falling rates of growth, rising unemployment and sated markets – in fact destroy jobs and add to overproduction. The structural crisis of industrial society is explained away as merely a passing malady, curable by the traditional medicines of Keynesianism or monetarism. But although more and more people are beginning to see that these old explanations and remedies have had their day, no new explanation has yet emerged. A mood of apocalypse haunts the White Man's metropoles. Those responsible for economic and political life are revealed like the emperor in the fairy tale – naked, but behaving as if still elegantly and decently clad.

The really basic questions are now being asked by others: the ecology movement, the 'alternative' social movement, and the women's movement: Can there be a truly human existence in a despoiled nature? Can we develop models of social and economic organization which are not rooted in the exploitation of people and of nature? Yet even the prefigurative models proposed mainly by the ecology and alternative movement remain trapped within the mental – and real life – horizons of the White Man: the industrial nations, of both East and West (Bahro 1979, Ullrich 1979, Huber 1980, 1982, Gorz 1980).

Virtually all these more recent models and blueprints systematically exclude two areas of reality which continue to serve as the unseen foundation for the entire social edifice of industrialism: women and the colonies or underdeveloped societies. Our view is that no comprehensive, valid, and hence realizable alternative theory of science will emerge as long as the question of women and of the colonies continues to be shut out of both public discussion and the development of models for future societies. This book is intended as a contribution towards making these spheres visible and incorporating their interrelations and their connection to the whole into the development of a new social theory.

The realization that the women's question is related to the colonial question and that both are related to the dominant, global capitalist–patriarchal model of accumulation, did not dawn upon us suddenly or in our studies. Our perception of the systematic relationship between these questions is the result of many years of experience and observation in the Third World (in India and Latin America) and involvement in women's struggles in Europe. In turn, this led to a new perception of reality which was accompanied by a tide of new questions, or to put it another way: old questions had to be asked anew; and this led us to realize that most of the existing answers proved far from satisfactory.

The inadequacy of existing explanations of the existence and increase of poverty in the Third World became evident as soon as we turned to the position of women and peasants in these countries – that is, the majority of the population. Both women and peasants might figure in national or international statistics – especially women – but they were absent from theoretical analyses. Not until the 1970s did studies on the position of women in the Third World begin to reveal that the effect on women of what had generally been held to be development was deeply negative (Boserup 1970). Women's position at work, in education, health and political participation had all worsened. How could this be reconciled with the claims of a development policy that sought to improve the lot of the peoples of the underdeveloped countries?

Conversely, our involvement in women's struggles here in the North – in a so-called developed country – showed us that the exploitation and oppression of women, and in particular sexist violence against women, were by no means vestiges of a bygone, backward era. Rather, they were the necessary components of the present-day operation of capitalism. How was it that a social and economic system supposedly based on the freedom of the individual, promising happiness and prosperity for all, could perpetuate the unfreedom and inequality of women? How was it that violence against women was increasing within this supposedly peaceful system? Bourgeois and Marxist theoreticians seemed to have little to say on this matter. The absence of whole areas of reality – the Third World and women – from analyses of developed and underdeveloped societies led us to ask 'Why?'.

Studying the 'other women', that is, Third World women, enabled us to develop a critical stance towards our own situation. Whereas we set out by believing that the various forms of machismo and patriarchy which we encountered in Asia and Latin America were characteristics of under-development, we soon came to realize that our own situation was not entirely different. And it was while undertaking a more detailed study of the historical roots of male dominance that we made our most important discovery, namely that far from being signs of backwardness, sexism and patriarchy are central ideological and institutional props of the industrial system and its model of accumulation.

Our own concerns as women enabled us to better appreciate the position of women (and peasants) in the Third World. We were able to witness their oppression and exploitation not only as something totally alien or outside our own experience, but to see both what united us and what separated us. This perception of 'the other' also gave us the critical distance to question the supposed naturalness and normality of social relations in the developed world and the supposed abnormality of social relations, especially those between men and women, in the Third World. This view from the outside hence led to a view from within – and from below: in fact, this is the only standpoint from which the prevailing relationship between the sexes can be perceived and criticized.

Our understanding is not, however, greatly advanced as long as we continue to view the various parts of the world, and the two sides of the man–woman relationship, in isolation rather than as *relations*. This implies that development would not exist without underdevelopment, wealth would not exist without poverty, and the domination of men would not exist without the subjection and submissiveness of women. The contributions which make up this book seek to examine these relations and linkages.

In this endeavour, however, we cannot simply add the hitherto neglected areas – women and the colonies – on to the existing theories; to tack on women and the colonies cannot make an incomplete theory whole. The inclusion of these neglected spheres transforms previous social theories root and branch by placing new contradictions and relationships centre-stage. For example, the relation of wage labour and capital – once regarded as *the* central relationship – is now increasingly seen simply as one part of a much more comprehensive contradiction between human labour in general (including non-wage labour) and capital, with an additional contradiction between waged and non-wage labour. Ecologists have centred their theories on the contradiction between economic growth and the destruction of the environment. Orthodox Marxism's theoretical and conceptual apparatus is, therefore, no longer adequate for the demands of this new critique of capitalism.

The Marxist theory of society is based, in essence, on the assumption that overcoming oppression and exploitation – hence procuring social progress and socialism – depends on the development and unfolding of the productive forces. The motor of this advance is the contradiction between the relations of production, that is, property relations, and the development of the productive forces, generally understood as technological progress. Within this process, propertyless wage-workers constitute the historical subject as, allegedly, they represent the most general interest. Their exploitation – that is, the appropriation of their surplus labour by the owners of the means of production – is seen as the source of the production of both surplus value and capital accumulation, or, to use conventional economic terminology, of growth. The exploitation of women and the colonies, the rapacious appropriation of their labour and products, do not play an integral part in this analysis. They are left out in the analysis of the 'central' production relation, namely wage labour–capital, and labelled 'marginal groups', 'the periphery', 'backward', and so on, depending on the specific point of view. Behind this lurks the notion, shared by both Marxist and bourgeois theoreticians, firstly, that such 'groups' can establish contact with 'development' only through the forward march of the productive forces, and secondly, that any such development will be modelled on the European precedent – that is, will take the form of industrialization and modernization.

The main contemporary criticism of this position comes from the women's movement and the ecology and alternative social movements. These contend, quite correctly, that a social model based on the unfettered development of the productive forces and unlimited growth will destroy the foundations on which a 'socialist' life might develop. They have recognized that there are limits to human action upon nature, that nature strikes back because it is not limitless, and because humans are also limited and part of nature. They criticize the exploitative character of the development of the productive forces and the reduction of nature to mere matter to be dominated and exploited. Otto Ullrich has acutely observed that there is no *lower* limit to the 'development of the productive forces' which would render socialism impossible: however, there certainly is an upper limit (Ullrich 1980, 102).

The ecology and alternative movement's critique of the industrial system and growth model, however, also overlooks the relationship between men and women and between the industrialized countries and the Third World. The universal destruction wrought by the industrial system is often merely countered by a desire for a 'whole' and 'pure' nature, sought either in alternative forms of production in the North or more frequently in the poorer countries of Southern Europe and the Third World. But this implicit romanticization of nature serves more to obscure than to illuminate. The 'natural' products sold in wholefood and Third World shops, the handwoven clothes from Asia and Africa, are *commodities* too. They crystallize and embody relations of exploitation, and in particular the extreme exploitation of women and children in so-called 'cheap labour countries'. This 'alternative market' is part of a capitalist world market in which women and the colonies are the cheapest producers. 'Alternative tourism', too, is possible only because of the high international purchasing power of the Deutschmark, US dollar, or pound sterling.

Similarly, ecological analyses also exclude the exploitation of women's labour power. Restructuring the social and sexual division of labour is not a central concern. Ecologists and the alternative movement typically see relations between men and women, and between the industrialized countries and the Third World, as *moral*, not material relations, not as *relations of production*. In this respect they do not differ essentially from conventional economic or Marxist analyses. In their analyses they may point out that poverty in the Third World has to be borne in mind *as well* – with women, if they are mentioned, tacked on at the end. Any mention of women appears to be more the result of an uneasy conscience than of the realization that the exploitation of women and the colonies lies at the heart of the abundance and overproduction of the industrial system.

What do these excluded beings – women and the colonies – have in common? First, both are defined out of so-called social production and placed within – or more accurately demoted to – the 'realm of nature', because prior to capitalism the idea of a supposedly 'backward' nature did not exist. The view that women are closer to 'nature' than men originated with the rise of bourgeois societies and had its heyday in the 19th and 20th centuries (Guillaumin 1978, Griffin 1978).

In this process, women were divided into those who were 'good' and 'bad', 'civilized' and 'savage', 'tamed' or 'domesticated' (Heinsohn et al 1979). As Ehrenreich and English (1975) and Bock and Duden (1977) have shown, the domesticated housewife was created as the universal model of the 'good' woman. 'Bad' women (wild, savage, uncivilized, and backward) were originally seen as the womenfolk of workers and peasants. This label later passed on to women of the colonized peoples. Paradoxically, however, women – tamed and untamed – along with external nature, became the focal point for expectations of happiness and well-being. They were expected to produce life in the widest sense. Not only were women to bear and care for the next generation of wage-workers, but also to maintain the home and private sphere as a 'nature' reserve in which the exhausted and alienated wage-workers could regain their humanity.

This same mechanism of division into 'good' and 'bad', 'civilized' and 'savage', 'progressive' and 'backward' was also applied to the conquered and subjugated areas of Asia, Latin America and Africa. These, too, were 'defined into nature', *made* into the 'nature' of the white rulers of the earth and of capital, whose ascent to 'civilization' and status as 'civilized' nations required that other territories and societies be declared 'primitive'. Martha Mamozai's study of the relationship of German colonial rulers to 'their' subjects, and especially the women amongst them, has shown how the 'naturalization' of African and Asian women was closely connected with the 'rise' of white German women to the status of 'civilized' bourgeois ladies (Mamozai 1982).

This process is not an instance of backwardness, but of systematic exclusion or *colonization*. Women and subjugated peoples are treated as if they did not belong to society proper, as constituted from (male) wage-workers and capitalists. Instead, they are treated as if they were means of production or 'natural resources' such as water, air and land. The economic logic behind this colonization is that women (as the 'means of production' for producing people) and land, are goods that can in no way be produced by capital. Control over women and land is, therefore, the foundation of any system based on exploitation. What is paramount is to *possess* these 'means of production'; the relationship with them is one of *appropriation* – the prerequisite for the emergence of the central relation of production between wage labour and capital, which in turn allows women and the colonies to be appropriated as 'natural resources'.

For those at the receiving end of this process of colonization, this relation of appropriation constitutes robbery, expropriation, and the destruction of the basis of their lives. The ubiquitous means for imposing and maintaining this relation is *violence*. Moreover, it is overwhelmingly direct violence which becomes structural violence only superficially and in only a few centres of 'civilization'. We should, therefore, look to these processes of the colonization of women and conquered peoples for the causes of racism, sexism and fascism. Violence towards the colonized – that is, the appropriated – will increase in pace with the extent to which the growth model, that is supposedly 'fertile' in itself, breaks down.

The chapters in this book follow a certain chronological order that reflect the process by which our analysis developed. The first five were written between 1978 and 1980; the four last appeared in the years 1980 to 1983. The theoretical dimensions of this analysis are reflected in the themes within which the essays are grouped:

1. Capitalism and Women's Work;
2. Colonization of Women and Nature; and
3. Women's Struggles and Politics of Capital.

The first essays were written in the context of the debate in the women's movement on housework, but also of the discussions on imperialism, underdevelopment and dependency which took place among leftists in the 1970s. In contrast to the West's debate on housework we were not mainly concerned with the integration of housework into Marxist theory in which, so far, it had been 'forgotten'. Our main concern was to show that capitalism was *more* than the relation between wage labour and capital. The analysis of housework and of other non-wage work of subsistence producers in the colonies leads to a fundamental critique of the common perception of capitalism.

Apart from our involvement in the women's movement and its debates, and our experience in Third World countries, we received an important impulse for the development of our analysis from Rosa Luxemburg's work on capital accumulation. In trying to fit imperialism into the Marxian schema of accumulation she had found that capital accumulation or extended reproduction of capital was possible only on the basis of what she called non-capitalist strata and milieux. In this process these strata and milieux were both exploited and destroyed. She had thought mainly of the 'natural economies' of the peasants in Europe and the USA, and of the colonies as representatives of these.

But in the Marxian schema of accumulation these milieux and classes had no place. We observed a similar omission with regard to housework in Europe and the USA. And yet, there could be no doubt that the non-wage work of the Western housewife and the unpaid or low-paid work of small peasants and other subsistence producers in the colonies, constituted the hidden foundation upon which the classical capital–wage labour relation could be built up. We extended Rosa Luxemburg's analysis by recognizing that capitalism always had combined a process of 'ongoing primitive accumulation' based on direct violence, robbery and overexploitation with its process of so-called 'capitalist accumulation', based on the 'scientific' exploitation of the wage worker, by 'economic coercion'. Women, colonies and nature were the main targets of this process of ongoing primitive accumulation.

As their super-exploitation was and is the precondition for the exploitation of the wage workers, it is not correct to say that they are 'non-capitalist' strata and milieux, as Rosa Luxemburg does. Capitalism comprises both processes, and capital accumulation is based on a number of interrelated production relations, of which the wage labour relation is only the most privileged one. These ideas were first spelt out by Claudia von Werlhof in 'Women's Work, the Blind Spot in the Critique of Political Economy' (Chapter 1). She argues that housewives in the 'centres' and small peasants in the 'peripheries' were not just 'forgotten' in Marxist analyses of exploitation and accumulation, but that their systematic exclusion from what was defined as 'economy' was the necessary precondition for the 'rise' of the (male) white wage-worker and the capital-wage labour relation as a so-called 'dominant' relation. Such an analysis also puts into question the common two-class schema. Capitalist society does not only consist of (basically) capitalists and the (male) wage workers, mostly white. There are at least three tiers in the capitalist pyramid of exploitation: capitalists, wage workers (mostly white and male) and non-wage workers (mostly female), housewives and subsistence producers in the colonies (male and female).

On the basis of this analysis, Maria Mies, in 'Capitalist Development and Subsistence Production: Rural Women in India' (Chapter 2), examines the effects of capitalist development on the life- and work-conditions of poor rural women. The most important result of her analysis of the development process in India is the conclusion that the integration of ever more areas of life and economy into the capitalist market economy has not improved the situation of women but, on the contrary, their chances for survival and a human life have deteriorated everywhere. This applies particularly to poor, rural subsistence producers. This deterioration is not the result of some 'pre-capitalist backwardness' or of 'feudalism', but is the inevitable effect of capitalist modernization.

In Chapter 3, 'Investment in the Poor', Veronika Bennholdt-Thomsen shows how the policies of international development agencies – here the World Bank – have become aware of the 'value' of the non-waged work-force, especially of small peasants, including peasant women. In this respect the theoreticians and policy makers of international finance and their practices are far ahead of the limited insights of their left-wing critics. Under the cover of a strategy against absolute poverty, not only international, but also governmental agencies, are, with small financial investment, able to gain a secure hold of and control over both subsistence resources and the subsistence work of Third World peasantry. The primary aim of this strategy is not the abolition of absolute poverty, but as far as possible to use all 'under-utilized or unutilized' labour capacity of the poor in a 'productive' way, which means profitability for the accumulation process. The main instrument for the implementation of this policy is the small credit provisions for 'income generating activities' and other projects. Veronika Bennholdt-Thomsen argues that the exploitation of non-waged, low or unpaid work is not at all a new phenomenon, but, since its beginning has been an intrinsic part of capitalist development everywhere. In her opinion recognition of this fact has so far been impeded by the sexist and racist biases of social theory. With detailed theoretical arguments she offers a way out of this blind alley.

The second part of this book focuses on the analysis of the historical and social origins of the sexual division of labour, on the theoretical roots of the contemporary concepts of 'nature' and 'society', and on the role of violence in the establishment and further development of patriarchal–capitalist relations. The concept of colonization plays an important role in the analysis of these processes and structures.

In Chapter 4, 'Social Origins of the Sexual Division of Labour', Maria Mies offers an explanation of the origins of the asymmetric and hierarchical sexual division of labour which attempts to transcend the biological and sexist biases usually found in anthropological and sociological theories of the sexes. She argues that, ultimately, the emergence of male dominance over women is due to the historical fact that some men or groups of men were able to establish a monopoly over arms. By virtue of arms they finally changed their relationship to nature, to women and also to their own bodies, from one of co-operation and reciprocity to a one-sided relationship of exploitation and predation. This predatory mode of appropriation – because it was *not* a mode of production – proved to be 'more successful' than the productive and co-operative interaction with nature that women had established, in the sense that robbery and warfare became the quickest ways of accumulating wealth and 'surplus' without work. This predatory relationship, first established between men and women, became the paradigm of all exploitative relationships to emerge throughout history. Under capitalism this basically violent relationship was not abolished but only modified. Historically, this violence was used in Europe in the witch-hunt to destroy women's autonomy over their bodies, and in the colonies to destroy peoples' autonomous relation to their own land and subsistence production. Both processes took place around the same time. Only after this 'prelude' could the white, male wage-worker 'rise' to the status of a formally 'free' proletarian, but only by way of the housewifization of the women and the colonization of other peoples. The 'extra-economic violence' against women and colonies has remained the basis for the establishment of the wage–labour relation, based on 'economic coercion'.

In the context of this analysis, Chapter 5, Claudia von Werlhof's 'The Concept of Nature and Society under Capitalism', discusses the contradictory relationship between the concepts of 'nature' and 'society' as they emerged in capitalism. She argues that the concept of 'nature' which was created with the rise of capitalism was based on an economic definition of nature: everything that was to be free of costs, that is, free for unrestricted appropriation, was defined as 'nature'. This concept then included women, the earth, water, other 'natural resources' and also the native peoples, the land and the peoples in the colonies. This 'nature', on the other hand, was the eternal supplier of 'life', of living people and substances, to be transformed into dead capital. In this process more and more of nature is destroyed, but this is seen as the precondition for the creation of civilized society. As nature, however, remains the precondition for the capitalist accumulation process and the 'growth' of ever more dead capital, capitalism itself has to re-create 'nature' anew; this is what is constantly being done through natural science and technological innovation. Yet the basically antagonistic relationship between capital and nature, or 'society' and 'nature' cannot be transcended in this mode of appropriation.

Veronika Bennholdt-Thomsen continues this discussion on the role of violence in civilized society in Chapter 6,'Women's Work and Violence against Women'. Violence in modern society is not an extra-economic factor, but constitutes an intrinsic part of the economy. This has not ended with (classical) colonialism. She shows that in its command over women's work capitalism cannot operate without direct violence. Capitalist division of labour is in itself sexist; that is, sexism constitutes the foundation for the functioning of this mode of 'production' or, more precisely, appropriation. As in slavery or bonded labour its continuity is guaranteed by means of violence. Open and hidden, direct and structural violence, has forced women into an oppressed social position. Basically, their labour is, therefore, everywhere forced labour. These relations, and not some intrinsic male sadism, are the root causes of the increase of violence against women.

Part three focuses on the new tendencies of the policies of capital *vis-à-vis* women in general on the one hand, and on women's resistance and struggles against these policies, particularly in the Third World, on the other.

In Chapter 7, Maria Mies' 'Women's Struggle and Class Struggle in Rural India', provides an account of the process of organizing poor, agricultural labourer women, and of their struggles both against sexual oppression by their husbands, and exploitation and harassment by the landlords, and illustrates the fact that, for poor, rural women class exploitation and oppression is closely linked to patriarchal oppression and exploitation and, therefore, their struggle against the one cannot be divorced from their struggle against the other. Contrary to the view commonly held by orthodox Marxist parties and organizations, namely, that resistance against male oppression should be subordinated to and separated in time and space from class struggle, this example shows that by combining both struggles the power of the poor peasants as a class was strengthened rather than weakened.

In Chapter 8 Veronika Bennholdt-Thomsen describes the mechanisms whereby the specific modern form of forced female labour, namely that of the housewife, is today spread all over the world and, particularly, also in the Third World. In 'Why is the Housewife Being Created in the Third World, too?' she demonstrates that the housewife model constitutes the theoretical core of most women-related development programmes and policies. To be defined as a housewife does not mean that women de facto work only in the home – in any case, what would 'home' mean? A wind-screen, a hut, a pavement? It means that they have to do any work at any time and at any place, not paid or poorly paid, and that this low pay is justified by the fact that they are considered to be materially dependent on a male 'breadwinner', irrespective of whether or not there is such a man, or whether or not he is capable of providing 'bread' for the family. Housewifization of women in this respect also means stealing from women their own resources, which they need for their subsistence, destroying their social networks and thus atomizing them.

In the final chapter of this book: 'The Proletarian is Dead, Long Live the Housewife', Claudia von Werlhof argues that the structures and relations we had observed in Third World countries are increasingly reintroduced into First

World countries. International and national capital, in order to solve its accumulation crisis, is now openly propagating the hitherto hidden production relations of the housewives, this time not for the reproduction of labour power alone but for the production of commodities, as a panacea for its growth crisis. Rationalization and automation increasingly render the 'free' proletarian superfluous, and concomitantly the 'image of the future', based on the universalization of the model of the free, democratic, male, white wage-worker, the historical subject for the revolutionizing of capitalism, disappears. The proletarian disappears, because he is: a) too expensive, b) not 'productive' enough. He is increasingly being replaced by housewifized labour, that is, labour that bears the characteristics of housework, namely, labour not protected by trade unions or labour laws, that is available at any time, for any price, that is not recognized as 'labour' but as an 'activity', as in the 'income generating activities', meaning isolated and unorganized and so on. Under the slogan of 'flexibilization of labour' capital today follows a policy of restructuring labour according to this model. Housewifization of labour is particularly propagated with regard to the new computer technology and the old/new strategy of homeworking. Women will constitute the bulk of this new labour force outside the 'formal sector'. But men, also, will increasingly find themselves in such housewifized labour relations. The motives for this new strategy of capital are not only economic. Housewifization of labour in this sense is also a political strategy to break the power of the organized (male) proletariat. The trade unions, which never included housework in the definition of work, are not in a position to counter this strategy of capital.

Since these essays were written, the consequences of this perspective, also with regard to other areas, have become clearer to us. Some of these are: the role of the state in the establishment; maintenance and further restructuring of capitalist–patriarchal relations and the subordination of women; a fundamental critique of the methodology used in social science research and social theory from a feminist point of view; a feminist critique of technology and particularly of the patriarchal–capitalist concept of progress prevalent both in capitalist and in socialist societies. The latter became particularly relevant with the appearance of the new reproductive technologies and genetic engineering. Moreover, on the basis of this analysis a discussion has started between feminists and the ecology and alternative movement and a critique of those who see the way out of today's crisis in a dualization of the economy. In this context the development of a feminist perspective of a future society, a perspective which comprises the totality of reality, has become the urgent task for today and tomorrow.

Maria Mies

Part 1:
Women's Work and Capitalism

1. Women's Work: the Blind Spot in the Critique of Political Economy*

Claudia von Werlhof

> Political economy as the science of the conditions and forms under which different human societies produce and exchange, and under which products are accordingly distributed each time – political economy in this expanded sense is yet to be created. The scientific knowledge we possess of economy so far is almost totally restricted to the evolution and development of the capitalist mode of production.
> (MEW 20, 139; transl. J. M.)

We would like to examine whether this statement by Engels is applicable to the position of women throughout the course of history. What is described as the 'women's question' concerns not only the individual, micro-social relationships, but all macro-social relationships too, including the international and historical aspects.

These aspects will receive special attention in the following pages: a) because a characterization and typification of the logic of various modes of production in history is not possible without reference to the division of labour based on sex; and b) because unless the 'women's question' is seen as fundamental, the understanding of the development of non-European societies and their relationship to Europe since the end of the Middle Ages (and later to the USA and other countries of the so-called centre) has to remain superficial.

So far, discussions within the parameters of both the classical and modern critique of political economy have paid scant attention to these two aspects. Feminists, too, have hardly taken notice of them.

It is not surprising, therefore, that the current discussion about the definition of modes of production and of international relations has continually circled around the women's question without really being aware of it. Although so close, the main cause of the present epistemological gaps remains hidden, perhaps because the social relations accompanying it 'seem the more self-evident the more their internal relationships are concealed from it, although they are understandable to the popular mind.' (Marx 1959:77, 817).

*This chapter was originally published in: Beiträge für Feministischen, *Theorie und Praxis*, No. 1, 1978, pp. 18–32. The English translation here is by Janet Martin.

Indeed, there even seems to be an unconscious resistance towards exactly this liberating insight that many of the questions raised in this context are, in fact, women's questions. (This is true even for Meillassoux (1976), although he explicitly makes the women's question his topic, unlike many other authors.) Further examples of this resistance are the attempted explanations of: 'heterogeneity' (A. Córdova), 'hierarchy' (S. Amin), inter-relation or 'articulation' (P.Ph. Rey, E. Terray et al.) and 'unequal development' (E. Mandel) of modes of production – we would say production relations – in the Third World.

The progressive element of the so-called 'modes-of-production discussion' (see also the latest debate on the 'Asiatic' mode of production), which nevertheless is reminiscent of the positivist dualism of 'traditional' and 'modern', stops exactly at the point at which the question should be raised: *who are*, in fact, the people working in production relations that deviate from the supposedly capitalist norms?

Surprisingly, the question of 'heterogeneity' has not been raised with reference to the so-called First World where, supposedly, there are only 'homogeneous' production relations (Amin 1975, 236).[1] The assumption of 'homogeneity' is not only Euro-centred and a glorification of capitalism, because all other production relations appear to be 'deformed' and 'underdeveloped' (Mandel 1970:25) in comparison to the 'homogeneity' of production relations in the First World, but it is also sexist, because it mystifies – even denies – that in the First World, too, labour power is 'over'-exploited in the sense that less than its reproduction costs are covered by wages. Indeed, aside from other peculiarities of production in these spheres, half of all the working hours are not paid for at all. Our 'deformed' and 'underdeveloped' people are women.

As a counterpart of the modes-of-production discussion, which argues from the point of view of the social relations in the Third World itself, the theory of imperialism considers, then as now, only production relations in the wage labour sphere (Busch et al. 1971; Neusüss 1972) and above all is fixated on the circulation sphere, the world market. By that it has not only failed to go beyond Rosa Luxemburg's early approach but neither has it really assimilated her theory of imperialism. Paradoxically, Rosa Luxemburg, who was also unaware that she had written about the women's question in *The Accumulation of Capital*, had already anticipated much of the present discussion. She not only stated a continuing historical coincidence of 'capitalist' and 'non-capitalist' spheres in both the First and the Third World, but she also based her theory on the logic of the relations existing between the two spheres and the two worlds:

> The decisive fact is that the surplus value cannot be realised by sale either to workers or to capitalists, but only if it is sold to such social organisations or strata whose own production is not capitalist. (Luxemburg 1963:351–2)

But who are these 'non'-capitalist producers, these people who do not produce commodities for a wage? They are the majority: housewives throughout the world, peasants of both sexes, mainly in the Third World producing for their own subsistence, and the army of male and female so-called 'marginalized' people, most of whom also live in the Third World (unfortunately, Luxemburg considered only the peasants). According to Luxemburg, however, capitalists and wage labourers are simply responsible neither for the realization of surplus value nor for its origin:

> Non-capitalist organisations provide a fertile soil for capitalism; more strictly: capital feeds on the ruins of such organisations, and although this non-capitalist milieu is indispensable for accumulation, the latter proceeds at the cost of this medium nevertheless, by eating it up. Historically, the accumulation of capital is a kind of metabolism between capitalist economy and those pre-capitalist methods of production without which it cannot go on and which, in this light, it corrodes and assimilates. Thus capital cannot accumulate without the aid of non-capitalist organisations, nor, on the other hand, can it tolerate their continued existence side by side with itself. Only the continuous and progressive disintegration of non-capitalist organisations makes accumulation of capital possible. (Luxemburg 1973:416)

What is defined here is simply a process of continuing 'original' accumulation as a logical and fundamental part of capital relations; the Third World and/or the agricultural areas – we would add: and the households – being locations for this process which has the purpose of facilitating accumulation in the First World and/or the urban areas.

This discovery, that the so-called original or primitive accumulation is far more than simply a historical and isolated occurrence of locally limited importance for Europe during its transition from feudalism to capitalism, is also one of the central points in current debates:

> Parallel to the mechanisms of accumulation, which are peculiar to the capitalist mode of production – the extended reproduction – a mechanism of original accumulation still continues. This characterises the relations between the centre and the periphery of the capitalist world system. (Amin 1971:51.)[2]

The term 'parallelism' of different accumulation mechanisms would, however, have to be replaced by the notion of a process in which different phases of capital accumulation are based on one another (Marx 1939:504). The production relations within the periphery and within the centre, and those between the periphery and the centre, are equally affected by this process, a phenomenon Luxemburg has already analysed. This process could be traced straight to the last micro-relationship between a man and a woman, irrespective of whether inside or outside the household. Luxemburg did not go as far as this, although nothing in her argument would have prevented her.

On the other hand, however, the debate on 'women's work' has not yet been related to the mode of production and accumulation as a whole and their international determinants. For if we ask ourselves what these so-called 'non'-capitalist producers and consumers (the housewives, subsistence-peasants and marginalized people of urban and rural areas in general) really do, we can note their common characteristics: whether they earn an additional wage or not, they are forced to produce (also) goods for their own direct consumption without payment, as they would be unable to survive on their often minimal wage alone, much less without it. (For example they keep animals or allotments, make use of waste products by recycling them, often sell a part of their agricultural product and handicrafts, produce and maintain their houses and clothes themselves, ('do-it-yourself'), and do all the housework including child care and so on.)

What serves to preserve their life from their own point of view is, from the point of view of capital, the reproduction of labour power. Even if capital has no need for this labour, or not all of it, or needs it only periodically (usually in the best years of life, that is, in youth) as wage labour, it can still make use of this reserve pool of the 'marginal mass' at any time and in any way, and indeed cheaply, by not having to provide for its production and reproduction.

This supposedly 'non'-capitalist relation ('non'-capitalist because it is outside wage labour), that is, a production relation in which life (for capital the potential-commodity labour power) is (re-)produced by unpaid, use-value orientated subsistence work; this relation is very convenient for capital, precisely because of its difference from the wage labour relation. Without risking or paying anything, capital appropriates (it robs) the surplus labour made day in, day out by these subsistence producers, whose labour has been transformed into labour power usable for capital as wage labour, or in other forms. Only on this very basis does the 'real' process of capital valuation and accumulation begin.

The production and perpetual reproduction of this basis, therefore, correspond to a kind of continuing process of original accumulation, which is characteristically the same whether it concerns the macro-relation First World/Third World or the micro-relation of man/woman.

A comparison of the different groups of producers in this sphere of production and reproduction of the commodity labour power (the sphere which typically establishes the 'heterogeneity' mentioned) shows that quantitatively, women not only constitute the majority of these rural and urban subsistence producers, but also qualitatively the present form of housework, which arose with capitalism, is the 'classical', typical, although reduced to its essence, form of subsistence work, which so far capitalism has needed, and this form of (re-)producing labour power has been and is being relegated exclusively to women.

This is not the place to discuss how the contribution of continuing original accumulation is to be measured in relation to total accumulation. It is nevertheless certain that exactly this (female) subsistence work for the (re-)production of labour power is all the more important as a precondition for completion of wage labour, the lower the wage costs as a result of the presence of women in such work the greater the possibility of its accomplishment; and/or it is in the interests of capital not only to have sufficient labour power but also to have available qualified and not easily replaceable workers. Conversely, when wages are low and unstable, or when there are periods with little, or no possibility of wage labour (this is true for the poor classes and generally for the Third World) then female subsistence labour is of greatest importance, particularly from the point of view of those directly affected.

If, in fact, a continuing process of original accumulation is a constant prerequisite for the accumulation of capital, we arrive at a completely new understanding of capitalism, which consequently makes possible the frequently sought 'totality' of perception. For, in the long run, how can production relations, which are the means for the accumulation of capital, be or remain non-capitalist, or in other words, how can capital accumulation result from a different mode of production still existing? (Biermann and Kössler 1977:54) How can relations be non-capitalist, when capital itself creates them outside the sphere of wage labour, in order to enforce the continuation of original accumulation, especially where all pre-capitalist relations have already been absorbed? (Bennholdt-Thomsen 1976) This aspect could not have been observed to the same extent in Luxemburg's time although it must have been known to her, above all in the form of the capitalist nuclear family.

If, then, capitalism is viewed in its totality, relations must, therefore, be regarded not only as economic but also as indispensable for accumulation relations which, until now, have been falsely considered 'extra-economic', or even 'natural' and, therefore, universally independent from historical changes, simply because they did/do not exist as a wage labour relation. An example for this is women's work: bearing and bringing-up children, satisfying men's need for food, sexuality and communication. (Werlhof 1977b)

In total, it can be seen that an accumulation theory of the nature described is preferable to Euro-centred, sexist theories of imperialism, and to the world market analyses. Also because of their generally structuralist, static and non-dialectical approach, it is preferable to theories of 'articulation' of various modes of production, all the more so because we need a theory applicable both to the macro- and micro-spheres of society. The modes-of-production discussion is more concerned with a differentiation between a growing number of modes of production which are homogeneous in themselves (Banaji 1972),[3] and its mosaic-like compilation does not help in defining the character of a social and economic formation. The latter, which has often been treated like a residual category, must be released from its 'closet-like' existence where all 'inexplicable' and uncomfortable phenomena, such as women's work, have so far been deposited. On the other hand, the concept of 'society in permanent transition' would be most suitable for a theory of accumulation because the movement of appropriation and absorption corresponds most closely to it.

The scope of the question of 'heterogeneity' and the perpetual merging of contradictory relations becomes further apparent when one considers that we are not dealing exclusively with phases during the origin and development of capitalism. Already the first-class societies in history, collectively seen as having had an 'Asiatic' mode of production apparently had heterogeneous production relations. (Thanh-hung 1975:37/48) Some researchers are still surprised by this today, for instance in the case of the Aztecs. (Bartra 1969)[4]

The empires of the Incas and Aztecs, as the first large, class societies on the American continent, were based on the appropriation of the surplus product and the surplus labour, drawn from the forced public labour of the subjugated tribal societies (for the construction of the drainage system, the building of houses for the ruling class and for the wars of conquest). These largely pre-civilized, pre-patriarchal tribal societies, which practised virtually no form of social division of labour (Meillassoux 1972), once subjugated, became the material basis for the empire, but their internal social relations remained basically unchanged (compare also China, India, the Middle East and the Near East). As a result of this fusion between the production relations of tribal societies and those of a class society, which first and foremost practised a division of labour based on sex, it was specifically women and agricultural producers who constituted the economic foundations at that time, too. (Werlhof 1976)

If it is true that all class societies to date have accumulated by means of contradictory ('heterogeneous') production relations, the creation of the necessary basis and preconditions (simple reproduction) being extorted mainly from women, and 'real' accumulation (extended reproduction), that is the production of a visible surplus product for the rulers, being extorted mainly from men, then we must ask, and examine the implications of, some systematic questions about our own present-day situation.

1. What if the prevailing production relation under capitalism were not simply the wage labour relation, but a *two-fold relation*, composed of: wage labour; and non-wage labour? What if, then, the typical aspect of a production relation were that one of its part relations has to be complemented by at least one other relation, which would thereby be contradictory to the first? In the case of capitalist relations, the non-wage labour side would correspond to the phase of continuing original accumulation, and the wage labour side would correspond to the following phase of 'real' accumulation, in other words, the end phase.

As the basis of accumulation the non-wage labour side would have the following kind of importance: as it ensures the reproduction of labour power and living conditions it must 'necessarily be continual, if it is to fulfill the duty of providing and maintaining human energy. Production ["real" accumulation] on the other hand, need not necessarily fulfill this condition.' (Schiel 1977, 2; transl. J. M.)

2. What would be the consequences for the analysis of class structure of this two-fold production relation being not only contradictory with respect to capital but also in itself?

It is fundamental and typical for women to be non-wage labourers and typical for men to be wage labourers. (A female wage labourer is always simultaneously a non-wage labourer.) Their relationship to one another would be complementary and contradictory. *Complementary*: for the accumulation of capital, including its preconditions concerning the (re-)production of labour power, and complementary also for the wage labourers, who, as human beings, want to reproduce their existence. *Contradictory*: firstly, in favour of capital, because it divides the exploited (Lenin 1971, 115)[5] and, secondly, also in favour of the wage labourer, because he would be better compensated for his exploitation, but at the costs of the (female) non-wage labourer. The result would be a general hierarchical (Sacks 1977, 61)[6] class structure of a *three-, not two-fold* nature, which would repeat itself within all formations normally labelled as 'classes' (Werlhof 1977a), and this would also be the case for the relation between industrial and agricultural production, between wage labourers and peasants, between town and country, and between the First and the Third World. (Baxandall et al. 1976, 11)

3. Which methods of implementation of this double-faced production relation, contradictory in itself and toward capital, would have to be observable?

It is, in fact, possible to quite easily ascertain that the method of using 'extra-economic' violence, in other words direct, political violence, usually associated with the process of original accumulation, has been maintained until today, although according to classical theory, the phase of original accumulation has long since passed.

Typically this *not* 'extra'-economic (in the superstructural sense) and *not* non-capitalist form of violence is to be found wherever original accumulation continues: in the family, and violence against women in general; in the reproduction sphere as a whole, and outside the family, as well as in the Third World.

The simultaneous expansion of 'economic' violence, that is to say indirect, structural violence, being internationalized by the exploited themselves, corresponds to the expansion of capitalist commodity production. This has led more to a general increase of violence than to a substitution of one form of violence by another.

4. Which forms and combinations of exploitation would be observed with respect to our assumption about the double character of the capitalist production relation?

Initially, it must be remembered that exploitation in the form of slavery was not confined solely to the ancient Greek and Roman mode of production. Slavery celebrated its 'heyday' only *within* the capitalist mode of production, when between the 16th and 19th centuries 30 million Africans were shipped as slaves to North and South America. When we see, therefore, that the advance of civilization and its modes of production did not necessarily lead to the dissolution of all earlier forms, and that these might even have received a confirmation in a new guise, thereby only now being able to develop fully, then the question arises as to whether such events merely represent coincidents of history or whether they represent an inherent logic.[7]

Under the capitalist production relation, on the one hand, there is the form of exploitation in which wage labour produces surplus value. Without considering that there are even differences here, at least with respect to the rate of surplus value (low wage groupings for women, migrants and foreign workers as against the labour 'aristocracy' of skilled workers, for example) we are mainly interested here in the form and rate of exploitation of non-wage labourers, that is to say, of women (housewives), subsistence peasants and, generally, 'marginalized' people in the Third World.

Surplus labour can be appropriated as such (unpaid services), as surplus product, or as surplus value. Revenues, coming to the appropriators in cash, in kind and through work, are called profit and rent. Profit, as a form of revenue, is bound to the capitalist production of surplus value; whereas rent (and in particular ground-rent) was the predominant form of revenue in pre-capitalist times (money-, labour-, and product-rents).

While the capitalist draws his profit from the surplus value produced by the wage labourers, the pre-capitalist landowner draws his rent from the surplus labour and/or surplus product of his slaves and/or serfs. After the general implementation of capitalist relations, profit increasingly usurped ground-rent as the main form of revenue, and the serfs and slaves became wage labourers and tenants. Marx, nevertheless, found that ground-rent did not disappear with the expansion of capitalist relations, rather it succeeded in retaining a modified importance alongside, against, and even within these relations, so that rent could now be defined as an excess revenue above the average profit (surplus/extra-profit) and as a part of the surplus value itself. (MEW 25, 838)

Thus, two questions arise: a) were slavery and serfdom really abolished under capitalism? b) Possibly rent not only acquired a specific importance as a form of revenue within capitalist relations, but also retained a general importance, which means that the part it plays in the production of surplus value is, in fact, far greater than has hitherto been assumed.

The wage labourer's living labour capacity is part of himself. He can dispose of it by exchange, although under duress (because he is forced into it and by exchange). However:

In the slave relation, he [the slave] belongs to the individual, particular owner, and is his labouring machine. As a totality of force-expenditure, as labour-capacity, he is a thing belonging to another, and hence does not relate as subject to his particular expenditure of force . . . In the serf relation he appears as a moment of property in land, as an appendage of the soil, exactly like draught-cattle. (Marx 1973, 464–5)

Until today, no one either wanted, or was able, to define the class-position of women. In any case, women are not, or not only, wage labourers.

What if women have a class position that simultaneously encompasses slavery and serfdom, and which, furthermore, would be comparable to the position of a tenant or small scale peasant, a *combined* class position in which work as a whole would be subsumed under capital?[8] That work would correspond to the fact that, 'an accumulation must have taken place prior to labour [wage labour] and not spring out of it – which enables him [the capitalist] to put the worker to work and to maintain his effectiveness.' (Marx 1973, 504)

In *The German Ideology* Marx himself refers to women and children as the slaves of the male family head. (MEW 3, 1959, 32–3.) In 'Capitalism and Women's Work' (Lenin 1962, 206–7) Lenin calls women 'domestic slaves' and on another occasion he notes:

> the base, mean and infamous denial of rights to women, or inequality of the sexes, that disgusting survival of feudalism and medievalism, which is being renovated by the avaricious bourgeoisie and the dull-witted and frightened *petite-bourgeoisie* in every other country in the world without exception. (Lenin 1968, 647)

Unfortunately this phenomenon was not investigated systematically and there remained only moralistic appeals; or the women's question was analysed exclusively within the limitations of the wage labour question. (Marx et al. 1976)

On the other hand, without Marx really noticing it, there are very clear parallels between the position of women and the position of tenants and small scale peasants in his ground-rent theory.

What if the land-owner continues to exist in the form of the wage labourer himself, because his 'ownership' of a woman ('land', his wife) – which means that he has her labour/body at his disposal – absolves capital from the need to make deductions from the surplus value produced by the wage labourers, in order to maintain their labour power? What if the ownership of women corrupts the wage labourers, and splits the exploited as a whole into two large groups? The question regarding what can be owned as property and how property has developed historically has not yet been adequately answered. According to Marx, there can be ownership of products – that is objects – and ownership of means of production – this being a social relation, namely, 'having the command over labour'. (Marx.)

The *ownership of human beings themselves* has received only scant attention with reference to slavery and serfdom, not, however, as a possibly *logical* ingredient of all class societies, or even as the first-ever form of ownership. (Engels 1968.) The proletariat is even expressly characterized as having:

> a complete absence of all property, for the safeguarding of inheritance for which monogamy and male domination were established. Here all the foundations of classical monogamy are removed . . . Therefore, there is no stimulus here to assert male domination. (Engels 1968, 499)

Supposedly the proletariat would also be able to abolish the family with ease, for what could possibly be inherited here?

All the political and theoretical errors that have been made in this context can be traced back to the fact that the proletarian man's ownership of his wife has never been recognized. In his ground-rent theory Marx observes that ownership of slaves or serfs is comparable to ownership of land, but he fails to systematically follow this through. (MEW 25, 817.) Is the ownership of women comparable to the ownership of slaves/serfs and land? Only on signing the marriage contract can a woman at least become the *possessor* (not the *owner*) of herself:

> It is furthermore evident that in all forms in which the direct labourer remains the 'possessor' of the means of production and labour conditions necessary for the production of his own means of subsistence, the property relationship must simultaneously appear as the direct relation of lordship and servitude, so that the direct producer is not free: a lack of freedom which may be reduced from serfdom with enforced labour to a mere tributary relationship. (Marx 1959/77, 790)

A woman who is not the owner but only the possessor of herself, would be comparable to a tenant/small scale peasant with, simultaneously, the characteristics of a slave/serf. She has the house and herself as 'land', and, at the same time, she has her labour capacity to work the 'land', but not, however, within a wage labour relation.[9] She supplies capital with labourers and her owner (husband) with the means to reproduce his labour power. Through the transformation of her labour into the labour power of her husband – the wage labourer – she provides capital with a higher absolute surplus value than would otherwise have been possible. She also provides her husband-owner with an absolute rent plus, in almost all cases, a differential rent, in the form of labour- and product-rents.

How large is the overall rent which all men appropriate from the ownership of their wives? How large is it in comparison to profit? Is the increase in surplus value more lucrative if derived from rent rather than from profit?

It is certain that whatever may be the class position of women, it is not one-dimensional; also, that the wage labourer, as a type of 'land'-owner, would lead an additional existence with a special class position (although as an exploiter in this case). The position of a woman, however, can incorporate everything simultaneously: perhaps encompassing all previous forms of exploitation combined with, and strengthened by the capital relation.

The general reason for this may lie in *women*'s historically caused *double character*, as labourers on the one hand, and as a fertile resource (like land) on the other: in women, the general production condition – 'unity of labour with its material preconditions' (Marx 39/40, 375) – has already been realized.

It remains to be asked how the resulting different forms of woman's double exploitation, as labourers and as fertile resources, have been (re-)combined and shifted in the course of history – above all in the present age – especially in relation to the class position of men in general, and to their husbands' class position in particular. The increasing trend towards the psycho-social work and exploitation of women, must also receive careful attention. Research would also be required into the parallels between the small peasant and urban (Evers 1976) ownership of small plots of land, especially in the Third World. In this context, for example, it can be noted that it is these very housewives, small-scale peasants and 'marginalized' people who continue working in and maintaining activities which are no longer worthwhile, and even self-destructive. In fact, they expend enormous efforts in so doing, because they have no alternative means of existence. (MEW 25, 812 ff; Marx et al 1976, 55)

5. When the contradictory/complementary aspect of the capitalist production relation recurs in the corresponding class positions, forms of violence and exploitation, it is also valid for the development of the productive forces. 'In fact all production of surplus value, and thus all development of capital, has for its natural basis the productiveness of agricultural labour.' (Marx 1959/77, 785) . . . and of housework. Capitalist production in the form of wage labour is successful only in its slowest, most contradictory fashion both in agriculture and women's work where it comes up against limitations in the production of surplus value.

> Capital must always consider whether the additional costs in the form of wages, resulting from the release from housework, will not raise the total reproduction costs so much that they detract from the surplus value additionally produced. (Schiel 1977, 22)

This would also be true for agriculture.

In general, it seems that the falling tendency of the profit rate is curbed by those labourers who work under conditions in which high productivity is not possible. (Deere 1976; Werlhof 1977c; Dierckxsens, therefore, put the term 'unproductive' in inverted commas, Dierckxsens 1977, 84) Furthermore, housework, and parts of the urban and agrarian sectors, are responsible for producing specific products, namely, those that satisfy basic needs for the reproduction of life, whereas, for example, luxury goods and weapons in particular are produced in the sphere of wage labour and more highly developed productive forces. This is one reason for the wastefulness and perversion of capitalist commodity production, and for the general *confusion between productive forces and technology*. So far there is no problem-orientated study into this production for the dominant classes, production for domination, based on (female) forced labour for the satisfaction of basic needs. (Ehrenreich 1976, 20)

6. With regard to the institutional superstructure of capitalist production, presumably here too, a contradictory/complementary combination between older and newer forms must have occurred. More is known about the phenomenon of the continuing existence of the family and its reinforced presence in capitalist guise than is known about the functions of the state, for example. In any case, the state's importance has not been undermined, despite the opinions of liberal economists; rather the contrary is true. Also, Marx's assumption that the state would 'wither away' as socialism developed,

communism operating in a society without a state, has been almost forgotten. Even in China, for example, there is virtually no discussion of this issue. Instead of withering away under socialism at present, such as in the Soviet Union, the state has become more than ever before an 'asiatic despot' as Dutschke attempts to prove. (Dutschke 1974)

Where is the state situated in the process of accumulation? Is it the state that mediates between original and final phases in the accumulation of capital, forcing the former and protecting the latter?

7. Taking forms of ideology, social consciousness and behaviour, and finally taking class struggles and revolutionary movements into consideration, how does the capitalist production relation justify itself and what does it create? Is there a women's consciousness 'for themselves' towards men, state agents and capitalists who force, violate and exploit them? Is there such a consciousness among the small subsistence peasants and generally the 'marginal mass' in the Third World towards First World monopoly capital? Is it really just so simple that, with

> the slave's awareness that he cannot be the property of another, with his consciousness of himself as a person, the existence of slavery becomes a merely artificial, vegetative existence, and ceases to be able to prevail as the basis of production. (Marx 1973, 463)

It is necessary to re-examine revolutionary movements from within a different perspective. Most of those movements that have arisen during the last 50 years have been in the Third World, and these were mostly undertaken and fought by peasants, peasant-workers and women (?).

In conclusion the following theses could be formulated:

● Not only are women the first human beings in history to be exploited, their exploitation also provided a general pattern for subsequent forms of exploitation of man and nature; and women today experience a combination of parts of all these forms of exploitation.

● Historically, the class position of the male wage labourer is very recent compared to that of women. What chains him to history is his patriarchal aspect which makes him, simultaneously, an exploiter.

● Typical women's work is found in the sphere of continuing original accumulation, whether it is inside or outside the family. This part of the capitalist production relation is the basis of capital accumulation and, on the one hand the logical/contradictory complement to the wage labour relation, and on the other, from the point of view of the individuals, the basis for their personal reproduction of, not only their labour power, but also of their human life in general.

● Imperialism is the method of enforcing capital accumulation on a worldwide scale, and – in particular – of enforcing a continuation of original accumulation.

● Ultimately, an antagonistic relationship exists not only between wage labourers and capitalists but in a far more comprehensive sense, especially between the poor women of the Third World and First World monopoly capital.

● The situation of Third World rural and urban subsistence producers, the 'marginal mass', most closely resembles that of women.

● It is not women who have a colonial status, but the colonies that have a woman's status. In other words, the relationship between the First and the Third World corresponds to the relationship between man and woman.

> However, the reconciliation of irrational forms in which certain economic relations [e.g. the family] appear and assert themselves in practice, does not concern the active agents of these relations, in their everyday life. And since they are accustomed to move about in such relations, they find nothing strange therein. A complete contradiction does not offer the least mystery to them. They feel as much at home as a fish in water among manifestations [e.g. the ideology of women as 'nature'] which are separated from their internal connections and absurd when isolated by themselves. What Hegel says . . . applies here: that which seems irrational to ordinary common sense is rational, and that which seems rational to it is itself irrational. (Marx 1959/77, 779)

And:

> From the stand point of higher economic forms of society, private ownership of the globe by single individuals will appear quite as absurd as private ownership of one man by another. (Marx 1959/77, 776)

Why have neither Marx nor his followers applied these two findings to the 'women's question'?[10]

Notes

1. Senghaas-Knoblock is an exception here.
2. Compare A. G. Frank and E. Senghaas-Knobloch.
3. This is valid for the discussion about the so-called 'colonial mode of production' in Asia.
4. About the Asiatic mode of production in Mexico.
5. Compare this with his statement about the tendency of imperialism to divide the working class.
6. 'As a compensation for the loss of economic autonomy they [the ruling classes] – consigned a social adult status and tutelage over women to men exclusively.' (Sacks)
7. Even Marx was unsure about this question in the *Grundrisse* and at times his argument is contradictory.

8. Bennholdt-Thomsen differentiates between different forms of subsumption among agricultural producers.

9. Besides being a tenant of herself, women would also be the farm worker employed by the tenant; as a worker she would in turn be a slave/serf, since she receives no wage.

2.   Capitalist Development and Subsistence Production: Rural Women in India*

Maria Mies

All economic systems, modes of production, and all human history presuppose two types of basic human activities: production of the means of subsistence and production of new life or procreation. The first is necessary to satisfy basic human needs and to sustain life, the second to ensure the continuation of society from generation to generation. Engels correctly called both types of human activity *production* and stated that the institutions of a particular society or of a particular epoch are determined by the organization and the development of these two types of production.[1] As production of the means of subsistence is dependent on human co-operation in labour, so too production of new life or procreation is dependent on the co-operation of women and men in the sexual act. Both processes are closely interlinked, and as Marx noted, in both processes people enter into a double relationship.

> The production of life, both of one's own in labour and of fresh life in procreation, now appears as a double relationship: on the one hand as a natural, on the other as a social relationship. By social, we understand the cooperation of several individuals no matter under what conditions, in what manner and to what end. It follows that a certain mode of production, or industrial stage, is always combined with a certain mode of cooperation, or social stage, and this mode of cooperation is itself a productive force.[2]

In so far as the production of human life and of *living–working* capacity is the necessary precondition of all modes and forms of production, we shall call this the *subsistence production and reproduction*. In the sphere of use-value production the distinction between subsistence production and reproduction has little analytical value as both processes are hardly separated from each other. Therefore, in the following I use the term subsistence production to denote the continuum between the two processes. Subsistence production thus defined involves a variety of human activities ranging from pregnancy, the

* This article is a revised edition of a paper presented at a conference on Subsistence Reproduction at the Center for Development Studies and Planning, the University of Bielefeld, West Germany, in April 1978. It was first published in: *Bulletin of Concerned Asian Scholars*, Vol. 12, No. 1, 1980.

birth of children, to production, processing and preparation of food, clothing, making of a home, cleaning, as well as the satisfaction of emotional and sexual needs. In all this activity human energy is spent to transform 'nature' into human life. Therefore, I shall call this activity *subsistence work*. Most of this work is done by women.

Under capitalism the two processes involved in subsistence reproduction are not only being transformed and redefined, but they are increasingly separated from each other. The production of new life through the co-operation of men and women in the sexual act, formerly an important *social* act, is now relegated to the sphere of nature or called 'biological reproduction'. And the day-to-day restoration of the labourers, whose energies have been consumed in the capitalist production process, is defined as reproduction of the labour *force*. The capitalist is interested only in the latter, not in the labourer as a living human being, but the labour *force* can be extracted only from *living* (strong, healthy, etc.) human beings.

Capitalism has brought about another fundamental structural separation and redefinition: that between production and reproduction. The term production is now reserved for the production of exchange values only, which becomes the dominant type of production. The term reproduction is used to denote two related processes: (1) the reproduction of the capitalist production cycle over time or extended reproduction or accumulation. This process has also been called system reproduction; and (2) the reproduction of the labour force, as mentioned above. The first process has been analysed by Marx in *Capital*, Volume II, Chapter 21.[3] The analysis of the second, however, was taken up more recently, partly in connection with the international debate on housework which was initiated by the women's movement. Before we turn to the further theoretical implications of this debate, let us first have a look at the subsistence producers.

Subsistence production covers a wider range of human activity than unpaid household work in the capitalist centres. Statistically, housewives in the capitalist centres form only a small percentage of the world's subsistence producers. The majority of these subsistence producers are small peasants and artisans, both men and women, living in the capitalist peripheries in Asia, Africa and Latin America. My hypothesis is that capital accumulation, particularly in its present phase, creates an ever-increasing mass of relative surplus population which will not be absorbed into the formal wage labour pool, whose constituents will remain structurally non-wage labourers, and who have to produce their own survival in various forms of subsistence production. These subsistence producers constitute a pool of marginalized people.

The concept of marginality and marginalization was developed in the 1960s and 1970s in Latin America in the context of the dependency theory.[4] In contrast to the definition of an industrial reserve army as the production by capitalism of a relative surplus population to keep wages low, several authors have defined the large masses of pauperized peasants and urban poor in peripheral countries as marginalized or a marginalized pool.[5] Capitalist development in these countries will not lead to an absorption of these masses into wage labour proper. They are neither needed to keep the wages of other workers low nor is there a chance that further development will lead to their proletarianization. Hobsbawm attributes this inability of dependent capitalism to transform pauperized peasants into industrial proletarians to the capital intensive, labour-saving technology used in peripheral countries, in contrast to the much simpler technology prevalent in 19th century European industry which *could* absorb large masses of pauperized peasants.

Whereas these authors see marginalization as an inherent structural element of dependent capitalism, Bennholt-Thomsen, developing further the analysis of Kowarick,[6] sees pauperization or marginalization as an integral part of the capitalist mode of production proper. According to her, the production of marginalized masses who are not able to sell their labour power and therefore have to develop a number of forms of subsistence production are not an aberration of the capitalist accumulation process which will disappear with 'full-fledged' capitalism, but are a necessary precondition and result of this mode of production. The contradictory development of capitalism leads, at the same time, to a generalization of wage labour and to the generalization of non-wage labour. In the capitalist centres this generalized non-wage labour is mainly found in the form of housework.

With the further development of labour-saving technology, the marginal pool of non-wage labourers, who simply have to produce their subsistence, is also growing in the capitalist centres. This does not mean that they are 'outside' capitalism. According to Bennholt-Thomsen, their subsistence production, including that of housewives, is subsumed under capital accumulation.

Although capital 'does not take full responsibility' for the reproduction of these marginalized people and 'defines them back into nature' – where they are apparently reproducing themselves 'naturally' – it still taps their living labour power and integrates their products into a global accumulation process.[7] Whereas housewives in the capitalist centres are workers separated from any means of production, subsistence producers in the capitalist periphery often still control some marginal means of production: land, tools. This also applies to women who often perform the bulk of agricultural work in addition to their household work.[8]

Capitalist penetration in India and its impact on women

India's female population is one of the largest in the world. About 80% of this population live in rural areas, producing mostly in the subsistence sector.[9] The participation of women in the rural economy varies widely according to the specific form of subsistence production: they include tribal gatherers and hunters, slash and burn cultivators, settled peasants with plough cultivation, small proprietors, tenants or agricultural labourers without land, subsistence artisans, those engaged in household industries, and peddlars. No systematic research has been done as yet on the basic features of women's participation in this sector, or on the effects of capitalist development on their work and living conditions. But there is enough quantitative and qualitative data available to serve as a base for an analysis of the trends affecting women's lives under the impact of capitalist development. The following analysis is based on statistical data available from studies carried out between 1974 and 1978, and from qualitative observations which I carried out in some limited areas, mainly Andhra Pradesh, between 1977 and 1978.

Before the International Women's Year (1975), the Indian government set up a committee to investigate various aspects of the status of women. This Committee on the Status of Women in India (CSWI) based its inquiry on the statistical material available in the decennial Census reports – the last being the 1971 Census – the National Sample Surveys and other official statistical material, as well as on field studies in all states of the country. In December 1974 the CSWI presented its report. The picture that emerged from its 480 pages was gloomy, and understandably the government was not very eager to give this report wide publicity. The findings of this report have been consistent with those of the demographer Asok Mitra who writes:

> Accelerating a trend which started in the last century, the last thirty years after Independence reduced Indian womanhood more and more to an expendable commodity: expendable, demographically as well as economically. Demographically, the female is being reduced more and more mainly to a productive function, to be expendable as soon as this demand is fulfilled. Economically, she is being inexorably squeezed out of the productive sphere and reduced to a unit of consumption and therefore less socially desirable. The two streams of deterioration are two sides of the same coin.[10]

This deterioration extends into all spheres of women's life, and can be documented by analysing a number of mortality rates, health and nutritional standards, employment and education, as well as their political representation. Rural women and poor urban women – the vast majority of Indian women – are the worst hit by this trend. In the following analysis I will focus on two aspects of this trend, the sex ratio and the employment situation.

The sex ratio
An analysis of the sex ratio in the Indian situation reveals that there has been a steady decline in the proportion of women to men since the beginning of the 20th century. This period has also seen the penetration of capitalist relations in the economy, especially in the agricultural sector. My contention is that the nature of capitalist penetration played a significant role in the physical reduction of women. We shall try to illustrate this by considering the case in the All-India situation and then looking at some case studies.

The figures in Tables 2.1 and 2.2 show two important features of the sex ratio. First, the ratio of female to male population in India has been low for a long time, and secondly, this ratio has been declining since 1911, registering the steepest fall between 1961 and 1971. Asok Mitra has found that Indian female babies and girls (ages 0–9 years) have a much higher mortality rate than boys, and that this rate has gone up consistently between 1941 and 1971. This period also witnessed the increased mortality rate of women as compared to men in the other age groups, particularly in the age group between 20 and 45 years. A similar bleak picture emerges from an analysis of the maternal mortality rate. In rural India it was 573 per 10,000 live births in 1968, whereas in the USA it was 32 (1965), in the UK 29 (1968), Hong Kong 44 (1966), Malaysia 200 (1965) and Sri Lanka 300 (1968).[11]

The growing mortality rate of women and female children cannot be explained by the 'usual' neglect of females in the patriarchal Indian society. We have to ask further why this neglect is growing or intensifying. One concrete explanation may be found in the differential health treatment and nutritional standards of females and males. In a health survey carried out in 1957 in six rural communities it was found that 730 girls and 513 boys were ailing in the age group below 15. Whereas a doctor was consulted for 50.1% of the males, this was the case for only 25.4% of the females.[12] Moreover, when girls or women became ill, they generally received free, traditional or no treatment. The high mortality rate of women and girls is also connected closely with malnutrition. Seventy percent of pregnant women suffer from anaemia.[13] It may appear strange that those who prepare food are getting less food than those whom they feed, but in a typical Indian household women give food first to the men and the children, and usually eat what is left over themselves. However, the growing deficit of women *vis-à-vis* men, their growing mortality rate, their deteriorating health and nutritional standards cannot be explained only by referring to a sexist ideology or the current family structure. Both factors were no less dominant in earlier years. What needs to be explained is the relationship between the declining sex ratio and the development processes that have taken place in India.

There seems to be a close connection between the employment of women in production and their proportion in the total population. This pattern is further corroborated if one compares the population with the employment trends. Women seem to be increasingly losing ground in both since 1911 (see Table 2.2). Thus the Indian Council of Social Science Research (ICSSR) brochure, 'Critical Issues on the Status of Women', states:

> In the 40 years between 1911 and 1951, the gap between men and women in the population increased by 27 percent. During the same period, women's proportion to the total work force declined from 525 per 1000 males (1911) to 408 per 1000 males (1951). In the 20 years between 1951 and 1971, the gap between men and women in the population rose from 8.9 million to 19.9 million. In the same period the number of women workers in agriculture declined from 31 to 25 million, while [the number] of men increased by 34.3 million. In the non-agricultural sector, women workers declined from 9.3 to 6.2 million, while men increased from 32.8 to 48.4 million. The total number of men workers increased by 27 percent while women suffered a decline of 12 percent – reducing their ratio in the workforce to 210 per 1000 men.[14]

These figures are indisputable evidence of a growing disparity between the sexes with regard both to their chances for physical survival and employment. A closer analysis of female work participation will show how women in the rural sector are affected by these trends.

Women's employment in the rural sector

Tables 2.2 and 2.5 show that women have lost ground in all industrial categories where they had been employed since 1911 and that the sharpest decline was between 1961 and 1971. Eighty percent of female workers are employed in the rural sector. The most dramatic decline in female employment has been in the secondary sector, i.e. the industries, in trade and in commerce – sectors which had worked along capitalist lines since the colonial period. But between 1961 and 1971 this trend could also be observed in their traditional agricultural occupations, and household industries (see Tables 2.3 and 2.4).

Yet as Table 3.6 indicates, this process is not accompanied in the same proportion by growing proletarianization. Whereas the number of female cultivators dropped by 52%, the number of male cultivators increased by 6%.

Table 2.1
Sex ratio in states, 1921–71
(Females per 1000 Males)

State	1921	1931	1941	1951	1961	1971
Andrha	993	987	980	986	981	977
Assam	908	886	886	877	876	901
Bihar	1,016	994	996	990	994	956
Gujrat	944	945	941	952	940	936
Jammu & Kashmir	870	865	869	873	878	882
Kerala	1,011	1,022	1,027	1,028	1,022	1,019
Madhya Pradesh	974	973	970	967	953	943
Maharashtra	950	947	949	941	936	932
Mysore	969	965	960	966	959	959
Orissa	1,086	1,067	1,053	1,022	1,001	989
Punjab	821	830	850	858	864	874
Rajasthan	896	907	906	921	908	919
Tamilnadu	1,029	1,027	1,012	1,007	992	979
Uttar Pradesh	909	904	907	910	909	883
West Bengal	905	890	852	865	878	892
All-India	955	955	—	947	941	930

Source: Tables 2.1. 2.2, 2.3 and 2.4: 'Critical Issues on the Status of Women, Employment, Health, Education Priorities for Action', by Indian Council of Social Sciences Research, Advisory Committee on Women's Studies, New Delhi 1977.

Table 2.2
Females per thousand males of total population, all India workers in each industrial category and non-workers 1901–71

Year	In Total Population	Workers (I-IX)	Primary Sector					Secondary Sector				Tertiary Sector				Non-workers	Year
			I	II	I-II	III	I+II+III	IV	V	VI	IV+V+VI	VII	VIII	IX	VII+VIII+IX		
1901	972	504	431	1051	540	335	534	(639)*	553	400	543	405	65	325	350	1,707	1901
1911	964	525	427	1054	567	337	560	(500)	574	336	548	513	62	371	390	1,676	1911
1921	955	516	463	952	557	372	545	(562)	508	412	501	479	65	357	379	1,629	1921
1931	955	453	289	1006	476	337	466	(396)	440	303	423	396	41	484	410	1,656	1931
1951	947	408	357	857	469	491	470	(434)	288	248	291	187	61	332	257	1,580	1951
1961	941	460	498	819	565	297	552	—	110	134	348	119	22	287	210	1,581	1961
1971	930	210	135	498	249	210	248	(155)	88	101	142	59	34	165	108	1,726	1971

The industrial categories are: I. Cultivators; II. Agricultural labourers; III. Livestock, forestry, fishing, hunting & plantation orchards & allied activities; IV. Mining and quarrying; V. Manufacturing processes, (a) Household industry, (b) Other than household industry; VI. Construction; VII. Trade and commerce; VIII. Transport, storages and communications; IX. Other services; X. Non-workers.

* The parenthetical figures are for 'Mining and Quarrying'.

Table 2.3
Important manufacturing activities in which the ratio of female-to-male workers has shown long-term decline: 1911–1961

Manufacturing activities	Female workers per 1000 male workers				
	1911	*1921*	*1931*	*1951*	*1961*
Processing of foodgrains	12,075	7,779	7,065	1,520	331
Bread and other bakery products	1,644	1,466	1,662	447	64
Production of vegetable oils	688	656	595	347	458
Nets, ropes, cordage, etc.	1,962	1,295			1,236
Footwear and their repair	232	201	141	88	81
Earthenware and pottery making	572	540	490	402	507

Source: J. P. Ambannavar, *Demography India*, 4(2), December 1975, p. 353.

Table 2.4
Decline in women participation rate in rural India
age 15-59, 1961–71

	W.P.R. 1961	W.P.R. 1971
Cultivator	30.02	7.13
Agricultural labour	12.60	11.80
Plantations, etc.	0.92	0.58
Household industry	3.42	0.77
Manufacturing	0.37	0.34
Construction	0.13	0.09
Trade & commerce	0.51	0.22
Other services	2.70	0.77

Source: Asok Mitra, The Status of Women: Employment and Literacy.
Only Transport improved slightly from 0.02 to 0.03.

Table 2.5
Distribution of female workers by broad industrial categories, 1911–1971: (in thousands)

Year	Total female population	Total number of female workers	I Cultivators	II Agricultural labourers	III mining, quarrying, live-stock, forestry, fishing, hunting, plantation	IV household industry	V other than household industry	VI construction	VII trade & commerce	VIII transport storage & communication	IX other service	Total of I & II (ag. sec)	Total of III & IX (non-ag. sec)
1911	123,898	41,802	18,090	12,808	1,452	—	4,391	294	2,266	79	2,422	30,898 (73.9)	10,904 (26.1)
1921	122,749	60,085	20,276	10,003	1,431	—	3,689	289	2,189	67	2,151	30,279 (75.5)	9,816 (24.5)
1931	146,075	37,600	12,180	14,997	1,575	—	3,281	291	1,914	49	3,313	27,177 (72.3)	10,423 (27.7)
1951*	173,549	40,539	13,368	12,694	1,357	—	2,906	291	1,153	123	3,647	31,062 (76.8)	9,377 (23.2)
1961	212,467	59,402	33,103	14,171	1,187	4,665	789	243	815	65	4,364	47,274 (79.6)	12,128 (20.4)
1971 (P)	273,900	31,298	9,266	15,794	907	1,331	865	204	556	146	2,229	25,060 (80.1)	6,238 (19.9)

Source: Govt. of India: Towards Equality.

* Figures do not include Jammu and Kashmir.
(P) Provisional. The figures are based on 1% sampling.

Table 2.6
Employment in 1961 and 1971
Using Adjusted* Census Figures

Cultivators	Males		Females	
	1961	*1971*	*1961*	*1971*
Cultivators	66,465	70,005	33,156	15,976
Agric-labourers	17,324	32,535	14,198	20,272
Other workers	45,382	49,876	12,151	8,343
Total workers	129,171	152,531	59,505	44,591
Non-workers	96,975	131,531	153,286	219,412
Total population	226,146	283,937	212,791	264,013

Source: Gail Omvedt: 'Women and Rural Revolt in India', based on 1971 Census figures) in *Social Scientist*, Trivandrum, October 1977.

* These figures are adjusted. The figures in Table 5 are not adjusted.

This is a clear indication of the fact that women are losing control over land as a means of production, i.e. they are gradually becoming *pauperized*. Similarly, the female agricultural labourers increased by 43% whereas the male agricultural workers increased by more than double that rate (88%); women are also not becoming proletarianized at the same rate as men.

More revealing still is the data in Table 2.2. Whereas until 1961 the proportion of women among cultivators had been between 289–498 per 1,000 men (with the exception of 1931), this ratio fell steeply between 1961 and 1971 to a mere 135 women to 1,000 men. Similarly, the female ratio among agricultural labourers had been relatively stable since 1901, but between 1961 and 1971 it dropped from 819 women per 1,000 men to 498 women per 1,000 men, a decline of about 40%. What happened between 1961 and 1971 can be seen as the accentuation of a long-term tendency towards both proletarianization and marginalization.[15] The tendency towards proletarianization is revealed in the fact that the percentage of agricultural labourers to total workers in agriculture *rose* from 24.04 to 38.04%, while the percentage of workers to the total population declined from 49.73 to 35.95%. When analysing the development of work-participation since 1901, Asok Mitra remarks that there has:

> practically been no transfer from agriculture to non-agriculture . . . The primary sector has held firm, almost unchanged, providing the great bulk of employment. It also shows distressingly enough how little manufacturing, including household industry, has been gaining since 1901 despite the steady rise in industrial production, demonstrating that the displacement of human labor has been occurring with the rise in production along with a possible distortion in the production of wage goods.[16]

The fact that more than 50% of all female workers in 1971 are agricultural labourers[17] does not contradict this statement. Every observer of Indian villages knows that the status of the agricultural labourer is itself a marginal one. She/he is neither a 'free' wage labourer nor does she/he have the 'security' of a feudal serf. What is more important, she/he is a wage labourer only for a limited time of the year, and this time is shrinking due to the introduction of new technology. Nevertheless, these labourers are not 'free' to leave the land and become proletarians in the classical sense.

The polarization between men and women in rural India becomes more evident if one considers that, even as wage earners, women generally get one third less than the male agricultural labourer. Thus, Pandey observed that in 1975 women in agriculture got only 68.8% of the earnings that males received.[18]

Pauperization and marginalization: the case of tribal women in Andhra Pradesh

So far the analysis has focused on the all-India trend of increasing pauperization and marginalization of women in the subsistence sector. In order to understand more concretely how these processes take place, it is necessary to supplement the quantitative analysis with at least some evidence of a qualitative nature. I recorded the following examples in 1977 in Andhra Pradesh when I had the opportunity to visit two tribal areas,[19] the Visakhapatnam Tribal Agency Area, and the West Godavari Tribal Agency Area. It had been the strategic policy of the British colonial administration to keep the tribal belts isolated as buffer zones and to prohibit non-tribals from entering these areas as moneylenders, traders and land speculators. These areas were controlled mainly by the forest department.

Although these areas were never sealed off totally, the tribes which I saw were still following partly a traditional mode of subsistence production in its 'pure' form:

● Hunting and gathering (men doing the hunting, women the gathering) supplemented by slash and burn cultivation, called *podu* in this area;
● A concept of 'territory' rather than individual land ownership;
● Little or no vertical stratification of the society;
● Sexual division of labour unaccompanied by social asymmetry; women enjoy both more freedom and power than Hindu women and a higher rate of participation in the productive process;
● Absence of 'puritanical' Hindu concepts and morality regarding drinking, dancing, eating of meat, sexuality;
● Absence of the work ethic; tribals work only as much as they need for their subsistence;
● Absence of 'overpopulation'; zero population growth;
● Absence of poverty, of orphans, of destitute women, etc.

Since Independence, particularly after 1960, it has been the policy of the Indian government to integrate the tribals or *girijans* (hill people) into the so-called national mainstream. This policy, carried out mainly by the Tribal Welfare Department, would wean the tribals away from *podu* cultivation, thus getting control over the rich mineral and other resources in the hill areas. It would also depopulate the forest over one or two generations and resettle the tribals outside the forest, establish a cash economy among them, and establish individual ownership of the land and a capitalist market system. Finally it would break up the social cohesion of the tribes by putting the tribal children into boarding schools (*ashram* schools) where they are subjected to a process of Hinduization by non-tribal teachers and taught to give up their 'bad' tribal habits.[20] In my 1977 visit I noted the following developments:

1) *Rapid deterioration of the ecology:* The prohibition of *podu* cultivation and the establishment of a market economy and of cash-crop cultivation of coffee, oranges, pharmaceutical plants, ground nuts, tobacco, etc., have driven the tribals further up into the hills. Ironically, they *have* to continue *podu* cultivation because the government gives neither adequate land or work to all tribals, nor sufficient wages or prices for their products. Thus the ecological balance, which the tribals had maintained for centuries, is being destroyed. The hills are barren and rainfall has decreased by 10–15 inches in the last few years. Afforestation done by the government only serves the government-controlled development projects like coffee or teak plantations or other cash crops raised mainly for export.

2) *Growing dependence on the fluctuations of the national and international market:* Apart from coffee plantations, the Integrated Tribal Development Agency (ITDA) distributed some acres of land for coffee cultivation to some tribals. (In one village 30 families got 1–2 acres of land; 30 families did not get land.) These small tribal holdings are seriously affected by all fluctuations of the international coffee price.

3) *Break-up of the tribes into classes (differentiation):* The authorities have created a landed/landless differentiation, giving individual grants of land, cattle, sheep, sewing machines, coffee, seeds, fertilizers, etc., to *some* tribals but not to all.

4) *Land alienation:* In most tribal areas all the fertile land has been alienated by non-tribal immigrants. In one area which I visited in 1978, these non-tribals had established themselves as a new landed class and the tribals had become their share croppers or agricultural labourers. These non-tribals produced Virginia tobacco for export (to Russia, USA, Europe) and chillies for the home market.

5) *Growing dependence on government or other welfare agencies:* The old tribal autonomy is being destroyed.

6) *Growing dependence on externally produced items:* In many villages rice has replaced millet as the staple food. But rice is not produced by the *podu* cultivator. It is usually supplied by the non-tribal traders or landholders who give rice as wages for labour.

7) *Growing inequality between men and women with greater pauperization of*

women: The penetration of capitalism has often witnessed the removal of women from their means of production and from their productive functions. It has further brought about a change in the sexual division of labour to their disadvantage. This can be illustrated by the following two cases:

  i) In the traditional tribal economy in West Godavari, producers had control over the marketing of their product which they would exchange at the market place. But wherever depots for the collection of the tribal products have been established by the Girijan Cooperative Corporation, the marketing function has been taken over by non-tribal men and the marketing role of the women has been undermined. A few sewing machines have also been given to them by the Mahila Mandals (womens' clubs) but they produce items which they never use and the marketing is done by non-tribal men.

  ii) Introduction of new technologies has also adversely affected the tribal women. One of the methods to 'integrate the tribals into the national mainstream' is to settle them on the plains, on unreclaimed land in special colonies. In one such colony in West Godavari one of the new technologies introduced was seri-culture. But the training in this new technology (which in China and Bengal had been a traditional women's domain) was imparted only to men. As the women had been removed from the forest which provided the raw material for their earlier production (baskets, mats, etc.) they were left with nothing to produce in the colony. Even occasional seasonal work did not give them economic independence and the entire nature of the 'integration' process left them dependent on the men in the colony.[21]

Production for the world market: A house industry and marginalization

The following example, recorded in 1977, shows how women in house industries are being exploited in export-oriented production. In the villages around Narsapur, West Godavari district, Andhra Pradesh, about 150,000 women are engaged in the crochet lace industry. This industry – or rather the crocheting – was introduced by missionaries around 1860. They encouraged the local women to earn their livelihood by this new skill. In 1900 the lace goods began to be exported and there are now more than 50 such lace exporters or manufacturers, as they call themselves, in Narsapur. By 1970 they exported between $1 and $1½ million worth of lace goods every year to Australia, West Germany, Italy, Denmark, Sweden, Britain and the USA. By 1976–77 the export had gone up to $5 million and in 1977–78 it was $8 million. Another $1–2 million worth of lace goods are being sold in the big cities of India (1977–78).[22]

  This industry is a classical case of the putting-out system. The crocheting is done entirely as a house industry by girls and women of all ages. These women are mainly the daughters and wives of agricultural labourers and poor peasants who have lost their land in the course of the Green Revolution. Lace-making is a means by which they try to supplement the insufficient income of their husbands and hence they fall into the category of subsistence producers as discussed earlier. Three companies supply the thread to three stockists in the region. The exporters buy the thread from these stockists who themselves have become big exporters in the course of the last years. The exporters give this raw material to the middlemen/agents who then take the thread to the lace-makers, pay the wages to them (half the amount of wages is advanced by the exporters and the other half is invested by the agents), and they also collect the lace goods: tablecloths, luncheon sets, lace shirts and dresses etc. – all materials which have become fashionable in Western boutiques. The middlemen are employed full time. The women artisans, who earn less than one rupee per day,* are paid piece-work rates. For lace made of 2,000 meters of thread they get Rs.4, one woman usually needs a week to finish 2,000ms. This means she earns Rs.4 per week. Her daily earnings come to Rs.0.56 on average. (The women also work on Sundays and have no leisure time or holidays). This is less than one third of the minimum wage fixed for female agricultural workers.[23]

It is estimated that 95% of the foreign exchange earnings from the export of handicrafts of the state of Andhra Pradesh are earned by these women. The government introduced a quality marking office in 1960, the officer in charge of which controls the quality of the lace made by the women – he is, of course, a man – and he rejects bad or dirty lace goods. The women start crocheting as little girls and continue to do so until they are old and blind. They receive from the middlemen one pattern or design which they are supposed to crochet, often throughout their entire life. The women have no organization whatsoever, and they complained immediately to us about how they are being exploited by the male exporters who live in big bungalows. The exporters, in turn, said that their business was prospering and that they had not been affected by the crisis of the textile industry in the 1970s. In the chain of accumulation the exporters may invest their profits in other lucrative projects such as land, tractors, taxis or cinemas.

Consequences for women

Although we need a much broader and deeper study of the present processes affecting rural subsistence-producers, the above analysis of available data permits the formulation of a thesis: namely, *that capitalist penetration leads to the pauperization and marginalization of large masses of subsistence producers in India, the capitalist periphery*; and secondly, *that women are more affected by these processes than men*, who may still be partly absorbed into the actual wage labour force. Women in India, in particular, seem to face the following consequences.

1. Capitalist penetration into the rural areas leads to the gradual erosion of the material base of women's subsistence production. Although they may produce

* Rs. 8 = approximately $1.

for a worldwide capitalist market, the *form* of production and the *organization* of production usually remain the same as it had been for producing use values. The capitalists need no constant capital except for the yarn. They need no machinery or factories or sophisticated technology. In other words, capitalist accumulation can take place even when the organization of work is not changed. These forms are mainly private. On the other hand, the women remain largely excluded from the circulation of commodities. They receive low prices for their goods and low wages for their work. Eventually, the family may be forced to take out loans, or to sell their land (or they may lose it to the moneylenders). Yet often, before the family loses the land, the women lose their own poor belongings: gold, utensils, implements. They are still responsible for the satisfaction of the basic needs of the family, but since part of their product is being extracted as surplus product and the material base of subsistence production is getting smaller, the women have to fall back on older forms of securing a livelihood. They gather roots and leaves from the forest, collect firewood as fuel for themselves and for sale, walk many miles to fetch water, etc.

2. There is a growing inequality and polarization between the sexes. Capitalist penetration, far from bringing about more equality between men and women – as had been the fond hope of so many who have seen in capitalism the midwife of democracy – has, in fact, introduced new elements of patriarchalism and sexism. Although many subsistence societies, in India as elsewhere, had a very clearly defined sex-specific division of labour, capitalist penetration invariably upsets this pattern in the direction of enhancing male dominance and power.[24]

When production for exchange is introduced, men are recruited as labourers, whereas women remain responsible for subsistence or household production.[25] When capitalist *market relations* begin to replace the old local market systems, men push women out of the market sphere where they used to sell or barter their products.[26] Women may still continue in some local markets to sell vegetables, pottery or other goods which they have produced over and above their own use, but marketing – and the profits – along capitalist lines is invariably in the hands of men.[27]

3. This polarization between the sexes in rural areas is not an isolated process. It is closely related to the overall process of *class* polarization taking place under the impact of capitalist farming. Growing commercialization of agriculture, a rise in production of cash-crops, the rise in agricultural prices, and the introduction of new technology, all have strengthened the economic position of rich farmers. This class has also benefited most from government expenditure on rural development and has largely dominated the credit institutions. Even the various schemes devised for the uplift of the poor and marginal peasants eventually end up in the hands of the rural rich. On the other hand, more and more small farmers lose their land through indebtedness. In recent years this has led to a growing number of bonded labourers who, for the repayment of a small loan borrowed from their landlord or a rich peasant, are forced to work for long periods.

Though no systematic study has yet been done about the inter-relation between class differentiation and polarization between the sexes or increasing sexism, a few features of this ongoing process can be observed in the Indian context. For example, some of the so-called 'backward classes' (service castes like shepherds, potters, etc.) have been able to rise in recent years to the status of middle peasants or even rich peasants. Previously their women did agricultural labour, but once they have achieved a certain economic status they subject their women to seclusion and strict patriarchal norms. The women cease to work on the land as a sign that they are no longer of the inferior class. They become 'housewives'.

Another example of the combination of class differentiation and polarization between the sexes is the spread of the dowry-system (bridegroom-price) even among poor peasants and agricultural labourers. These classes did not know the dowry before, but used to demand a nominal bride-price. This is logical in communities where women are productive workers. But when men of these communities migrate to the cities, or are able to rise in economic status, they, too, demand dowries from their prospective fathers-in-law. Other families, wanting to prove their 'higher' social status, begin to imitate such practices. The patriarchal dowry system spreads, and the result is that many poor peasants become indebted because they have to take loans to marry off their daughters.

4. The integration of subsistence production and subsistence producers into the process of capital accumulation is not a peaceful affair, but is accompanied by violence, compulsion and extra-economic coercion, all of which go towards greater extraction of surplus labour from the producers. Very often this violence has a distinct sexual dimension. On the one hand there is the 'feudal' violence of the land-owning classes. Rape and sexual humiliation of tribal women and poor peasant women are a common feature in rural India. This type of violence seems to be increasing as former feudal landlords take to capitalist farming.[28] But there is also the patriarchal violence of the husband against his wife. The more women have been excluded from the productive sphere, the more they have become dependent on their husband's income, the more the men seem to be using their power to harass and beat their wives.

Capitalist penetration has added yet another dimension, that is, the *state's* violence against the biological reproductive capacities of men and women. Since capitalism is not able to satisfy the subsistence needs of the masses of pauperized and marginalized people in India, the masses have to depend on procreation to safeguard their own survival. As has been well-publicized, however, the government's neo-Malthusian population policies and sterilization programmes have periodically been enforced with coercion and direct violence.[29]

5. Another consequence of capitalist penetration in India for women in the subsistence sector is the break-up of the traditional family as the location for reproduction. Pauperized men migrate to the cities and leave their wives in the village. Therefore, the women, often without any means of production, turn to begging, to prostitution, or to employment for less than the minimum wage. In any case, they become the main breadwinners of the broken family.

Theoretical implications

In attempting to understand the relationship between subsistence production and capitalism, the classical argument has been that the capitalist mode of production will ultimately 'free' all non-capitalist spheres and modes from their structural isolation and backwardness and integrate them into one homogeneous world system ruled by the laws of capital accumulation. Thus, development of these spheres and regions is seen as the repetition of the historic process of development which took place in the West, starting with the take-off point of the so-called primitive accumulation in the mercantile era. Yet, both a look at history and at an analysis of the inherent contradictions of the capitalist mode of production teach us that 'primitive accumulation' does not necessarily precede the process of capital accumulation. Rather, it is an ongoing process by which non-capitalist and structurally heterogeneous spheres are being tapped for the extraction of surplus labour and surplus product.

The recent discussion[30] on the modes of production and on 'ongoing primitive accumulation' and the reanalysis of Rosa Luxemburg's work (1913) on capital accumulation,[31] have gone a long way to explain the relationship between subsistence reproduction and capital accumulation. According to Rosa Luxemburg, capitalist penetration means both the destruction *and* the preservation of subsistence economies, or to use her expression, of natural economies. Her argument is that capital accumulation, i.e. the reproduction of capital, is not possible without the existence of non-capitalist strata and regions. The realization of surplus value is possible only if the means of consumption and the means of production produced, over and above the requirements of the workers and the capitalists in the capitalist centres, can be sold to non-capitalist strata and countries, that is to subsistence peasants and colonies. Similarly, capital accumulation requires that the means of production be constantly renewed and extended, even if this is not done within the classical wage labour capital relationship. Thirdly, the increase of capital accumulation is possible only with an increase of labour power. In sum there must always be non-capitalist spheres of production for the extension of the market, extension of the means of production and extension of labour power.

Rosa Luxemburg thought only of peasants and colonies as the non-capitalist strata and regions to be tapped in the process of capital accumulation.[32] C. K. Werlhof has extended her analysis to the area of female labour *both* in the capitalist centres (housework) and in the capitalist periphery. She argues that the dominant production relation of capitalism is not simply the relation between wage labour and capital, but that this relation itself has a double-faced character, one side being represented by the wage labour relation and the other by the non-wage labour relation of subsistence reproducer, particularly of women. Women form the basis for the process of ongoing primitive accumulation as the precondition for accumulation proper.[33] Primitive accumulation presupposes an ongoing process of use-value production, and women are, according to K. Sacks, typically the producers of use-values whereas men in all class societies produce for exchange.[34]

In the capitalist centres the household is the typical sphere for ongoing primitive accumulation and use-value production. As the 'free' wage labourer under capitalism has been robbed of the means of subsistence production she/he is dependent on a wage for the satisfaction of her/his basic needs. The wage, however, covers only the price of food, clothes, housing, etc. *not the work* that is necesary to transform these commodities bought from the wage into use-values. Housework under capitalism, therefore, means much more than what is usually termed as reproduction of the labour force. It is, in fact, the ongoing process of the production and reproduction of life which is still the material base for the reproduction of the labour force, to be bought and exploited in the process of capital accumulation. This work constitutes the hidden base on which the classical exploitation of wage labour by capital can take place.[35] Without the unpaid 'consumption work' and 'relationship work' of millions of housewives, no labourer would be able to sell 'living' labour force to the capitalist.[36] The labour of the housewife has typically *not* been transformed into wage labour.

Following this analysis it may be said that capitalist penetration does not mean the transformation of all non-capitalist subsistence production into capitalist production units and of the use-value producers into 'free' wage labourers. Even in the capitalist centres such a transformation has not happened. This preservation of strata and regions of subsistence production does not mean, however, that they remain unaffected or that they can retain control over their product and means of production once capitalist penetration has started. Capitalist penetration in fact, means a violent attack on these subsistence producers and their real or formal or marginal subsumption under capital.[37]

The classical process of pauperization and proletarianization of subsistence producers which took place in the capitalist centre is not repeated in the capitalist peripheries. The proletarianization of pauperized tribals, small peasants, and small artisans is marginal because the industrial sector in the periphery is frequently stagnant. The effect of capitalist penetration, therefore, is a rapid deterioration of the *living conditions* of these classes in general, and of the women in particular. In order to be able to survive the women either flock to the overcrowded cities and try to make a living in the slums with occasional jobs as house-servants, peddlars, beggars, petty criminals, prostitutes, etc.; or they remain in the rural areas – and this is the majority – and work for a wage below the subsistence level. As agricultural labourers they move about as migrant labour, recruited and exploited both sexually and as workers by labour contractors, landlords, and even the police. In many countries they have been deserted by their husbands who have migrated to the cities in search of work and are not able or willing to send any money back to their villages. They form an inexhaustible source of cheap labour, which may be tapped whenever some sporadic capitalist expansion may take place. It is characteristic of the present phase of development that the 'formal subsumption' of this vast pool of marginalized female labour under capital forms an important part of a global capitalist strategy.[38]

What can be done?

It is beyond the scope of this paper to draw the necessary strategic conclusions from the above analysis. Yet a few hints can be given for the development of a strategy aimed at the emancipation of subsistence reproducers.

First, if the thesis is accepted that capital accumulation, particularly in its present phase, produces an ever-increasing mass of marginalized population, above all of women, who simply have to struggle for survival, and that this marginal mass forms the hidden base for extra-profits, then it is inadequate to dismiss these subsistence reproducers as lumpen proletarians and expect all structural change only from the classical wage labourers. In view of the fact that in most peripheral countries it is a *privilege* to be able to sell one's labour power in the market,[39] the wage labour class may strive for economic betterment rather than for an overthrow of the system. A unity of all exploited can be brought about only when the classical proletarians understand that they themselves are continually threatened by marginalization.

Secondly, it is equally inadequate to juxtapose, mechanically, class-contradictions and the man–women contradiction and to ask: What comes first, what comes second? Imposition of capitalist production relations does not only lead to a deterioration of women's status. The fight against sexism must, therefore, become an integral part of any strategy aimed at eliminating all class rule. To define women's liberation only as a tactical goal in the process of class struggle misses the main point.

Thirdly, if the exploitation of women's subsistence work forms the main base on which wage exploitation can take place, then this exploitation cannot be fought unless the sexist reproduction relations, mainly in the family, are revolutionized. In order to unveil the hidden character of these exploitative relations it is necessary to give up the *family* as the basic unit in our analysis and strategy. We have to ask rather what happens to individuals – women, children and men – in the process of capitalist penetration. Most studies of the rural class structure are based on the household as the basic unit. The economic status of the household, however, is usually defined by the status of the male head, whose status is mostly higher than that of the women and children.

Finally, if the family is abandoned as the unit for defining economic and political status and the analysis is done along sex-specific lines, the relationship between sex- and class-polarization would become clearer. At the present stage of my research, it is not possible to present enough factual evidence to further our understanding of this relationship. Yet, the Indian example and even some of the material presented here may give us some clue. The social history of the caste system teaches us that hierarchical caste divisions have been used to uphold hypergamous marriage relations.[40] This means that upper-caste men could always have access to lower-caste or 'untouchable' women – within or without marriage – but their own women were 'protected' from the men of the lower castes. In this non-reciprocal relationship, sanctioned by Hindu religion, low-caste women were exploited sexually and economically to enhance the upper-castes' population, and their political and economic power. Their wives were protected to guarantee that the property thus accumulated could be inherited by the 'real' sons only. If we look at contemporary India and the class differentiations taking place under the impact of capitalism, we find similar mechanisms at work. Whenever tribal men and women in India are being proletarianized, i.e. recruited as labourers for plantations, coal mines, etc., the women are not only exploited as labourers along with their men, but caste Hindus usually make them into prostitutes because of the freer and more egalitarian relationship prevailing between tribal men and women. They are less 'protected'. (The case of Santhal women in the coal mines of Chota Nagpur is the best known example.)

In this process the relationship between tribal men and women is also transformed. If the women want to defend themselves against the sexual exploitation of non-tribal men, they have to imitate the 'decent' behaviour of the women of the upper castes; they have to accept patriarchal behaviour patterns. But then their husbands also may imitate the sexist behaviour of their masters or overlords. A consequence of this analysis would be to fight the sexist norms, customs and institutions of the dominant classes and their claim to be advanced or progressive compared to the 'backward' castes and classes.

Notes

1. F. Engels, 'Der Ursprung der Familie, des Privateigentums und des Staates' (1884) (Verlag Marxistische Blätter, 1969).

2. K. Marx, *The German Ideology*, (1844) (ed.) C. J. Arthur (New York, 1970), p. 356.

3. H. D. Evers, 'Subsistence Reproduction': Introductory paper for the Conference on Subsistence Reproduction in Southeast Asia, the University of Bielefeld, West Germany, 1978; K. Marx, *Capital*, Volume II (London: 1974) Chapter 21.

4. V. Bennholt-Thomsen, *Marginalität in Latin Amerika. Eine Theorie-kritic in Latinamerika, Analysen and Berichte 3, Verelendungsprozesse und Widerstandsformen* (Berlin: Olle and Wolter, 1979). (Hereafter, Benholt-Thomsen, *Marginalität.*)

5. Anibal Quijano, 'Notas sobre el concepto de marginalidad social', (CEPAL, Oct., 1966), and Jose Nun, 'Superpoblacion relativa, ejercito industrial de reserva y masa marginal', in *Revista Latinamericana de Sociologia*, No. 2. 1969; Eric Hobsbawm, 'La marginalidad social en la historia de la industrializacion europea', also in *Revista*, 1969; Fernando Henrique Cardoso 'Comentario Sobre los Conceptos de Sobrepoblacion Relativa y Marginalidad' in *Revista Latinamericana de Ciencias Sociales*, Volume 1/2, 1971, pp. 57–76.

6. Lucio Kowarick, *Capitalismo e Marginalidade na America Latina* (Rio de Janeiro, 1975).

7. F. Frobel, J. Heinrichs and O. Kreye, 'Die neue internationale Arbeitsteilung: strukturelle Arbeitslösigkeit in den Industrieländern und die Industrialisierung der Entwicklungs-länder rororo aktuell' (Reinbeck, 1977). Maria Mies, 'Social Origins of the

Sexual Division of Labour', paper given at the Conference on Subsistence Reproduction, the University of Bielefeld, West Germany, 1978.

8. Esther Boserup, *Women's Role in Economic Development* (New York: St. Martin's Press, 1970). Meillassoux, (ed.) *L'esclavage dans L'Afrique pre-coloniale* (Paris: Maspero, 1975). In stressing the importance of women in these 'economies domestiques', Meillassoux has asserted that the wealth of these societies depends on the control over additional women whose reproductive functions as bearers of children are being appropriated by men. Though it is correct that these economies are interested in the increase of labourers and therefore need women as child-bearers, Meillassoux seems to reduce women to their biological functions only and to underestimate their role as primary producers of the means of subsistence. In fact, what distinguishes women in subsistence reproduction in the capitalist periphery from their sisters in the capitalist centres is the fact that they are still actively involved in the production of food, of clothes, of fetching water and fuel, of making utensils, etc., in short, in the production of use-values. They have not been reduced to 'mere housewives' dependent on the wage of the husband.

9. Government of India, 'Towards Equality'; Report of the Committee on the Status of Women in India, 1974.

10. Asok Mitra, 'The Status of Women', in *Frontier*, June 18, 1977.

11. Asok Mitra, *India's Population: Aspects of Quality and Control* (New Delhi, 1978) p. 393.

12. K. Dandekar, cited in Mitra, *ibid.*, 390–2.

13. *Ibid.*, 393.

14. ICSSR, 'Critical Issues on the Status of Women in India' (New Delhi: Advisory Committee on Women's Studies, 1977).

15. Gail Omvedt, 'Women and Rural Revolt in India', in *Social Scientist*, Trivandrum, October–November, 1977.

16. Mitra, 1978, pp. 449–50.

17. Mitra, 1978, p. 441.

18. Kanti Pandey, 'Unprotected Rural Workers' in *Economic Times*, 24 August 1975. A recent study, *Bonded Labor in India*, (done by the National Labor Institute and the Gandhi Peace Movement in 1978 and edited by Sharma Marla) has revealed that almost 5% of the agricultural labour force are caught up in debt-serfdom and are not free to sell their labour in the open market. The commercialization of agriculture seems to lead to an increase of bonded labor: 56% of the bonded labourers went into bondage only in the last three years. A bonded labourer is a cheaper and more reliable worker for a landlord or rich peasant.

19. Tribes constitute 6.94% of the total Indian population (*Statistical Abstracts*, 1976). They are the descendants of the original inhabitants of the land who were driven into inaccessible hill tracts. They do not form part of the Hindu caste system.

20. For example, one of the 'bad' habits of tribal women is not to wear blouses, but to cover their breasts only with the loose end of their sari. In the *ashram* schools all girls are to be taught to wear sari-blouses given to them free by the government. As the sari-blouse has become a symbol of progress among tribal women, they need money to buy the material and to have the blouse stitched by a tailor.

21. Another instance of marginalization of rural women was brought to my attention in a study on the impact of development measures on women in the command area of the Nagarjunasagar dam. This study is being carried out by the Administrative Staff, College of India. Since the last years of the Fourth Five Year Plan, Command Area Development (CAD) has emerged as the leading strategy for agricultural development in areas covered by irrigation schemes. The objective of CAD is to 'maximize the agricultural production in tons as related to the volume of water available'. S. Sarupria and K. V. S. Sastri, 'Regional Development Planning for Command Areas in Andhra Pradesh' (Hyderabad: The Indian Institute of Economics, 1977). The emphasis is clearly on capitalist farming. In the newly irrigated areas, cash crop production – particularly rice cultivation – was started on a large scale. Many of the small peasants in the Nagarjunasagar area lost their land to the rapidly expanding rich peasants who were able to get the credits and other development inputs. The population in the irrigated areas grew faster than in the non-irrigated areas as both the rich peasants who bought the irrigated land and agricultural labourers have immigrated.

In one block of the Nagarjunasagar command area I was told that the men had taken over rice transplantation which, since time immemorial, has been a 'women's job' in the whole of India. This is the first instance I have heard in which this pattern of division of labour between the sexes has been upset. (In West Godavari, one of the centres of rice cultivation along capitalist lines [tractors are much in use], women are still used for rice transplantation.) Men have also taken over weeding which had been a 'woman's job' before. Further changes in the sexual division of labour to the disadvantage of women may be expected in the future.

22. It is very difficult to get exact figures on the volume of export of lace for the exporters. Most of them deal directly with the importing firms. The figures cited were given by the Director of Industries, Hyderabad. They cover those exporters who have approached the government for the export incentive of 15%. According to an estimate of the manager of the leading bank in Narsapur, the export of lace amounts to Rs.5–10 million per year (1977–78).

23. The minimum wage for female agricultural labourers ranges between Rs.2 and Rs.4, according to the area and the type of work.

The manufacturers contend that the women are sitting in their house and do not want to work outside. If they, the manufacturers, were not to give the women employment, the latter would have nothing to do. They argue further that the women belong to castes – mainly the Kapu and the Agnikulakshatriya – who have always kept their women in the house or under seclusion. In fact Kapu women themelves confirm this view regarding their caste, but it is very doubtful whether this statement is totally correct. Most of the Kapus are small agriculturists. In the whole of Andhra Pradesh, women have had a tradition of working in the fields and so have Kapu women in other areas. The Agnikulakshatriyas are fishermen and traditionally in these communities women do the selling of the fish. Now they have given up this activity and have become 'women sitting in the house'.

24. Boserup, 1970. This example illustrates how capital accumulation and integration of local industries into the world market finds its best precondition in a situation where masses of pauperized women can be exploited and where the ideology of the housewife, the 'woman sitting in the house' is propagated. The male exporters who market their products and make tremendous profits then appear as benefactors, 'giving' work to women who would otherwise starve. The building-up of capitalist production relations in this area was identical with, and inseparable from, the strengthening of patriarchal and sexist men–women relations.

25. Karen Sacks, 'Engels Revisited: Women, the Organization of Production, and Private Property' in E. Z. Rosaldo and L. Lamphere (eds.) 'Women, Culture and Society (Stanford, CA: Stanford University Press, 1973). This is usually the case when poor rural men migrate to the cities in search of jobs and leave their families behind. This process can be observed mainly in Africa and Latin America but also in India. In some parts of South-East Asia, however (Singapore, Taiwan, South Korea, Thailand), where Free Production Zones and World Market Factories are established, young women form up to 80% of the industrial labour force. The polarization of the sexes takes place in these zones through extreme exploitation of women. It is facilitated, as in the Narsapur case, by the diversification of the production process and the strengthening of a patriarchal and sexist ideology. Women have to leave the job when they get married or have children. Carmen D. Deere, 'Rural Women's Subsistence Production in the Capitalist Periphery' in *Review of Radical Political Economics*, Volume 8, No. 1, 1976. Also Frobel, Heinrichs and Kreve, 1977.

26. Technology is another field where women are losing out to men. Whereas men and women's technology in the subsistence economy, though different due to the traditional pattern of sexual division of labour, was mainly used for the production of use values, the new technology which is aimed at the production of exchange values is frequently controlled by men. Women's old technology and skills are rendered obsolete as new, labour-saving, capital-intensive equipment is introduced. When such technology is introduced into spheres which were traditionally women's jobs, the women are pushed out and replaced by men.

Due to the contradictions of the capitalist accumulation process in these dependent economies, the replacement of 'traditional' labour-intensive, low-productivity technology by capital-intensive labour-saving technology, can never be absolute. The old technology may become obsolete, but it remains in the hands of women who continue to use it to supplement their men's low income. Therefore, we find the most primitive technology still being used by women alongside highly sophisticated modern technology that is controlled by men. This is the case, for example, in construction, in sweeping factories, and in agriculture. In their homes women have to stick to their old ways of producing, preserving and preparing food. The proverbial conservatism of women may have its roots in the fact that they are excluded from the control over new technologies which are used for exchange value production.

27. In most coastal fishermen's communities in Andhra Pradesh, fish selling had always been a women's job. When fish-canning factories and freezing centres were introduced, the men began selling the fish to these centres. A similar process could be observed in the Anand Dairy Cooperative Scheme in Gujarat where milk and milk products were produced along capitalist lines and marketed in the cities (Operation Flood I and II). Women, who had formerly done not only most of the work in the feeding and milking of the buffaloes but had also marketed the milk, are now completely out of the picture in the Anand complex. (Cf. Rami Chabra, *Indian Express*, 15 July 1978.)

28. Hardly a day passes without reports on so-called atrocities against the rural poor appearing in the newspapers. These atrocities invariably include rape of women. Though rape is definitely on the increase, the newspaper-reading public has become so used to these reports and so callous, that rape and sexual violence hardly provoke any reaction.

29. Maria Mies, 'Frauen–das überflüssige Geschlecht' and 'Der Kampf gegen die Armen' in Mies, Daibler, v. Werlhof and Lenz (eds.) *Frauen in der Dritten Welt*, 1978.

30. In West Germany this new debate started when some women and men linked up the dependency theory with the discussion on housework in capitalism. The Center for Development Studies at the University of Bielefeld has provided a forum for this debate through a series of seminars on subsistence reproduction in Asia, Africa and Latin America. The main participants of this debate are: C. v. Werlhof, Veronika Bennholt-Thomsen, T. Schiel, H. D. Evers, M. Mies, and E. Senghaas Knobloch.

31. Amando Cordova, 'Rosa Luxemburg und die Dritte Welt' in Claudio Pozzoli (ed.), *Rosa Luxemburg oder die Bestimmung des Sozialismus* (Frankfurt 1977). André Gunder Frank, 'On So-called Primitive Accumulation' in Frank, *World Accumulation, 1492–1789* (New York: Monthly Review Press, 1976; London: MacMillan Press, 1978). Eva Senghaas-Knobloch, 'Weibliche Arbeitskraft und gesellschaftlich Reproduktion' in *Leviathan* (4/4), 1976.

32. Rosa Luxemburg, *Die Akkumulation des Kapitals* (1913) (Frankfurt: Archiv sozialistischer Literatur, 1970).

33. Claudia v. Werlhof, 'Zu den Folgen der Einbeziehung der Frauenfrage in die Kritik der Politischen Okonomie' in Beiträge zur Feministischen Theorie und Praxis, 1, 1978.

34. Sacks, 1973.

35. v. Werlhof, 1978.

36. Batya Weinbaum and Amy Bridges, 'The Other Side of the Paycheck: Monopoly Capital and the Structure of Consumption' in *Monthly Review* (Vol. 28, no. 3) July–August, 1976, pp. 88–103. Eli Zaretzki, *Capitalism, The Family and Personal Life* (New York: Harper & Row, 1973).

37. Veronika Bennholdt-Thomsen, 'Probleme der Klassenanalyse des Agrärsektors in Staten weltmarktabhängiger Reproduktion' in *Bielefelder Stüdien zur Entwicklungssoziologie*, Nr. 5: Subsistenz-produktion und Akkumulation, Verlag Breitenbach, Saarbrücken, 1979). It is misleading to call these forms of subsistence production non-capitalist (as R. Luxemburg did) or pre-capitalist as is often done in the discussion on the mode of production. Capital accumulation thus takes place on the ruins of these economies. Capital has always used the same tactics in its attack on the subsistence economies. It first destroys the means of production of the producers or robs them, cheats them, etc. Then it recruits the 'freed' labourers as wage labourers and makes them dependent at the same time on the commodity market for their subsistence.

38. A critique of this strategy has been made by Veronika Bennholt-Thomśen in 'Investition in die Armen: Zur Entwicklungspolitik der Weltbank', unpublished manuscript, Bielefeld, 1978.

39. According to several informants, no one will get a job as an ordinary factory worker in IDL Chemicals, a reputed Indian chemical concern, unless he pays Rs. 2,000 as a bribe. In one

case a girl, who could not pay this sum, asked a contractor to advance her this sum. Yet since she is giving all her salary to her family she has no means to repay the loan. The contractor therefore uses her freely as an unpaid bonded prostitute. He does not even allow her to get married. These examples show what a 'privilege' it is to be able to sell one's labour power in India.

40. One of the more well known Indian examples of the inter-relation between sexual differentiation and class differentiation is the case of the matrilineal and polyandrous Nayars of Kerala. The Nayar men who were recruited by the British Administration as clerks and civil servants emerged as a new class who possessed money income whereas the large Nayar *taravad* (the matrilineal joint family) had common property or land. The British interpreted the Nayar men–women relationship as promiscuous and made the appropriate laws for these men to bequeath the self-earned income to their own sons and not to their sisters' children as had been the rule in this matrilinear and matrilocal community.

At the same time new marriage laws were introduced which imposed monogamy and patriarchal marriage relationships between men and women. Under the impact of the new concept of private property and the sexist bourgeois ideology, these Nayar men began to be ashamed of the polyandrous marriage relationships of their mothers and the practical absence of the concept of fatherhood. As this new form of patriarchalism served their own interests and appeared with a claim to modernity and progress, the Nayar men eagerly seized this opportunity to raise their class status. I. Karve, *Kinship Organisation in India* (Bombay, 1965); K. E. Gough, 'Is Family Universal? The Nayar Case' in N. W. Bell and E. F. Vogel (eds.) *The Family* Glencoe, Ill.: The Free Press, 1960).

It would be necessary to document further the interplay between sexism and class-formation with evidence from Africa and Latin America. At the moment I can only advise the reader to study Meillassoux's work on slavery in precolonial Africa and Karen Sack's 'Engels Re-visited' (1973). It seems obvious from these examples that 'private property' and a new class of owners of this private property was built up through *razzias* which included the kidnapping of women as slaves and producers of slaves. I would argue, therefore, that the first form of private property was not land or cattle but 'private' women – not born in the clan, but kidnapped and appropriated both as workers and producers of workers.

3. 'Investment in the Poor': An Analysis of World Bank Policy*

Veronika Bennholdt-Thomsen

The World Bank (International Bank for Reconstruction and Development/IBRD) is the most powerful development agency in the world.[2] Its policy strongly influences the course of events in Third World and its relation to the First World. There has been a shift in the World Bank policy since 1973. It is the attack on absolute poverty through 'investment in the poor' themselves, that is, in small scale production. Previously, only large scale industrial production had been considered a worthwhile investment as a development asset. 'In retrospect, it is clear that too much confidence was placed on the belief that rapid economic growth would automatically result in the reduction of poverty, corresponding to the "trickle-down" theory'. (Robert McNamara, President appears to be directed entirely towards the needs of the poor strata of 1977.) The strategy to achieve development now suggested by the Bank's President appears to be directly entirely towards the needs of the poor strata of the population. According to McNamara, the ways 'in which basic human needs can be met earlier in the development process' must be found . . . To the extent that the poor possess some tangible assets, however meagre, it is possible to help them become more productive.' (1977).

Surplus extraction from the poor or from wage workers only?

The concept of 'absolute' as against 'relative poverty' was first introduced by McNamara in his annual speech to the Board of Governors in Nairobi in 1973.

> Relative poverty means simply that a few countries are less well-off than others or that some citizens of a country have less wealth than their neighbours. Absolute poverty, on the other hand, is characterised by a state of degrading life conditions such as disease, illiteracy, malnutrition and

*The expression 'investment in the poor' stems from two World Bank experts themselves: Chenery and Ahluwalia, 1974.

This article was first published in English in: *Social Scientist*, Vol. 8, no. 7, Feb. 1980 (first part) and Vol. 8, no. 8, March 1980; in German in: Bennholdt-Thomsen et al (eds), *Lateinamerika, Analysen und Berichte 4*, Berlin 1980.[1]

neglect, and the victims of this poverty are unable to satisfy the most basic of their human needs.

Approximately 40% of the population in the developing countries, mostly in the rural areas, exist in this state of 'absolute poverty'. In some cases this is essentially owing to the peasants' low productivity and, therefore, in order to alleviate absolute poverty, it is necessary to increase their productivity. McNamara identified land and rent reforms, credits for the 'small farmers', the application of a cheap and simple technology and the construction of roads, storehouses, market places and schools as the most important measures to facilitate greater productivity.[3]

This shift to a concern for absolute poverty is astonishing, especially for the critics of the World Bank, who, from their knowledge of the Bank's policy, find it difficult to believe that the IBRD is suddenly concerned with the poorest of the poor, even though they constitute the majority of the world's people. The tenor of their analyses is, therefore, to prove that this new focus is mere eye-wash.

Ernest Feder argues that: 1) in reality the World Bank uses only a minimum portion of its credit for agricultural programmes; 2) even this portion may in no way actually be intended for the 'small farmers'. Rather it is meant to benefit the middle to the larger farmers, because only in this way can a good bargain be made. Credits for 'small farmers' would mean losing money. Hence, Feder sees the programme to combat absolute poverty as weak, since the actual operation would only lead to a greater differentiation within the rural population with enterprise and accumulation on the one side and further marginalization on the other. (Feder, 1976)

Susan George sees the new style of the World Bank as politically motivated, namely, to contain the socially explosive potential of the impoverished masses by giving them hope. In her opinion, this is a middle course between total breakdown and revolution. It will not work, however, since the programme is aimed at the creation of development enclaves. It may bring about a rural progress which is unachievable for the country as a whole, and with which the country has no cogent relationship. (George 1978)

My own opinion is that the World Bank's policy of investment in the poor is not 'eye-wash' but in fact *is* directed at absolute poverty and especially the peasants; the goal to increase the productivity of these 'self-employed producers' actually exists. Contrary to the opinions of Feder and George, I think the programme fits very well into the World Bank's overall political and economic function and ideology; and in accordance with this economic function the programme will work successfully. Feder's and George's error is that they fail to see the ideology of the Bank's apologists as a reflection of economic interests, because they do not appreciate, as does the World Bank, that investing in the poor can be profitable.[4]

Apart from the resonating undertone of beneficience, the World Bank theoreticians provide sufficiently numerous arguments for the profitability of such investments. Lester Brown, of the Overseas Development Council, the

United States development agency, which co-operates closely with the World Bank, makes clear what constitutes the main reason for the interest in the poor: 'Indeed, idle manpower constitutes a valuable but wasted resource . . . That this will simultaneously help to meet world food needs (keeping food prices lower for everyone) . . . is a further incentive for pursuing such a strategy.' Under the title, 'The Need for Investment in the Poor', Ahluwalia and Chenery (1974, 225) write: 'While this strategy has shortrun cost to the upper-income groups, in the long run they may even benefit from the "trickle-up" effects of greater productivity and purchasing power of the poor.' (1974, 48) In his 1973 speech, McNamara mentions not only the political but also the economic side of this phenomenon: 'A continual increase in inequality gives rise to a growing danger for the political stability . . . In the long run this development will be an advantage for the privileged, as also for the poor.'

It is obvious that investment in the poor is supposed to benefit the privileged. What has to be explained is the mechanism through which these benefits are realized. Feder and George assume that the World Bank representatives are deliberately raising false hopes for the poor because they cannot believe such a mechanism might exist. They continue to believe solely in a model of capitalist profit and accumulation through wage labour, concentration of production, big enterprises and big technology which, however, does not accord with reality.

This problem not only emerges in relation to the World Bank policy; it refers in general to the evaluation of the function of peasants, other private-owning producers and the so-called surplus population in capitalist accumulation. Neither neoclassical nor Marxian economics have any categories which enable them to come to grips with the subordination of these workers under capital and capitalist valuation. This absence of concept has to be understood – especially in the Marxist–Leninist approach to political economy – against the background of the thesis that peasants and craftsmen are private-owning producers who, as remnants of the pre-capitalist mode of production, would disappear with capitalist penetration. But this contradicts historical evidence. These sectors in the developing countries, in the form in which they exist today, have emerged only with capitalist development. If one refrains from treating the majority of the world population as an economic residual category as Marxism and neoclassical theory does, then its simultaneous expansion with capitalist expansion points to the need to analyse it together with the capital valuation process.

From this point of view it is significant that the new strategy of the World Bank is not to create jobs in industrial plants, rather, it seems to revert to pre-capitalist forms of production, in so far as the direct producers should become owners. The implications of this are threefold:

1. It is apparently clear from this developmet policy itself, that an absorption of the unemployed through wage contracts is not possible, and also, as we shall see, not even opportune, contrary to what is generally implied.

2. For reasons relating to the entire structure of the World Bank, this form of

production must also at least cover costs, if not be profit-generating. Otherwise, such a programme would not be implemented.

3. The fact, that the World Bank promotes the re-establishment of workers, who at the same time are owners of the means of production, should help to make clear that these forms of production do not always imply pre-capitalist forms of production. Rather, they are forms of production particularly exploitable for the accumulation process.

This World Bank policy is aimed at increasing the productivity of the private- or self-owning producers.[5] As already indicated, to doubt this aim, or that it can be achieved, is wrong. What can justifiably be questioned is whether it would result in a simultaneous increase in consumption for the producers. Nevertheless, the belief that this would be the result persists, based on the conception that under capitalism self-owning producers are small, independent entrepreneurs, because they themselves own the means of production and shoulder the responsibility. Investment in their enterprise would, therefore, mean higher level returns for them. This appearance of independence is, however, deceptive. Indeed, the actual production process is not under the direct management and control of their little 'capital', but indirectly is subjugated by big capital. Hence, the surplus product realized through productivity increase, manifests itself not as profit for the producers but as profit for the various (really entrepreneurial) capital factions.

Forms of subordination of work under capitalism

In order to grasp the specific relationship between these workers and capitalism, new categories need to be introduced. Following Marx's terminology I opt here for a differentiation of forms of 'subsumption' or 'subordination' of workers under capitalism.

In the case of wage labour, the subordination arises from the fact that labour power itself is sold. Marx has called this 'real' subsumption, as he considered wage labour in the final form in which all work would be done under capitalism; which would thus be 'real' capitalism. In the case of the small producers, themselves owning the means of production, the subordination under capital arises from the fact that they sell their product. Here two forms can be distinguished: market subsumption and formal subsumption. Marx recognized only 'formal subsumption' and that only as transitional towards 'real' subsumption which, we now know is erroneous. I, therefore, shall use 'formal' along with 'market subsumption' as actual and non-transitional forms.

Market subsumption means that the small producers have free access to the market and can decide to whom, when and how to sell. Hence it is the 'blind mechanism' of circulation that subordinates them under capitalism, because they cannot influence the prices they get for their products. They are, in fact, in a disadvantaged position *vis-à-vis* the price-building process, because they produce the same commodities for the same market as those produced by industrial entrepreneurs. It is these entrepreneurs who can dictate the prices, who can sell at lower prices than small producers (because of their exploitation of wage labour together with mechanization) and who can react with more flexibility to price changes or production failures (because of their capital support). But peasants are not capitalists who orientate their production according to expected average profit; they produce not to accumulate but to survive. In contrast to capitalist entrepreneurs, it is not possible for them to respond to market changes by productivity increasing through investments since the returns from the commodities are first needed for consumption. Neither can they invest in other, more lucrative production sectors, as their 'capital' is tied to land. The alternative of hiring themselves out as wage labourers is similarly unlikely because of the lack of work. Hence, they are forced to produce under extremely disadvantageous conditions: circulation's 'blind mechanism' treats them as it does capital, even though their method of operation is not the same as capital's. For the craftsmen who are forced to enter into these exchange relations, the costs of the physical reproduction of labour power have to be minimized in order that their products can be sold at all. It means, above all, the so-called phenomenon of 'self-exploitation': under-nourishment, malnutrition and early death. The equal treatment of the unequal leads to their exploitation. This exploitative relationship rests on a capitalist relation of production, since the independent value-generating law of the capitalist market asserts itself behind the back of the producer and manifests itself in the production sphere.

The same process which spontaneously gives rise to market subsumption, when controlled, results in formal subsumption. The control arises from granting of credits to the small producers. Mediated through the credit, a given capital obtains control over the producers and that means a direct hold over their surplus labour. Unlike in the case of an enterprise, the administration of the credit is not considered to be the business of the credit recipients; it remains in the hands of the credit-giving institution. In most cases the credit is given by instalments and has to be used for specific inputs and labour processes that have been fixed beforehand. In addition, the credit recipients are obliged to sell to a specific wholesaler, at a price which can be fixed in advance or can be unfavourable because of abundance at peak seasons. These additional conditions are introduced because with small producers there exists the danger of their using the credit for subsistence goods and not for the aimed surplus product. Because of a minimum investment, which the producer himself bears additionally, capital is in a position to determine the course of the production process and to dictate the quality criteria since the credits are deducted from the returns from the products. In this form of subordination under capital, market mechanisms, such as the exchange of commodity against money, orientation to market prices and so on are used. However, this is more apparent than real. Hence the differentiation towards the form of free, or mere market access is necessary. The exchange that consequently emerges is more a hidden form of wages, comparable to piece-rate wages, since payment takes place through the product. Yet, it is not the labour power of the producers themselves but the whole production process, for which they are responsible, which is subordinated under capital; this is why I call it not *real* but *formal* subsumption. The investment in the formally subsumed production process is subjected to less risks for the investor than that under real subsumption; at the same time, the entire course of the production process is more controllable than in market subsumption. Thus fluctuations in market prices can be used to benefit the credit-givers, while production errors and crop failures are a charge on the producers.

In agriculture the subordination of small producers through credit mechanisms has become the predominant form throughout the world within the last 40 years. Contrary to Marx's opinion, market, not formal subsumption can be considered as transitional, because as a dominant form it belongs to the past; but it re-emerges with every so-called self-employed activity of the informal sector, but will certainly be transformed into formal subsumption as soon as it promises to be profitable. That this will happen much earlier or more easily than the founding of an enterprise with wage-workers is obvious. In formal subsumption the responsibility and thus the commitment of the immediate producer differs from that of wage-workers. The risk for a potential investor is, therefore, much lower; the return quicker and higher.

With the formal subordination of the peasants under capital a 'wonderful way' which allows capital to invest profitably in poverty, has been found. The profit realizes itself as such in the spheres of inputs and outputs and not in the actual production process. Nevertheless, it is produced within the peasant family operation itself. Indeed, capital does not undertake responsibility for the production process. The living labour power of the peasant family is absorbed through repayment by working; a system that Lenin thought to be already disappearing in Russia at the turn of the century. This is different from wage labour where the wages, regulated by entrepreneurs, have to cover the reproduction costs of the labour power. The employer is thus made directly responsible for the reproduction of the workers, since there is a direct relation between wages and reproduction level. In contrast the formally subsumed producers can be made responsible even for the low level of their reproduction which in reality is not caused by them.

IBRD is a capitalist bank: Profits are secured

The aim of the rural development programmes is at its clearest in so far as the repayment of credits is concerned. The credit experts of the World Bank speak of 'the farmers' failure to use borrowed funds for productive purposes'. (World Bank, Agricultural Credit 1975:41) 'Low interest rates may also encourage delinquency . . . ' (Ibid) 'The farmer's lack of enthusiasm [sic!] toward repayment is worsened by the unwillingness of governments to impose sanctions, through their credit institutions, on those whose debts are overdue.' (Ibid) But already state repression seems to be functioning sufficiently well, since 'experience shows that except for a few countries, recuperation of large portions of arrears is usually possible over a large number of years. On bank-assisted projects, losses resulting from defaults have seldom exceeded 5% of loans outstanding.' (Ibid)

The concern is also to reduce the cost of control by keeping down the number of bank employees. The World Bank experts speak of a 'waste of manpower' in this connection. In order to avoid this, the peasants should not be made individually liable; credit should, instead, be given to a larger group within which the individuals control each other. 'The best prospects, in the future, will lie in some form of group responsibility for individual borrowings . . . ' (Ibid) When this is still not effective the responsibility for the administrative costs should be shifted to the farmers: 'Farmers should generally be required to contribute to the costs of the investment for which they are borrowing. This would emphasize their responsibility for making it a success . . .' (ibid) And if this still does not work, because the peasants have no money, then there is yet another possibility: 'great flexibility is necessary with regard to small farmers, such as acceptance of a contribution in labor'. (Ibid) Big international capital thus uses the system of repay-work to pay off!

The 'feasibility' of credit programmes, however, is linked not only to repayment guarantees, but is fundamentally based in several extractive mechanisms. Thus, this agricultural development policy builds a package which is summarized below:

> The farmers use the funds to purchase productive inputs – fertilizers, seeds, pesticides, livestock, tubewells, machinery – which are combined with family labor to produce more output. The *additional output* is sold, the proceeds being sufficient to repay the loan and still leaving the farmer better off. The payments received from the farmers by the agricultural bank are adequate to cover administrative costs, to pay the interest on the government loan and to regenerate lending capacity. (Ibid. emphasis mine)

Thus:

1. *The peasants should buy the international monopolist firms' inputs.* That is, the inputs of the actual farm production process.

2. In the actual production process *as much labour power as possible should be mobilized*.

3. Through this, *the marketable quantity of the products should be increased*.

4. *The consumption fund of the farmers* is considered only, if at all, *a marginal problem*. This means: get as much as possible out of the farmers by leaving the reproduction of this labour power to them.

5. The total credit operation must be able at least to *cover the costs for the bank*.

Paradoxically, the 'farmers' from whom all this is to be squeezed are defined as absolutely poor.

It should be asked how 'additional output' in this context is to be understood, that is, additional to what? A paradox runs throughout the whole argument: on the one hand the target group is identified on the basis that their living conditions are at mere or subsistence level or below it; and on the other, in the formulation of the programme, this consideration is completely disregarded. As the minimum subsistence level has been identified as the basic problem, presumably the strategy would be aimed at raising that level. But in reality the concern is not to increase the peasants' consumption but to increase the *marketable output*!

The goal is 'to draw farmers from subsistence to commercial agriculture' (World Bank 1975:20), meaning: how can the production of a commercially viable product be increased at the expense of a subsistence product? 'Delinquencies have also been reduced when repayment has been coordinated with the marketing of crops that are centrally processed, e.g. tobacco, cotton, cocoa, tea and coffee.' (Ibid:43) Monocultural products clearly pose fewer problems *vis-à-vis* repayment, as the peasant family cannot feed itself with all of them.

The consequences arising from monoculture for subsistence have been impressively analysed in the study by the *Comité d'information Sahel* (1975), which demonstrates that it was not climatic conditions that were primarily responsible for the famine in the Sahel zone, but rather the reduction of foodstuff production in favour of groundnut cultivation. But the World Bank experts have suggested how responsibility for climatic variations and other environmental risks can be shifted on to the peasants:

> Following a bad harvest, credit agencies frequently adjust repayment terms either through renewals or postponement of maturity dates. However, most of the available data indicate that once a loan is in arrears, collection is both difficult and costly. This attests that in areas where output is highly variable, it might be possible to employ contracts whereby the credit agency would be paid a percentage of the farmer's output rather than a fixed amount. Such share-cropping arrangements are quite common for land rentals. (World Bank, 1975)

In short, big international finance capital, which supposedly brings modernization and development, falls back on production relations that have commonly been labelled as traditional or pre-capitalist. But it is, in fact, more accurate to recognize that this seeming backwardness is, in reality, modernity.

When the first goal of credit policy consists in drawing peasants away from subsistence to commodity or market production, then the second goal consists in maintaining them in the market. The credit is intended to prevent them being completely forced out of competition.

Subordination under capital, mediated through the market, leads to a situation in which, finally, the peasants are no longer able to reproduce themselves by means of the sale of their produce. The consequence is either to increase production for their own consumption or to abandon their peasant enterprise and become under- or unemployed wage labourers. It means that not only must the existence of the peasants be guaranteed, but also their existence as commodity producers. For this purpose, their production must be capitalized so that their productivity adjusts to that of the larger enterprises, without, of course, becoming equal. What must be guaranteed is the co-existence of marketable commodities of big enterprises *and* peasants.

Alternatively, according to some theoretical models, agricultural production will be entirely taken over by big enterprises because peasants and small farmers will be forced out of the market. According to such models this should long since have happened. That it has not is owing to four main reasons:

1. Peasant production guarantees cheap agricultural products, since neither rent nor profit, nor even the reproduction costs of labour power, are realized here. In contrast, the factory- and business-type agricultural production would rapidly lead to foodstuffs becoming more expensive.

2. Also the demand for agricultural products is limited. Hence, it often does not pay to invest in marginal land. Nevertheless, a surplus product can always be extracted in these areas from small peasant production. (cf. Martine Alier 1967)

3. The structurally narrowed labour market makes it politically advisable to prevent peasant production from disintegrating. In this way the potential explosiveness of the pauperized sub-proletariat can be diverted. Agrarian reform cannot give land to everyone, but it does give hope and this works as a pacification mechanism. (Duran 1968:60f)

4. Finally, the above three advantages accruing from peasant production for a national economy can be combined with profit-making, as peasants can, through credit, be drawn from (relative) independence into the orbit of specific capital.

The baseline of this design is, however, the nuclear family with its specifically patriarchal structure. The nuclear family, consisting of women and children under the command of a male 'head of household', provides the cheapest reservoir of labour which can be mobilized simply by the exercise of patriarchal power. National and international policy can rely on the patriarchal family structure which has been established throughout the world by colonialism and reinforced by development policy in the last decades. And where this family does not yet function in the required form it will be installed by means of the agricultural programme to combat absolute poverty: the programme of credit to small-scale farms also called 'family units'. (Boserup 1970; Rogers 1980)

In a comparative study of five Latin American countries (Bolivia, Chile, Mexico, Peru and Venezuela) and data from South-East Asia, Africa, and the Middle East, World Bank authors conclude that all factors considered, small family units are the most efficient. (Eckstein et al 1978) They argue that it is short-sighted policy to favour large-scale enterprises on the basis that they show the highest value per hectare and, in the case of Mexico, have contributed most to agricultural production. Rather than evaluating on the basis of the output value per hectare and quantity of sales, the criteria they advocate for evaluation are: the best application and use of resources, with labourintensiveness regarded as the most important. The argument is well known:

> The smaller farmers . . . were found to be using less capital and fewer purchased non-labor inputs per hectare, but more man-days per hectare than were the larger farm units . . . if one has, as a shorter-run objective, research for the productive use of excess rural manpower which cannot be employed in towns and cities, then labor intensity takes on the virtue of employment generation. Another virtue of labor intensity in farming is that it can provide an economy with agricultural products in ways that use up fewer of those sources which, in developing countries, are generally more scarce than farm labor: financial capital, capital goods (often imported), and other manufactured inputs. In this sense labor-intensive methods may be more efficient overall as a use of society's resources, even though 'efficient' farming is normally thought to result from the use of non-labor inputs to enhance the productive efforts of the farmer. (Ibid:113–14)

In other words, the unpaid labour, which in cost benefit analysis is labelled 'owner's family labor shadow-priced at zero', makes the small family enterprise very efficient. It is easy to imagine that the mobilization of family work through some minor inputs improves their productivity; that is, the goal of the programme will be reached. But the benefit of increased productivity does not necessarily remain with, or satisfy the stomachs of, the producers themselves. On the contrary, they must pay back the input value which has already been shadow-priced at zero in advance. Against this background the absurd situation, which is widely observed among Third World peasants, can be clearly understood. They produce the food necessary for their own consumption and for the nourishment of their underfed children, but are forced to sell it.

A further aspect emphasized is the reduction of food prices for the working population.

> Another way of looking at the question of efficiency, given the divergence between product per hectare and total hectare productivity in these groups, is to consider the relative importance of two questions . . . : Either, who can extract the most value from a hectare of land? Or, who can produce staple food for the poor for lowest cost to society? The rich farmers, in Mexico and elsewhere, would often perform best for the first criterion, while the poor farmers would frequently qualify as superior by the second. (Ibid: 116–117)

The peasants, however, should not cultivate only essential foodstuffs. It is further argued that large enterprises' high returns can be traced back to the expensive production methods employed for the high-value cultivated products. 'If so, this production could perhaps be as well done in small units if the same access would be extended to them.' (Ibid)

Better use of land resources is identified as another decisive advantage of peasant production.

There is . . . a strong tendency in developing countries for land to be used more intensively by small than by large farmers . . . In particular, the greater application of family labor to given land areas by the smaller farmers is both logical and demonstrable . . . And this in itself constitutes a reasonable strong argument for subdividing large estates into smaller units as a means of increasing national output. (Ibid: 118)

Finally, the question of why should one of the most unreservedly capitalist agencies as the World Bank plead for such a revolutionary goal as land reform can be answered: not land reform itself, but the manipulation of the patriarchal nuclear family and its profitability is the revolutionary, modernizing and developmental end.

In summary, the main aim of this chapter is to show that the wage form is not the only – and certainly not the most important – means of extracting profit. Other forms of subordination of labour exist under capital which are even more profitably exploitable. The World Bank's policy towards Third World poverty is not window-dressing, but an appropriate project for such a large financial enterprise: investment in the poor is profitable. The main profit-procuring instrument is the granting of credit by means of which the poor can be drawn away from subsistence to commercial production. Thus, subsistence production and, in general, time for subsistence work – time and work for one's own immediate use and consumption – were and remain the battlefield of profit-making. In contrast to what is generally assumed, this applies not only or mainly to necessary (subsistence) work time and surplus work time within the wage relation but to any production relation upon which capital, by means of money, has obtained control. Further, more money, that is, greater money flow, does not mean higher consumption. 'Investment in the poor' by means of offering them credit facilities means, therefore, robbing them not only of the products of their labour but also of the time they may have devoted to subsistence production.

For the peasantry, however, there is the possibility of liberation (see note 2): once aware of the betrayal, they can consciously struggle to withdraw from commercial to subsistence production.

Notes

1. The first notes for this chapter were written in 1974; followed by a first draft in 1976 and two further versions in 1978 and 1979. It became increasingly obvious that: the peasants do not disappear; wage work does not become the single nor the overall form of capitalist relation of production and exploitation; non-wage forms are much more profitable for several of the different fractions of capital; circulation (i.e. market) is a means of extracting and appropriating surplus; subsistence production is *the* battlefield of profit-making. Investment in the rural poor can be profitable and must not at all be seen as a predominantly social policy. This was the conclusion drawn from my empirical research in different regions of Mexico. In Mexico the early agrarian reform had already created conditions which appeared only much

later elsewhere. So, when in 1973 the then President of the World Bank, McNamara, announced the new IBRD policy, I was both afraid and pleased. I saw that the IBRD was on the way to make out of 'my' experience an international strategy; and so it turned out.

2. Structure of IBRD: Members are made up of about 130 industrial and development countries; the influence and vote-quota of each member country correspond to its share of the Bank's capital. The USA has over 23% of the votes, Canada, Great Britain, West Germany, France, Japan and the USA together form a majority block. In sum, the World Bank may be seen as representing the interest of the big multi- or transnational corporations. The Bank's statutes stipulate that it must support private enterprises in the donor and recipient countries. The refinancing of the World Bank takes place through private bond-issues in the international capital market, which contribute over half the credit volume.

The Bank is therefore not a welfare institution. Rather, it operates on the basis of general financial and economic criteria, even though a department of the Bank, the IDA, gives especially favourable loans to particularly poor countries – loans financed mainly through taxation by the national governments of the highly industrialized countries. Membership of the IBRD is tied to that in the International Monetary Fund (IMF). These two sister organizations together control the international policy and are able to manipulate national political interests. This is made easy through the increasing debts of the recipient countries. (Payer 1974, George 1976)

3. The programme for the attack on absolute poverty has so far concentrated mainly on the agricultural sector. In 1977, however, McNamara announced greater consideration for the non-farmers, poor rural and slum population, in the World Bank programme, but this will not be seen as of equal importance with measures for the 'small farmers'. Both the developing countries themselves and the Bank, have had less experience in creating off-farm earning opportunities and in assisting cottage industries and small-scale entrepreneurs. (McNamara, 1977) My analysis of this section of McNamara's speech will concentrate on the agricultural sector and peasant production. However, many of the mechanisms employed to draw small handicraft producers (eg. housewives) or slum-dwellers involved in petty commodity production and trade, away from their subsistence orientation towards commercial orientation, will probably be similar.

4. Feder also assumes that in future the Bank will spend only a small portion on the agricultural sector, and even that mainly for large enterprises and middle and rich peasants. Contrary to this, the programme for rural development has received more funds than any other. (World Bank Annual Report, 1977) Also the proportion for the 'small farmer' projects seems to be considerably higher than Feder had expected. In 1970 the funds for agricultural projects constituted 18.1%, in 1972, 14.7% of the total funds, rising to 32.7% in 1977. As McNamara pointed out in 1978, the 40% increase in credits for the agricultural sector, targeted for the last five-year period, had been far surpassed, reaching 145%. Similarly, the projected 70% of agricultural projects, which should include a component for peasants, had also been surpassed, reaching 75%, with the component for peasants amounting to more than half of the funds. (World Bank Annual Reorts)

5. 'Self-owning' producer is used in analogy to 'self-employment', meaning, for example, members of co-operatives who are neither private owners nor employees of foreign capital.

Sources

Boserup, Esther, (1970) *Women's Role in Economic Development*, London.
Brown, Lester R., (1974) *By Bread Alone*, New York/Washington.
Brown, Lester R., (1970) *Seeds of Change*, New York.
Chenery, Holis, Monteh S. Ahluwalia, C. L. G. Bell, John H. Duloy, Richard Jolly (1974) *Redistribution with Growth*, Oxford.
Comité d'information Sahel (1975) *Qui se nourrit de la famine en Afrique?*, Paris.

Durán, Marco Antonio (1968) 'Los problemas agrarios mexicanos', in *Revista del México Agrario, No. 3.*

Eckstein, Shlomo, Gordon Donald, Douglas Horton, Thomas Carroll (1978) 'Land-reform in Latin America: Bolivia, Chile, Mexico, Peru, Venezuela', World Bank Staff Working Paper, No. 275, April.

Feder, Ernest (1976) 'McNamara's Little Green Revolution. The World Bank Scheme for the Liquidation of the Third World Peasantry', in *Comercio Exterior De México*, Vol. 22, no. 8, pp. 296–306.

—————(1976) 'The New World Bank Programme for the Self-Liquidation of the Third World Peasantry', in: *Journal of Peasant Studies*, Vol. 3, no. 8, April.

George, Susan (1976) *How the Other Half Dies.*

Martinez Alier, Juan (1967) 'Un edificio capitalista con una facheda feudal? El latifundio en Andalucía y en America Latina', in *Cuadernos del Ruedo Ibérico*, no. 15, Paris, pp. 3–53.

Marx, Karl (1970) Resultate des unmittelbaren Produktionsprozesses, Archiv sozialistischer Literatur 17, Frankfurt.

McNamara, Robert, Address to the Board of Governors, World Bank: Nairobi 24.9.1973; Washington D. C. 30.9.1974; Manila 4.10.1976; Washington D.C. 26.9.1977.

Payer, Cheryl (1974) *The Debt Trap. The IMF and the Third World*, Penguin Books.

Rogers, Barbara (1980) *The Domestication of Women. Discrimination in Developing Societies*, London and New York.

World Bank (1975) Agricultural Credit, Sector Policy Paper, May.

—————(1978) Agricultural Land Settlement. A World Bank Issue Paper, Washington, January.

—————(1978) Rural Enterprise and Nonfarm Employment. A World Bank Paper, Washington, January.

Part 2:
Colonization of Women and Nature

4. Social Origins of the Sexual Divisions of Labour[1]

Maria Mies

The search for origins within a feminist perspective

Since the rise of positivism and functionalism as the dominant school of thought amongst Western social scientists in the 1920s, the search for the origins of unequal and hierarchical relationships in society in general and the asymmetric division of labour between men and women in particular has been tabooed. The neglect and even systematic suppression of this question has been part of an overall campaign against Marxist thinking and theorizing in the academic world, particularly in the Western world. (Martin and Voorhies 1975: 155ff) Only now is that question being asked again. Significantly, it was not asked first by academics, but by women actively involved in women's struggle. Whatever the ideological differences between the various feminist groups, they are united in their rebellion against this hierarchical relationship, which is no longer accepted as a biological destiny but seen as something to be abolished. Their search for the social foundations for this sexual inequality and asymmetry is the necessary consequence of their rebellion. Women who are committed to struggle against the age-old oppression and exploitation of women cannot rest content with the indifferent conclusion put forward by many academics, who say the question of origins should not be raised because we know so little about them. The search for the social origins of this relationship is part of the political strategy of women's emancipation. (Reiter 1977) Without understanding the foundation and the functioning of the asymmetric relationship between men and women it is not possible to overcome it.

This political and strategic motivation fundamentally differentiates this new quest for origins from other academic speculations and research endeavours. Its aim is not merely to analyse or to interpret an old problem but rather to solve it.

The following discussion should, therefore, be understood as a contribution to 'spreading the consciousness of the existence of gender hierarchy and collective action aimed at dismantling it'. (Reiter 1977:5)

Problems of biased concepts

When women began to ask about the origins of the unequal relationship between the sexes they soon discovered that none of the old explanations put forward by social scientists since the last century was satisfactory. This is because, in all explanations, whether they stem from an evolutionist, a positivist–functionalist or even a Marxist approach, the problem which needs explanation is, in the last analysis, seen as biologically determined and hence beyond the scope of social change. Therefore, before discussing the origins of an asymmetric division of labour between the sexes it is useful to identify the biologistic biases in some of the concepts we commonly use in our debates.

This covert or overt biological determinism, paraphrased in Freud's statement that anatomy is destiny, is perhaps the most deep-rooted obstacle for the analysis of the causes of women's oppression and exploitation. Although women who struggle for their liberation have rejected biological determinism, they find it very difficult to establish that the unequal, hierarchical and exploitative relationship between men and women is due to social, that is, historical factors. One of our main problems is that not only the analysis as such, but also the tools of the analysis, the basic concepts and definitions, are affected – or rather infected – by biological determinism.

This is largely true of the basic concepts which are central for our analysis, such as the concepts of nature, of labour, of *the sexual division of labour*, of the *family* and of *productivity*. If these concepts are used without a critique of their implicit ideological biases, they tend to obscure rather than to clarify the issues. This is, above all, true for the concept of *nature*.

Too often this concept has been used to explain social inequalities or exploitative relations as 'natural', inborn, and, hence, beyond the scope of social change. Women, particularly, should be suspicious when these terms are used to explain their status in society. Their share in the creation and maintenance of life is usually defined as a function of their biology or 'nature'. Thus, women's household and child-care work are seen as an extension of their physiological make-up, of the fact that they give birth to children, of the fact that 'nature' has provided them with a uterus. All the labour that goes into the production of life, including the labour of childbirth, is seen not as the conscious interaction of a human being with nature, that is, a truly human activity, but rather as an activity *of* nature, which produces plants and animals unconsciously and has no control over this process. This definition of women's interaction with nature – including her own nature – as an act *of* nature has had and still has far-reaching consequences.

What is mystified by a biologically determined concept of nature is a relationship of dominance and exploitation, dominance of the (male) human being over (female) nature. This dominance relationship is also implicit in the other concepts mentioned above, when applied to women. Take the concept of labour: Due to the biologistic definition of women's interaction with nature her work both in giving birth and raising children as well as the rest of domestic work does not appear as work or labour. The concept of labour is usually reserved for men's productive work under capitalist conditions, which means work for the production of surplus value.

Women also perform such surplus-value generating labour, but under capitalism the concept of labour is generally used with a male bias, because under capitalism, women are typically defined as housewives, that means as non-workers.

The instruments of this labour, or the bodily means of production implicitly referred to in this concept, are the hands and the head, but never the womb or the breasts of a woman. Thus not only are men and women differently defined in their interaction with nature but the human body itself is divided into truly 'human' parts (head and hand) and 'natural' or purely 'animal' parts (genitalia, womb, and so on).

This division cannot be attributed to a universal sexism of men as such, but is a consequence of the capitalist mode of production which is interested only in those parts of the human body which can be directly used as instruments of labour or which can become an extension of the machine.

The same hidden asymmetry and biologistic bias, which can be observed in the concept of labour, also prevails in the concept of sexual division of labour itself. Though overtly this concept seems to suggest that men and women simply divide different tasks between themselves, it conceals the fact that men's tasks are usually considered as truly human (that is, conscious, rational, planned, productive and so on) whereas women's tasks are, again, seen as basically determined by their 'nature'. The sexual division of labour, according to this definition, could be paraphrased as one between *human labour* and *natural activity*. What is more, however, this concept obscures the fact that the relationship between male (that is, 'human') and female ('natural') labourers or workers is a relationship of dominance and even of exploitation.[2] Yet, when we try to analyse the social origins of this division of labour, we have to make clear that we mean this asymmetric, hierarchical and exploitative relationship and not a simple division of tasks between equal partners.

The same obfuscating logic prevails with regard to the concept of *family*. Not only is this concept used and universalized in a rather Eurocentric way, presenting the nuclear family as the basic and timeless structure of all institutionalization of men–women relations, it also hides the fact that this institution's structure is hierarchical and unegalitarian. Such phrases as 'partnership within the family' serve only to veil the true nature of this institution.

This brief discussion of the biologistic biases inherent in some of the important concepts has made clear that it is necessary to systematically expose the ideological function of these biases, which is to obscure and mystify asymmetric and exploitative social relations.

This means, with regard to the problem before us, namely the analysis of the social orgins of the sexual division of labour, that we are *not* asking: When did a division of labour arise between men and women? (Such a division is the necessary consequence of all human interaction with nature.) But rather: How did this division of labour become a relationship of dominance and exploitation; and why did this relationship become asymmetric and hierarchical? These questions still loom large over all discussions on women's liberation.

Suggested approach

What can we do to eliminate the biases in the abovementioned concepts? Not use them at all, as some women suggest? But then we would be without a language to express our ideas. Or invent new ones? This is what others feel is better. But concepts summarize historical practice and theory and cannot voluntaristically be invented. We have to accept that the basic concepts we use in our analysis have already been 'occupied' – like territories or colonies – by dominant sexist ideology. Though we cannot abandon them, we can look at them 'from below', not from the point of view of the dominant ideology but from the point of view of the historical experiences of the oppressed, exploited and subordinated and their struggle for emancipation.

It is thus necessary, regarding the concept of *productivity of labour*, to reject its narrow definition and to show that labour can be productive only in the sense of producing surplus value as long as it can tap, extract, exploit, and appropriate labour which is spent in the *production of life*, or subsistence production which is non-wage labour mainly performed by women. As this *production of life* is the perennial precondition of all other historical forms of productive labour, including that under conditions of capital accumulation, it has to be defined as *work* and not as unconscious, 'natural' activity. Because human beings do not only live; they *produce* their life.

In what follows, I shall call the labour that goes into the production of life *productive labour*. The separation from and the superimposition of surplus-producing labour over life-producing labour is an abstraction which leads to the fact that women and their work are being 'defined into nature'.

The search for the origins of the hierarchical sexual division of labour should not be limited to the search for the moment in history or prehistory when the 'world-historic defeat of the female sex' (Engels) took place. Though studies in primatology, prehistory and archaeology are useful and necessary for our search, we cannot expect them to give an answer to this question unless we are able to develop non-biologistic concepts of men and women and their relations to nature and history. As Roswitha Leukert puts it: 'The beginning of human history is primarily not a problem of fixing a certain date, but rather that of finding a materialist concept of man [the human being] and history.' (Leukert 1976: 18, transl. M. M.)

If we use this approach, which is closely linked to the strategic motivation mentioned earlier, we shall see that the development of vertical, unequal relationships between women and men is not a matter of the past only.

We can learn a lot about the actual formation of sex-hierarchies if we look at 'history in the making', that is, if we study what is happening to women under the impact of capitalism both in its centres and its periphery, where poor peasant and tribal societies are now being 'integrated' into a so-called new national and international division of labour under the dictates of capital accumulation. Both in the capitalist centres and in the peripheries a distinct sexist policy was and is used to subsume whole societies and classes under the dominant capitalist production relations.

This strategy usually appears in the guise of 'progressive' or liberal family laws (for example, the prohibition of polygamy), family planning and development policies. The demand to 'integrate women into development', first voiced at the International Women's Conference in Mexico (1975), is largely used in Third World countries to recruit women as the cheapest, most docile and manipulable labour force for capitalist production processes, both in agri-business and export-oriented industry (Fröbel, Kreye, Heinrichs 1977) as well as in the unorganized sector.[3]

This also means that we should no longer look at the sexual division of labour as a problem related to the family, but rather as a structural problem of a whole society. The hierarchical division of labour between men and women and its dynamics forms an integral part of the dominant production relations: that is, class relations of a particular epoch and society and of the broader national and international divisions of labour.

Appropriation of nature by women and men

To search for a materialist concept of men/women and history, however, means to search for the *human nature* of men and women. But human nature is not a given fact. It evolved in history and cannot be reduced to its biological aspects, but the physiological dimension of this nature is always linked to its social dimension. Human nature cannot, therefore, be understood if we separate its physiology from its history. Men's/women's human nature does not evolve out of biology in a linear, monocausal process, but is the result of the history of women's/men's interaction with nature and with each other. Human beings do not simply live as other animals live. Human beings must *produce* their lives through work. This production takes place in a historical process.

In contrast to the evolution in the rest of the animal world (natural history) human history is social history right from the beginning. All human history is characterized, according to Marx and Engels, by 'three moments' which existed at the beginning of mankind and also exist today: 1) People must *live* in order to be able to make history; they must produce the means to satisfy their needs. food, clothing, a shelter. 2) The satisfaction of needs leads to new needs. Human beings develop new instruments to satisfy their needs; and 3) Men who reproduce their daily life must *make other men*, must *procreate* – the relationship between men and women. Marx characterizes this 'production of life' as a process of 'appropriation of nature' through sensuous, objective activity. (Marx/Engels *The German Ideology*, 1970)

Later Marx uses the expression 'appropriation of the natural matter' to conceptualize 'work' in its broadest sense: work, as appropriation of nature for the satisfaction of human needs:

> Labour is, in the first place, a process in which both man and nature participate, and in which man on his own accord starts, regulates, controls the material reactions between himself and nature. He opposes himself to nature as one of her own forces, setting in motion arms and legs, head and hands, the natural forces of his body, in order to appropriate Nature's productions in a form adapted to his wants. By thus acting on the external world and changing it, he at the same time changes his own nature. (Marx *Capital* I:173).[4]

We must stress that this 'appropriation of nature' is the characteristic of *all* human history, including its earliest, primitive stages. Engels identifies these earliest stages as prehistory, separated from actual human history, which, according to him, begins only with civilization. This means it begins with full-fledged class and patriarchal relations. Engels is not able to answer the question of how humanity then jumped from prehistory to social history; moreover, he does not apply the method of dialectical historical materialism to the study of these primitive societies which have 'not yet entered history'. He thinks that the laws of evolution prevailed up to the emergence of private property, of family and the state. (Engels 1973)

But if we want to find a materialist concept of women and men and their history we must first analyse their respective interaction with nature and how, in this process, they built up their own human or social nature. If we followed Engels, we would have to relegate women's interaction with nature to the sphere of evolution. (This, in fact, is being done by functionalists and behaviourists all over the world.) We would have to conclude that women have not yet entered history (as defined by men) and still basically belong to the lower animal world, because history, for Engels, begins with civilization, the exploitation of woman by man and man by man.

Women's/men's appropriation of their own bodies
According to Marx, the labour process, in its elementary form, is a conscious action with a view to producing use-values. In a wider sense, it is 'the appropriation of natural substances for human requirements'. This 'exchange of matter' (Stoffwechsel) between human beings and nature is the everlasting nature-imposed condition of human existence, or rather is common to every historical phase. (Marx, *Capital* I: 179) In this 'exchange of matter' between human beings and nature, human beings, women and men, not only develop and change the external nature with which they find themselves confronted, but also *their own bodily nature*.

The interaction between human beings and nature for the production of their human requirements needs, like all production, an instrument or a means of production.

Their own body is the first means of production with which human beings act upon nature. It is also the eternal precondition of all further means of production. But the body is not only the 'tool' with which human beings act upon nature, it is also the aim of the satisfaction of needs. Human beings use their body not only to produce use-values, they also keep their bodies alive – in its widest sense – by the consumption of their products.

In his analysis of the labour process, in its widest sense, as appropriation of natural substances Marx makes no difference between men and women. For our subject, however, it is important to stress that men and women act upon nature with a qualitatively different body. If we want to be clear about the asymmetric division of labour between the sexes, it is necessary to talk not of MAN's (the abstract generic being) appropriation of nature, but of women's and men's appropriation of nature. This is based on the assumption that women and men appropriate nature differently. This difference is usually obscured because 'humanness' is identified with 'maleness'.[5]

Maleness and femaleness are not biological givens, but rather the result of a long historical process. In each historical epoch maleness and femaleness are differently defined. This definition depends on the principal mode of production in these epochs. This means that the organic differences between women and men are differently interpreted and valued according to the dominant form of appropriation of natural matter for the satisfaction of human needs. Men and women, therefore, have developed a qualitatively different relationship to their own bodies. Thus in matristic[6] societies femaleness was interpreted as the social paradigm of all productivity, as the main active principle in the production of life.[7] All women were defined as 'mothers', but 'mothers' meant something other than it does today. Under capitalist conditions all women are socially defined as housewives (all men as breadwinners) and motherhood has become part and parcel of this housewife syndrome. The distinction between the earlier, matristic definition of femaleness and the modern one, is that the modern definition has been emptied of all active, creative, productive, (that is, human) qualities.

The historically developed qualitative difference in the appropriation of the male and female bodily nature has also led to 'two qualitatively different forms of appropriation of external nature, that is two qualitatively distinct forms of relations to the objects of appropriation, the objects of sensuous bodily activity.' (Leukert 1976:41)[8]

Women's and men's relation to nature

First we must stress the difference between animal and human relation to nature. Human relation to nature is *praxis*, that is action + reflection, it becomes visible only in the historical process, and it implies social interaction or co-operation. The human body was not only the first *means* of production, it was also the first *force* of production. This means the human body is experienced as able to bring forth something new and hence change the external and the human nature. Human relation to nature is, in contrast to that of other animals, a productive one. In the appropriation of the body as a productive force the difference between woman and man has had far-reaching consequences.

What characterizes women's relation to nature, to their own as well as to external nature? First, we see that women can experience their *whole* body as productive, not only their hands or their heads. Out of their body they produce new children as well as the first food for these children. It is of crucial importance for our subject that women's activity in producing children and milk is understood as truly *human*, that is, *conscious, social activity*. Women appropriated their own nature, their capacity to give birth and to produce milk, in the same way as men appropriated their own bodily nature, in the sense that their hands and head and so on acquired skills through work and reflection to make and handle tools. In this sense the activity of women in bearing and rearing children has to be understood as *work*. One of the greatest obstacles to women's liberation is that these activities are still interpreted as purely physiological functions, comparable to those of other mammals, and lying outside the sphere of conscious human influence. This view that the productivity of the female body is identical with animal *fertility* – a view at present propagated and popularized worldwide by demographers and population planners – has to be understood as a *result* of the patriarchial and capitalist division of labour and not as its preconditon.[9]

In the course of their history women observed the changes in their own bodies and acquired, through observation and experiment, a vast quantity of experiential knowledge about the functions of their bodies, about the rhythms of menstruation, about pregnancy and childbirth. This appropriation of their own bodily nature was closely related to the acquisition of knowledge about the generative forces of external nature, about plants, animals, the earth, water and air.

Thus, they did not simply breed children like cows, but they appropriated their own generative and productive forces, they analysed and reflected upon their own and former experiences and passed them on to their daughters. This means that they were not helpless victims of their bodies' generative forces, but learned to influence them, including the number of children they wanted to have.

We are in the possession of enough evidence today to conclude that women in pre-patriarchial societies knew better how to regulate the number of their children and the frequency of births than modern women, who have lost this knowledge due to their subjection to the male civilizing process.

Among gatherers and hunters and other primitive groups various methods existed and partly still exist to limit the number of births and children. Apart from infanticide, which most probably was the earliest method (Fisher 1978:202) women in many societies used various plants and herbs as contraceptives or abortifacients. The Ute Indians used litho-spermium, the Bororo women in Brazil used a plant which made them temporarily sterile; missionaries persuaded the women not to use the plant anymore. (Fisher: 1979:204) Elisabeth Fisher tells us about methods used by women among the Australian aborigines, certain tribes in Oceania and even in ancient Egypt, which were predecessors of modern contraceptives. Women in Egypt used a vaginal sponge, dipped in honey, to reduce the mobility of sperms; acacia tips, which contained a spermicidal acid, were also used. (Fisher 1979:205)

Another method of birth control widely used among contemporary gatherers and hunters is a prolonged period of breast-feeding. Robert M. May reports about studies which prove that 'in almost all primitive gatherers and hunters' societies fertility is lower than in modern civilised societies. Through prolonged lactation ovulation is reduced, which leads to longer intervals between births'. He also observed that these women reached puberty at a much later age than civilized women. He attributes the much more balanced population growth, which can be observed today among many tribes as long as they are not integrated into the civilized society, to 'cultural practices which unconsciously contribute to a reduction of fertility'. (May 1978:491) Though he correctly criticizes those who think that the low rate of population growth in such societies is the result of a brutal struggle for survival, he still does not conceive of this situation as a result of women's conscious appropriation of their generative forces.[10]

Women's production of new life, of new women and men, is inseparably linked to the production of the means of subsistence for this new life. Mothers who give birth to children and suckle them necessarily have to provide food for themselves and the children. Thus the appropriation of their bodily nature, the fact that they produce children and milk, makes them also the first providers of the daily food, be it as gatherers, who simply collect what they find in nature – plants, small animals, fish and so on – or as agriculturists. The first division of labour by sex, namely that between the gathering activities of the women and the sporadic hunting of the men, most probably has its origin in the fact that, of necessity, women were responsible for the production of food for the groups' daily subsistence. Gathering plants, roots, fruits, fungi, nuts, small animals, and so on, was, right from the beginning, a collective activity of women.

It is assumed that the need to provide for the daily food and the long experience with plants and plant life eventually led to the cultivation of grain and tubers on a regular basis. According to Gordon Childe, this development took place in the Neolithic Age, particularly in Eurasia, where wild grains were first cultivated. He and many other scholars attribute the beginning of agriculture to women, who also invented the first tools for this new mode of production: the digging stick – already in use for digging out wild roots and tubers – and the hoe. (Childe 1976; Reed 1975; Bornemann 1975; Thomson 1960; Chattopadhyaya 1973; Ehrenfels 1941; Briffault 1952)

The regular cultivation of food plants, mainly tubers and grains, signified a new stage and an immense increase in the productivity of female labour, which according to most authors, made the production of a surplus possible for the first time in history. Childe, therefore, calls this transformation the neolithic revolution which he attributes to the regular cultivation of grain. On the basis of recent archaeological findings in Iran and Turkey, however, Elisabeth Fisher argues that already in the gathering stage people had been able to collect a surplus of wild grains and nuts. The technological precondition for the collection of a surplus was the invention of containers – baskets and jars of leaves and plant fibres. It seems plausible that the technology of preservation preceded the new agricultural technology, and was equally necessary for the production of a surplus.

The difference between the two modes of production is, therefore, not so much the existence of a surplus, but rather that women developed the first truly *productive relationship to nature*. Whereas gatherers still lived in a society of simple appropriation, with the invention of plant cultivation we can for the first time speak of a 'production-society'. (Sohn-Rethel 1970) Women not only collected and consumed what grew in nature, but *they made things grow*.

Women's relation to nature was not only a productive one, but from the beginning, was *social production*. In contrast to adult men, who could gather and hunt only for themselves, women had to share their products with, at least, their small children. This means their specific relation to nature (to their own bodily nature as well as to the external nature), namely, to be able to let grow and make grow, made them also the inventors of *the first social relations*, the relations between mothers and children.

Many authors have concluded that the mothers–children groups were the first social units. They were not only units of consumption but also units of production. Mothers and children worked together as gatherers and in early hoe cultivation. These authors are of the opinion that adult men were only temporarily and peripherally integrated or socialized into these early matricentric or matristic units. (Briffault 1952; Reed 1975; Thomson 1960)

Martin and Voorhies argue that these matricentric units coincided with a vegetarian phase of hominid evolution. 'Adult males would maintain no permanent attachment to these mother–child units – except to the unit of their birth.' (Martin and Voorhies 1975:174) This would mean that the permanent integration of males into these units has to be seen as a result of social history. The productive forces developed in these first social units were not only of a technological nature – but were above all the capacity for human co-operation. The ability 'to plan for tomorrow', to anticipate the future, to learn from one another, to pass on this knowledge from one generation to the next and to learn from past experiences, or, in other words, to constitute history.

To summarize women's historically developed relation to nature we can state the following:

a) Their interaction with nature – their own as well as external nature – was a reciprocal process. They conceived of their own bodies as being productive in the same way as they conceived of external nature as being productive.

b) Though they appropriated nature, this appropriation did not constitute a relationship of dominance or a property relation. They were not *owners* of their own bodies or of the earth, but they co-operated with their bodies and with the earth in order 'to let grow and to make grow'.

c) As producers of new life they also became the first subsistence producers and the inventors of the first productive economy. This implies, from the beginning, social production and the creation of social relations, that is, of society and history.

Men's relation to nature

Men's relation to nature, as that of women, has both a material-bodily and a historical dimension. The material side of this relation – which exists at all times as long as men and women live – means that men appropriate nature by means of a qualitatively different body from that of women.

They cannot *experience* their own bodies as being productive in the same way that women can. Male bodily productivity cannot *appear* as such without the mediation of external means, of *tools*, whereas woman's productivity can. Men's contribution to the production of new life, though necessary at all times, could become visible only after a long historical process of men's action on external nature by means of tools and their reflection on this process. The conception which men have of their own bodily nature, the imagery they use to reflect upon themselves is influenced by the different historic forms of interaction with external nature and the instruments used in this work-process. Thus male self-conception as human, that is as being productive, is closely linked to the invention of tools and the control of technology. Without tools man is no MAN.

In the course of history men's reflection of their relation to external nature found expression in the symbols with which they described their own physical organs. It is interesting that the first male organ to gain prominence as the symbol of male productivity was the phallus, not the hand, though the hand was the main instrument for tool-making. This must have happened at the stage when the plough replaced the digging stick or the hoe of early female cultivators. In some Indian languages there is an analogy between plough and penis, and in Bengali slang, like English, the penis is called 'the tool' (*yantra*). This symbolism, of course, not only expresses an instrumental relationship to external nature, but also to women. The penis is the tool, the plough, the 'thing' with which man works upon woman. In the north-Indian languages the words for 'work' and 'coitus' are the same, namely *kam*. This symbolism also implies that women have become 'external nature' for men. They are the earth, the field, the furrow (*sita*) upon which men sow their seeds (semen).

But these analogies of penis and plough, seed and semen, field and women are not only linguistic expressions of an instrumental relation of men to nature and to women, but they also indicate that this object relation is already characterized by dominance. Women are already defined as part of the physical conditions of (male) production.

Little is known about the historic struggles which took place before the productivity of men's relation to nature could establish itself as superior to that of women. But from the ideological battles, described in ancient Indian literature, that went on for several centuries over the question of whether the nature of the 'product' (grain, children) was determined by the field (woman) or by the seed (man), we can assume that the subordination of female productivity under male productivity was by no means a peaceful process but was part and parcel of class struggles and the establishment of patriarchal property relations over land, cattle and women. (I. Karve 1964)[11]

It would be revealing to study the analogies between their sexual organs and the tools that men have invented in different historical epochs and for different modes of production. It is no accident that in our time men call their penis a 'screwdriver' (they 'screw' a woman) a 'hammer', 'file', 'gun' and so on. In the harbour of Rotterdam, a trading port, the male sexual organs are called 'the trade'. This terminology tells us a lot about how men define their relationship to nature, and also to women and to their own bodies. It is an indication of the close link in the minds of men between their work instruments and their labour process, and the self-conception of their own bodies.

Yet before men could conceive not only of their own bodies as more productive than women's, but also in reality establish a relationship of dominance over women and external nature, they had first to develop a type of productivity which at least *appeared* independent of and superior to women's productivity. As we have seen, the appearance of men's productivity was closely linked to the invention of tools. Yet men could develop a productivity (apparently) independent of women's only on the basis of developed female productivity.

Female productivity, the precondition of male productivity

If we keep in mind that 'productivity' means the specific capacity of human beings to produce and reproduce life in a historic process (see p. 71) then for our further analysis we can formulate the thesis that female productivity is the precondition of male productivity and of all further world–historic development. This statement has a timeless material dimension as well as a historical one.

The first consists in the fact that women *at all times* will be the producers of new women and men and that without this production all other forms and modes of production lose their sense. This sounds trivial, but it reminds us of the goal of all human history. The second meaning of the above statement lies in the fact that the various forms of productivity that men developed in the course of history could not have emerged if they could not have used and subordinated the various historic forms of female productivity.

In the following pages I shall try to use the above thesis as a guiding principle for the analysis of the asymmetric division of labour between the sexes during some of the major phases of human history. It will help to keep our feet on the ground and thus enable us to demystify some of the common myths that are put forward to explain the social inequality between women and men as nature-given.

The myth of man-the-hunter
Women's productivity is the precondition of all other human productivity, not only in the sense that they are *always* the producers of new men and women, but also in the sense that the first social division of labour, that between female gatherers (later also cultivators) and predominantly male hunters, could take place only on the basis of a developed female productivity.

Female productivity consisted above all in the ability to provide the daily subsistence, the guarantee of survival, for the members of the clan or band. Women, necessarily, had to secure the 'daily bread', not only for themselves and their children, but also for the men if they had been unsuccessful on their hunting expeditions, because hunting is an 'economy of risk'.

It has been proved conclusively, particularly by the critical research of feminist scholars, that the survival of mankind has been due much more to 'woman-the-gatherer' than to 'man-the-hunter', in contrast to the assertions of social-Darwinists, old or new. Even among existing hunters and gatherers women provide up to 80% of the daily food, whereas men contribute only a small portion by hunting. (Lee and de Vore 1976, quoted by Fisher, 1979:48) By a secondary analysis of a sample of hunters and gatherers from Murdock's Ethnographic Atlas, Martin and Voorhies have proved that 58% of the subsistence of these societies was provided by gathering, 25% by hunting and the rest by hunting and gathering combined. (1975:181) Tiwi women, in Australia, who are both hunters and gatherers, got 50% of their food by gathering, 30% by hunting and 20% by fishing. Jane Goodale, who studied the Tiwi women said that bush-hunting and collecting was the most important productive activity:

> The women not only could, but did, provide the major daily supply of a variety of foods to members of their camp . . . Men's hunting required considerable skill and strength, but the birds, bats, fish, crocodiles, dugongs and turtles they contributed to the household were luxury items rather than staples. (Goodale 1971:169)

It is obvious from these examples that among existing hunters and gatherers, hunting by no means has the economic importance usually ascribed to it, and that women are the providers of the bulk of the daily staple food. In fact, all hunters of big game depend on food supplied by their women (which is not produced by hunting) if they want to go on a hunting expedition. This is why the old Iroquois women had a voice in the decision-making on war and hunting expeditions. If they refused to give the men the necessary supply of food for their adventures, they had to stay at home. (Leacock 1978; Brown 1970)

Elisabeth Fisher gives us further examples of still existing foraging peoples among whom women are the main providers of the daily food, particularly in the temperate and southern zones. But she also argues that gathering of vegetable food was more important for our early ancestors than hunting. She refers to the study of coprolites, fossil excrements, which reveals that groups living 200,000 years ago on the French Riviera survived mainly on a diet of mussels, other shellfish and grains, but not of meat. Twelve thousand years old coprolites from Mexico suggest that millets were the main staple food in that area. (Fisher 1979:57–8)

Though it is obvious from these examples, as well as from common sense, that humanity would not have survived if man-the-hunter's productivity had been the base for providing the daily subsistence of early societies, the notion that man-the-hunter was the inventor of the first tools, the provider of food, inventor of human society and protector of women and children, persists not only in popular literature and films, but also among serious social scientists, and even among Marxist scholars.[12]

The man-the-hunter hypothesis has been popularized particularly by anthropologists and behaviourists who follow the line of thinking developed by the South African anthropologist, Raymond Dart, who maintained that the first hominids had made their first tools from the bones of members of their own kind. (Fisher 1979: 49–50) Following this hypothesis, Konrad Lorenz (1963), Robert Ardrey (1966, 1976), Lionel Tiger and Robin Fox (1976), argue that hunting had been the motor of human development and that the existing relationship of dominance between women and men orginates in the 'biological infrastructure' of stone- age hunters. (Tiger and Fox 1976) According to these authors the (male) hunter is not only the inventor of the first tools – which of course are weapons – but also of the upright gait, because man-the-hunter needed to have his hands free to throw projectiles. According to them, he is also the 'breadwinner', the protector of weak and dependent women, the social engineer, the inventor of norms and hierarchical systems which have only one aim, namely to curb the biologically programmed aggressiveness of the males in their fight for the control over the sexuality of the females. They draw a direct line from the observed behaviour of some of the primates to the behaviour of the human male and maintain that the male primates strive to come to the top of the male hierarchy in order to be able to subject the females for their own sexual satisfaction.

> The efforts of the human primate to get to the top of the male hierarchy, which apparently is only slightly, but in fact fundamentally, different from that of the apes, aim at gaining control over the female members of his own group *in order to exchange them against the women of another group* [emphasis Tiger and Fox]. Thus he gets for himself sexual satisfaction and political advantages. (Tiger and Fox 1976)

The cultural achievement of these human hunter–primates seems to be that they have risen (or 'evolved') from the stage of rape to that of exchange of women. The exploitative dominance relationship between men and women has been ingrained into the 'biological infrastructure' of the hunting behaviour. Men are the providers of meat, for which women have a craving. Therefore the hunters were able to permanently subject and subordinate the women as sexual objects and worker-bees. What gave the hunters this tremendous advantage over women was, according to these authors, the 'bonding principle', which evolved out of hunting in groups. In his book *Men in Groups* (1969), Tiger had already advanced the idea of the 'male bonding' principle as the root cause of male supremacy when the US was in the middle of another of man-the-hunter's adventures, the Vietnam War. Although he knew, as Evelyn Reed points out, that meat-eating constituted only a tiny portion of the baboon diet, he claims that hunting and meat-eating constitute the decisive factor in pre-human primate evolution and that male bonding patterns reflect and arise out of man's history as a hunter.

> So, in the hunting situation, it was the hunting group – male-plus-male-plus-male – which ensured the survival of the entire productive community. Thus was the male–male bond as important for hunting purposes as the male–female bond was important for productive purposes, and this is the basis for the division of labour by sex. (Tiger 1969:122, 126)

The man-the-hunter model as the paradigm of human evolution and development has been the basis for numerous scientific works on human affairs and has been popularized by the modern media. It has influenced the thinking of millions of people and is still constantly advanced to explain the causes of social inequalities. Feminist scholars challenged the validity of this model on the basis of their own research and that of others. They unmasked this model, including its basic premises of the male bonding principle, the importance of meat as food and so on, as a sexist projection of modern, capitalist and imperialist social relations into prehistory and earlier history. This projection serves to legitimize existing relations of exploitation and dominance between men and women, classes and peoples, as universal, timeless and 'natural'. Evelyn Reed has rightly denounced the hidden Fascist orientation underlying this model, particularly in the writings of Tiger and his glorification of war. (Reed 1978)

Though we are able to demystify the man-the-hunter hypothesis and show that the great hunters would have been unable even to survive had it not been for the daily subsistence production of the women, we are still faced with the question why women, in spite of their superior economic productivity as gatherers and early agriculturists, were not able to prevent the establishment of a hierarchical and exploitative relation between the sexes.

If we ask this question in this way, we assume that political power emerges automatically from economic power. The foregoing discussion has shown that such an assumption cannot be upheld, because male supremacy did not arise from their superior economic contribution.

In the following pages I shall try to find an answer to the above question by looking more closely at the various tools invented and used by women and men.

Women's tools, men's tools

The man-the-hunter model is in fact the latest version of the man-the-toolmaker model. In the light of this model tools are, above all, weapons, *tools to kill*.

The earliest tools of mankind, the stone axes, scrapers and flakes were of an ambivalent character. They could be used to grind, smash and pulverize grains and other vegetable food, and to dig out roots, but they could also be used to kill small animals, and we can assume that they were used by men and women for all these purposes. However, the invention of arms proper, of projectiles, of bow and arrow, is an indication that killing of animals had become a major specialization of one part of the society, mainly of men. The proponents of the hunter hypothesis are of the opinion that the first tools were invented by men. They ignore women's inventions connected with their subsistence production. But, as was mentioned before, the first inventions were most probably containers and baskets made of leaves, bark and fibres, and later, jars. The digging stick and the hoe were the main tools for gathering as well as for early agriculture. Women must have continued developing their technology while some men developed specialized hunting tools.

What is important to note here is that women's technology remained productive in the true sense of the word: they produced something new. The hunting technology, on the other hand, was not productive, that is, unlike the stone axe, hunting equipment proper cannot be used for any other productive activity. Bow and arrow, and spears are basically means of destruction. Their significance lies in the fact that they cannot only be used to kill animals, but also to kill other human beings. It is this characteristic of the hunting tools which became decisive in the further development of male productivity as well as of unequal exploitative social relations, not the fact that hunters as providers of meat were able to raise the standards of nutrition of the community.

Hence we conclude that the significance of hunting does not lie in its economic productivity as such, as is wrongly assumed by many theoreticians, but in the particular relation to nature it constitutes. The relation to nature of man-the-hunter is distinctly different from that of woman-the-gatherer or cultivator. The characteristics of this relation are the following:

a) The hunters' main tools are not instruments to produce life but to destroy life. Their tools are not basically means of production, but means of destruction, and they can also be used as means of coercion against fellow human beings.

b) This gives hunters a power over living beings, both animals and human, which does not arise out of their own productive work. They can appropriate not only fruits and plants (like the gatherers) and animals, but also other (female) producers by virtue of arms.

c) The object-relation mediated through arms, therefore, is basically a *predatory* or *exploitative* one: hunters appropriate life, but they cannot produce life. It is an antagonistic and non-reciprocal relationship. All later exploitative relations between production and appropriation are, in the last analysis, upheld by arms as means of coercion.

d) The relation to nature mediated through arms constitutes a relationship of dominance and not of co-operation between the hunter and nature. This relationship of dominance has become an integral element of all further production relations which men have established. It has become, in fact, the main paradigm of their productivity. Without dominance and control over nature men cannot conceive of themselves as being productive.

e) 'Appropriation of natural substances' (Marx) now also becomes a process of one-sided appropriation, in the sense of establishing property relations, not in the sense of humanization, but in the sense of exploitation of nature.

f) By means of arms, hunters not only could hunt animals, but they could also raid communities of other subsistence producers, kidnap their unarmed young and female workers, and appropriate them. It can be assumed that the first forms of private property were not cattle or other foods, but *female slaves who had been kidnapped*. (Meillassoux: 1975; Bornemann: 1975)

At this point it is important to point out that it is *not the hunting technology as such* that is responsible for the constitution of an exploitative dominance-relationship between man and nature, and between man and man, man and woman. Recent studies on existing hunting societies have shown that hunters do not have an aggressive relationship to the animals they hunt. The pygmies, for example, seem to be extremely peaceful people, who know neither war nor quarrels nor witchcraft. (Turnbull:1961) Also their hunting expeditions are not aggressive affairs, but are accompanied by feelings of compassion for the animals they have to kill. (Fisher 1979:53)

This means that the emergence of a specialized hunting technology implies only the *possibility* of establishing relationships of dominance and exploitation. It seems that as long as the hunters remained confined to their limited hunting-gathering context they could not realize the exploitative potential of their *predatory mode of production*. Their economic contribution was not sufficient, they remained dependent for their survival on their women's subsistence production.

Pastoralists

Though there may have been inequality between men and women, men were not able to establish a full-fledged dominance-system. The 'productive' forces of the hunters could be fully released only at the stage when pastoral nomads, who domesticated cattle and women, invaded agricultural communities. This means, the full realization of the 'productive' capacity of this predatory mode of production presupposes the existence of other really productive modes, like agriculture.

Elisabeth Fisher is of the opinion that a dominance relationship between men and women could be established only after men had discovered their own generative capacities. This discovery, according to her, went hand-in-hand with the domestication and particularly the *breeding* of animals as a new mode of production. These pastoralists discovered that one bull could impregnate many cows, and this may have led to the castration and elimination of weaker animals. The main (stud) bull was then put to impregnate the cows when the time seemed most appropriate to the pastoral nomads. Female animals were thus subjected to sexual coercion. This means, the free sexuality of wild animals was subjected to a coercive economy, based on breeding, with the object of increasing the herds. It is plausible that the establishment of harems, kidnapping and raping of women, the establishment of patriarchal lines of descent and inheritance were part of this new mode of production. Women were also subjected to the same economic logic and became part of the moveable property, like cattle.

Two things made this new mode of production possible: the monopoly of men over arms and the long observation of the reproductive behaviour of animals. As men began to manipulate the reproductive behaviour of animals, they may have discovered their own generative functions. This led to a change in their relation to nature as well as to a change in the sexual division of labour. For pastoral nomads women were no longer very important as producers or gatherers of food, as was the case among hunters. They were needed as breeders of children, particularly of sons. Their productivity was now reduced to their 'fertility' to be appropriated and controlled by men. (cf. Fisher, 1979:248 ff)

In contrast to the hunters' and gatherers' economy, which is mainly appropriative, the pastoral nomads' economy is a 'productive economy'. (Sohn-Rethel) But it is obvious that this mode of production presupposes the existence of means of coercion for the manipulation of animals and human beings and for the extension of territory.

Agriculturists
It is, therefore, most probably correct to say that the martial pastoral nomads were the fathers of all dominance relations, particularly that of men over women. But there are enough data which suggest that exploitative relations between men and women also existed among agriculturists, not only after the introduction of the plough, as Esther Boserup believes, (1975) but also among hoe-cultivators in Africa, where even today farming is done mainly by women. Meillassoux (1:1975), points out that in such societies, which he characterized as *economies domestiques*, the old men were in a position to establish a relationship of dominance over younger men and women, because they could acquire more wives to work solely for them. The marriage system was the mechanism by which they accumulated women and wealth, which, in fact, were closely related. Meillassoux, following Lévi-Strauss, takes the existence of an unequal system of exchange of women for granted and mentions only in passing the probable roots of this system, namely, the fact that due to the ongoing subsistence production of the women the men were free to go from time to time on a hunting expedition. For the men in these domestic economies, hunting was a sporting and political activity rather than an economic one. On such expeditions, the men also kidnapped lonely gatherer women and young men of other villages or tribes. In a recent study of slavery in pre-colonial Africa, edited by Meillassoux, there are numerous examples to show that such hunters not only kidnapped and appropriated people whom they surprised in the jungle, but also organized regular raids into other villages to kidnap women. The women thus appropriated did not become members of the community, but were usually privately appropriated by the leader of the expedition, who would either use them to work for him as his slaves, or sell them against bride-wealth to other villages. These kidnapped women thus became a direct source for the accumulation of *private* property.

Slavery, therefore, did not emerge out of trade, but out of the male monopoly over arms. Before slaves could be bought and sold they had to be captured, they had to be appropriated by a master by force of arms. This predatory form of acquisition of labour power both for work on 'private' plots and for sale was considered the most 'productive' activity of these warrior-hunters, who, it must be kept in mind, were no longer hunters and gatherers, but lived in an economic system based on women's productive agricultural work; they were the 'husbands' of female agriculturists. Their productivity was described by an old man of the Samos in Upper Volta as the productivity of bow and arrow, by which all other products – millets, beans, and so on, and women – could be obtained:

> Our ancestors were born with their hoe, their axe, their bow and arrow. Without a bow you cannot work in the jungle. With the bow you acquire the honey, the peanuts, the beans, and then a woman, then children and finally you can buy domestic animals, goats, sheep, donkeys, horses. These were the riches of old. You worked with bow and arrow in the jungle, because there could be always someone who could surprise and kill you.

According to this old man there were 'commandos' of five or six men who would roam through the jungle trying to surprise and kidnap women and men who were alone who were then sold. (Heritier, in Meillassoux 1975:491)

This passage shows clearly that the Samo men conceived of their own productivity in terms of arms, that they surprised lonely gatherers in the jungle in order to sell them. The reason for this was: what had been captured by surprise in the jungle was *property* (private property). This private property was appropriated by the lineage of the hereditary chief (formerly the rain-makers' lineage) who then sold these captives to other lineages, either as wives against bride-price (in this case against cowrie shells as money) or as slaves for agricultural work, or they were returned, against ransom money, to their own village. These raids were thus a means for some men to accumulate wealth.

Female slaves were preferred and fetched a higher price because they were productive in two ways: they were agricultural workers and they could produce more slaves. The Samo usually killed the men in these inter-village raids, because they were of no economic use to them. But women and children were captured, made slaves and sold.

Jean Bazin, who studied war and slavery among the Segu, calls the capture of slaves by warriors the 'most productive' activity of the men of this tribe.

> The production of slaves is indeed a production . . . , in the whole of the predatory activity this is the only activity which is effectively productive, because pillage of goods is only a change of hands and place. The dominant moment of this production is the exercise of violence against the individual in order to cut her/him off from the local and social networks (age, sex, relatives, alliances, lineage, clientele, village). (Bazin in Meillassoux: 2, 1975:142)

On the basis of his studies among the Tuareg, Pierre Bonte draws the conclusion that slavery was the precondition for the expansion of the *economies domestiques* into a more diversified economy, where there is a great demand for labour. He sees slavery as the 'result and the means of unequal exchange'. (Bonte in Meillassoux: 2, 1975:54)

The examples from pre-colonial Africa make clear that men's predatory mode of production, based on the monopoly of arms, could become 'productive' only when some other, mostly female, production economies existed, which could be raided. It can be characterized as *non-productive production*. They also show the close link between pillage, loot, robbery on the one hand, and trade on the other. What was traded and exchanged against money (cowrie shells) was not the surplus produced over and above the requirements of the community; but, in fact, that which was robbed and appropriated by means of arms was *defined* as 'surplus'.

In the last analysis we can attribute the asymmetric division of labour between women and men to this predatory mode of production, or rather appropriation, which is based on the male monopoly over means of coercion, that is, arms, and on direct violence by means of which permanent relations of exploitation and dominance between the sexes were created and maintained.

This non-productive, *predatory mode of appropriation* became the paradigm of all exploitative relations between human beings. Its main mechanism is to transform autonomous human producers into conditions of production for others, or, to define them as 'natural resources' for others.

'Man-the-hunter' under feudalism and capitalism

The full potential of the predatory mode could be realized only under feudalism and capitalism.

The predatory mode of appropriation of producers, products and means of production by non-producers was not abolished totally when new modes of production replaced older ones. Rather it was transformed and dialectically preserved, in the sense that it reappeared under new forms of labour control.

Similarly, so far, new forms of the sexual division of labour have not replaced the old, but only transformed them, according to the requirements of the new modes of production. None of the modes of production which emerged later in history did away with predation and violent acquisition of producers' means of production and products. Later production relations have the same basic asymmetric and exploitative structure. Only the forms of dominance and appropriation have changed. Thus, instead of using violent raids and slavery for acquiring more women as workers and producers than were born in a community, hypergamous marriage systems were evolved, which made sure that the BIG men could have access not only to more women of their own community or class, but also to the women of the Little men. Women became a commodity in an asymmetric or unequal marriage market, because control over more women meant accumulation of wealth. (Meillassoux 1:1975) The BIG men then became the *managers* of social reproduction as well as of production. In all patriarchal civilizations the relationship between men and women maintained its character of being coercive and appropriative. The asymmetric division of labour by sex, once established by means of violence, was then upheld by means of institutions like the family and the state, and also by means of powerful ideological systems, above all the patriarchal religions, which have defined women as a part of nature that must be controlled and dominated by men.

In this process first women, and later other exploited people and classes, were defined as 'nature' by the dominant class, which defined itself as 'human'.

The predatory mode of acquisition saw a renaissance during the period of European feudalism. Feudalism as a specific mode of production based on ownership of land was built up with extensive use of violence and warfare. In fact, but for the endogenous processes of class differentiation in peasant societies, feudalism might never have evolved, at least, not in its European version which figures as the 'model' of feudalism. The predatory form of acquisition of new lands and the large-scale use of plunder and looting by the armed feudal class form an inseparable part of, and a preconditon for, the rise and maintenance of this mode of production. (Elias: 1978, Wallerstein: 1974)

Later, not only were new lands thus acquired, but with the lands, the means or conditions of production – the peasants – were also appropriated and tied to the feudal lord in a specific production relation, which did not allow them to move away from that land; they were considered to be part of the land. Thus, not only the women of these peasants, but the male peasants themselves were also 'defined into nature', that is, for the feudal lord they had a status similar to that of women: their bodies no longer belonged to themselves, but to the feudal lord, like the earth. This relationship is exactly preserved in the German term with which the serf is described: he is *Leibeigener* that is, someone whose body (*Leib*) is the property (*Eigentum*) of someone else. But, in spite of this change over from direct violent acquisition of land and the peasants who worked on it, to a 'peaceful' relation of *structural violence*, or, which is the same, to a dominance relation beween lord and serf, the feudal lords never gave up their arms or their military power which they used to expand and defend their lands and their wealth, not only against external enemies, but also against rebellions from within. This means, even though there were 'peaceful' mechanisms of effective labour control, actually under feudalism these production relations were established and maintained through the *monopoly over the means of coercion* enjoyed by the dominant class. The social paradigm of man-the-hunter/warrior remained the base and the last resort of this mode of production.

The same can be said of *capitalism*. When capital accumulation became the dominant motor of productive activity in contrast to subsistence production, wage labour tended to become the dominant form of labour control. Yet these 'peaceful' production relations, based on mechanisms of *economic coercion* (structural violence) could be built up only on the base of a vast expansion of the predatory mode of acquisition. Direct and violent acquisition of gold, silver and other products, mainly in Hispanic America, and of producers – first the Indians in Latin America and later African slaves – proved to be the most 'productive' activity in what has been described as the period of primitive accumulation. As Marc Bloch saw this process:

> Experience has proved it; of all forms of breeding, that of human cattle is one of the hardest. If slavery is to pay when applied to large scale enterprises, there must be plenty of cheap human flesh on the market. You can only get it by war or slave raiding. So a society can hardly base much of its economy on domesticated human beings unless it has at hand feebler societies to defeat or to raid. (Bloch, quoted in Wallerstein 1974:87)

Thus capitalism did not do away with the former savage forms of control over human productive capacity, it rather reinforced and generalized them: 'Large scale slavery or forced labour for the production of exchange value is prominently a capitalist institution, geared to the early pre-industrial stages of a capitalist world economy'. (Wallerstein: 88) This institution was also based on the monopoly over effective weapons and the existence of breeding grounds of enough 'human cattle' which could be hunted, appropriated and subjugated. This involves a redefinition of man-the-hunter's, now the rising European bourgeoisie's, relation to nature and to women. Whereas under production relations based on ownership of land, women and peasants were/are defined as 'earth' or parts of the earth – as nature is identified with the earth and her plants – under early capitalism slaves were defined as 'cattle' and women as 'breeders' of these cattle. We have seen that pastoral nomads also defined women mainly as breeders, but what fundamentally distinguishes the earlier pastoral patriarchs from the early capitalists is the fact that the latter are totally concerned with the reproduction of the labour force and the 'breeders' of this labour force. In the first instance, the capitalist is not a producer, but an appropriator who follows the paradigm of predatory acquisition, the precondition for unequal exchange. Whereas the ruling classes among the pastoralists and the feudal lords were still aware of their own dependence on nature, including women (whom they, therefore, tried to influence by magic and religion), the capitalist class, from the beginning, saw itself as the master and lord *over* nature. Only now a concept of nature arose, which generalized man-the-hunter's dominance-relation to nature. The division of the world, which followed, defined certain parts of the world as 'nature', that is as savage, uncontrolled and, therefore, freely available for exploitation and the civilizing efforts, and others as 'human', that is already controlled and domesticated. The early capitalists were interested only in the muscle-power of the slaves, their energy to work. Nature for them was a reservoir of raw material and African women an apparently inexhaustible reserve of human energy.

The changeover from production relations based on a master–servant pattern to one of a contractual character between capital and wage labour, would not have been possible without the use of large-scale violence, and the 'definition into exploitable nature' of vast areas of the earth and their inhabitants. It enabled the capitalists 'to take off' and to give concessions to the European workers out of the looting of the colonies and the exploitation of slaves.

In fact, one could say, to the same degree that the workers of the European centre states acquired their humanity, were 'humanized', the workers – men and women – of the peripheries, that is Eastern Europe and the colonies, were 'naturized'.

'Pacification' of the European workers, the establishment of a new form of labour control through the wage-nexus, the transformation of direct violence into structural violence, or of extra-economic coercion into economic coercion, needed, however, not only special *economic*, but also *political* concessions.

These political concessions were/are not, as most people think, the male worker's participation in the democratic process, but his sharing the social paradigm of the ruling class, that is, the hunter/warrior model. But his 'colony' or 'nature' is not Africa, but the women of his own class. And within that part of nature, the boundaries of which are defined by marriage and family laws, he has the monopoly of the means of coercion, of direct violence, which, at the level of the state, the ruling classes invested in their representatives: the king and later the elected representatives.

The process of 'naturization' was not limited to the colonies and the women of the working class, but the women of the bourgeoisie were also defined into nature as mere breeders and rearers of the heirs of the capitalist class. In contrast to the African women, however, who were considered to be part of 'savage' nature, the bourgeois women were seen as 'domesticated' nature. Their sexuality, their generative powers as well as all their productive autonomy were suppressed and strictly controlled by the men of their class, on whom they had become dependent for their livelihood. The domestication of the bourgeois women, their transformation into housewives, dependent on the husband's income, became the model of the sexual division of labour under capitalism. It was also a political necessity in order to get control over the reproductive capacities of women, of all women. The process of proletarianization of the men was therefore accompanied by a process of *housewifization* of women.

In this process, the sphere where labour power was reproduced, the house and the family, was 'defined into nature' – private, domesticated nature – and the factory became the place for public, social ('human') production.

Just as 'naturization' of the colonies was not achieved by peaceful means but was based on large-scale use of direct violence and coercion, so also the process of domestication of European (and later of North American) women was neither peaceful nor idyllic. Women did not voluntarily hand over control over their productivity, their sexuality and their generative capacities to their husbands, and the BIG men (Church, State). Only after centuries of most brutal attacks against their sexual and productive autonomy did European women become the dependent, domesticated housewives that in principle, we are today. The counterpart of the slave raids in Africa was the witchhunt in Europe, and both seem to stem from the same dilemma faced by the capitalist version of man-the-hunter: However much he may try to reduce women to a condition of production, to nature, to be appropriated and exploited, he cannot produce living human labour power without women. Arms give him the possibility of an exclusively male mode of production, namely slavery (or war) which Meillassoux considers to be the male equivalent for the reproduction within a kinship system (Meillassoux: 1978:7), an effort of the men of a certain society to become independent of their women's reproduction. But this male mode of production has its natural limitations, particularly when the hunting grounds for human cattle are exhausted. It was, therefore, necessary to bring under control the generative and productive forces of the European women. Between the 14th and 18th centuries, the male guilds and the rising urban bourgeoisie managed to push craftswomen out of the sphere of production. (Rowbotham: 1974, O'Faolain and Martines: 1973) Moreover, for centuries, millions of women of mostly poor peasant or poor urban origin were persecuted, tortured and finally burnt as witches, because they tried to retain a certain autonomy over their bodies, particularly their generative forces. The attack of church and state against the witches aimed not only at the subordination of female sexuality as such, although this played a major role, but against their practices as abortionists and midwives. The feminist literature which appeared in recent years gives ample evidence of this policy. (Rowbotham: 1974, Becker-Bovenschen-Brackert: 1977, Dross: 1978, Honegger: 1979) Not only were women artisans pushed out of their jobs and their property confiscated by the city authorities, the state and the church, but women's control over the production of new life had to be abolished, that is, their decision to give birth or to abort. This war against women raged throughout Europe for at least three centuries. (Becker-Bovenschen-Brackert: 1977)

The aim of the witch-hunt was not only to effect direct disciplinary control over women's sexual and reproductive behaviour but also to establish the superiority of male over female productivity. These two processes are closely linked. The ideologues of the witch-hunt were indefatigable in denouncing female nature as sinful ('sin' is synonymous with 'nature'), as sexually uncontrollable, insatiable and ever ready to seduce the virtuous male. What is interesting is, that women were *not yet* seen as sexually passive or even as asexual beings as was the case later, in the 19th/20th century. On the contrary, their sexual activity was seen as a threat to the virtuous man, that is the man who wants to control the purity of his offspring, the heirs to his property. It is, therefore, man's obligation to guarantee the chastity of his daughters and his wife. As she is 'nature', 'sin', she must be permanently under his guardianship; she becomes a permanent minor.

Only men are capable of becoming adults in the true sense. To control their own women's sexuality the men were advised to resort to beatings and other violence. (Bauer: 1917) But all direct and ideological attacks on the sinful nature of women also served the purpose of robbing women of their autonomy over other, economically productive functions, and to establish the male hegemony in most economic and non-economic spheres.

Sexual autonomy is closely connected with economic autonomy. The case of the professionalization of male doctors who drove out and denounced women healers and midwives as witches is the best documentation of this onslaught on female productive activity. The new capitalist class rose on the subjugation of women. (Rowbotham: 1974)

At the end of this 'civilizing process' we have women disciplined enough to work as housewives for men or as wage labourers for capitalists or as both. They have learned to turn the violence used against them throughout centuries against themselves and to internalize it – they defined it as voluntariness, as 'love', the necessary ideological mystification of their own self-repression. (Bock: 1977) The church, the state and, above all, the family, provided the institutional and ideological props necessary for the maintenance of this self-repression. Women were confined to the institution of the family by the organization of the labour process (division of household from workplace), by law and by their economic dependence on the man as the so-called 'breadwinner'.

It would be an illusion, however, to think that with the full development of capitalism the barbarous features of its bloody beginnings would have disappeared and that fully developed capitalist production relations would mean the end of the social paradigm of man-the-hunter/warrior and the transformation of extra-economic coercion into economic coercion.[13]

On the contrary, for the maintenance of an asymmetric exploitative division of labour on a national and international plane (both are interlinked) full-fledged capitalism needs an ever-expanding state machinery of repression and a frightening concentration of means of destruction and coercion. None of the capitalist core-states has done away with the police or the military; they are, paralleling the hunters, warriors and warrior-nomads, still the most 'productive' sectors, because through the monopoly of now legalized violence these states are able to effectively curb any rebellion among the workers within their orbit and also to force subsistence producers and whole peripheral areas to produce for a globally interlinked accumulation process. Though exploitation of human labour on a world scale for profits has taken mainly the 'rational' form of unequal exchange, the maintenance of the unequal relationship is everywhere guaranteed by means of direct coercion: by arms.

To summarize we can say that the various forms of asymmetric, hierarchical divisions of labour which were developed throughout history, up to the stage where the whole world is now structured into one system of unequal division of labour under the dictates of capital accumulation, are based on the social paradigm of the predatory hunter/warrior who, without producing himself is able, by means of arms, to appropriate and subordinate other producers, their productive forces and their products.

This extractive, non-reciprocal exploitative object relation to nature, first established between men and women and men and nature, remained the model for all other male modes of production, including capitalism, which developed it to its most sophisticated and most generalized form.[14] The characteristic of this model is that those who control the production process and the products are themselves not producers but appropriators. Their so-called productivity presupposes the existence and the subjection of other, and in the last analysis, female producers. As Wallerstein puts it: '. . . crudely, those who breed manpower sustain those who grow food who sustain those who grow other raw materials who sustain those involved in industrial production.' (Wallerstein: 1977:86) What Wallerstein forgets to mention is that all those sustain the non-producers who control this whole process, in the last analysis by means of arms. Because, at the heart of this paradigm lies the fact that non-producers appropriate and consume (or invest) what others have produced. Man-the-hunter is basically a parasite, not a producer.

Notes

1. This article is the result of a longer collective process of reflection among women in the years 1975–77, when I conducted courses on the history of the women's movement at Frankfurt University. Many of the ideas discussed here emerged in a course on 'Work and Sexuality in Matristic Societies'. The thesis of one of my students, Roswitha Leukert, on 'Female Sensuality' (1976), helped to clarify many of our ideas. I want to thank her and all the women who took part in these discussions.

This chapter was first presented at the Conference 'Underdevelopment and Subsistence Reproduction', University of Bielefeld 1979; also published in Maria Mies, *Patriarchy and Accumulation on a World Scale*, Zed Books, London, 1986.

2. The term exploitation is used here in the sense that a more or less permanent separation and hierarchization has taken place between producers and consumers. The original situation in an egalitarian community, that is, that in which those who produce something are also (in an inter-generational sense) its consumers, has been disrupted. Exploitative social relations exist when non-producers are able to appropriate and consume (or invest) products and services of actual producers. (See: A Sohn-Rethel 1978; Rosa Luxemburg 1925)

3. Recent research on women workers in the Free Trade Zones in South-East Asia and Latin America reveals that multinational corporations not only use and reinforce existing patriarchal institutions but also use modern sexist advertising to manipulate their, mostly female, labour force in Malaysia, South Korea, the Philippines, Singapore, Mexico, Haiti. (Grossmann 1979: Pearson/Elson 1978: Lenz 1980) In the unorganized rural and urban sector the housewife-ideology is used to transform pauperized peasant women into a totally atomized labour force in export-oriented household industries. (Mies 1980)

4. 'Appropriation of Nature' (Aneignung der Natur) has a double meaning in German, and this ambiguity can also be found in the way Marx uses this expression: on the one hand he uses it in the sense of: 'making nature our own, to humanize nature'. In his earlier writings the formulation 'appropriation of nature' is used in this sense. On the other hand it defines a relationship of dominance between Man and Nature. This is the case in *Capital* where Marx has reduced the broader definition to mean 'dominance over, control over, mastership over nature'. As we shall see, such an interpretation of this formulation proves to be problematic for women.

5. This sexism prevails in many languages. English, French and all Romanic languages cannot differentiate between 'man' (male being) and 'man' (human being). In the German language this difference can still be expressed: *Mann* is the male, *Mensch* the human being, though *Mensch* has also assumed a male connotation.

6. With Bornemann I use the term 'matristic' instead of 'matriarchal', because 'matriarchal' implies that mothers were able to establish a political system of dominance. But not even in matrilineal and matrilocal societies did women establish such lasting politically dominant systems. (Bonnemann 1975)

7. The Indian mother-goddesses (Kali, Durga etc.) are all embodiments of this active and practical principle, whereas many of the male gods are passive, contemplative and ascetic.

8. For a discussion of the relationship between a certain concept of nature and the appropriation of female bodies see also Colette Guillaumin 1978.

9. A comparison of the terminology used in population research today with that of an earlier period would be very revealing. Until the 1930s the production of new life was still conceptualized as 'procreation', that is, it still had an active, creative connotation. But today the generative productivity is conceptualized in passive, biologistic, behaviouristic and mechanistic terms such as: 'fertility', 'biological reproduction', 'generative behaviour'. This definition of human generative productivity as passive fertility is a necessary ideological mystification for those who want to gain control over this last area of human autonomy.

10. This is not surprising as May also uses the concept 'fertility' in the same sense as most population researchers and family planners do, namely as the result of unconscious, physiological behaviour.

11. For a discussion of the seed-and-field analogy in ancient Indian literature, see also, Maria Mies: 1973, 1980; Leela Dube: 1978.

12. See for instance Kathleen Gough's 'The Origin of the Family' in Rayna Reiter, (ed.) *Toward an Anthropology of Women.*

13. At the present moment in history we can no longer share the opinion of the earlier Marxists, including Rosa Luxemburg, that warfare and extra-economic violence were necessary methods to solve conflicts of interest as long as the productive forces had not reached their highest development, as long as human beings had not achieved total control and dominance over nature. (cf. Rosa Luxemburg 1925: 155-6) Our problem is that this definition of 'development of productive forces' *implies* violence and warfare against nature, women and other peoples.

14. It would be appropriate at this point to extend our analysis to the sexual division of labour under socialism, but this would require a much broader analysis. From what can be gathered from information about the status of women in socialist countries we can only conclude that the division of labour by sex is based on the same social paradigm as in the capitalist countries. One of the reasons for this is that the concept of the 'development of productive forces' and man's relation to nature has been the same as under capitalism, meaning, namely, man's lordship over nature, which implies his lordship over women.

Sources

Ardrey, Robert (1966) *The Territorial Imperative*, Atheneum, New York.
—— (1976) *The Hunting Hypothesis*, Atheneum, New York.
Bazin, Jean (1975) 'Guerre et Servitude à Segou', in: Meillassoux (ed.) *L'esclavage dans l'Afrique pre-coloniale*, Maspéro, Paris.
Bauer, Max (1917) *Deutscher Frauenspiegel*, Georg Müller, München, Berlin.
Becker, Bovenschen Brackert et al (1977) *Aus der Zeit der Verzweiflung: Zur Genese und Akutalität des Hexenbildes*, e.s. Frankfurt.
Bloch, Marc. *Cambridge Economic History of Europe I.*
Bock, Gisela (1977) 'Arbeit aus Liebe – als Arbiet: Die Entstehung der Frauenarbeit im Kapitalismus' in: *Frauen und Wissenschaft*. Beiträge zur Berliner Sommeruniversität, Courage Verlag, Berlin.
Bonte, Pierre (1975) 'Ésclavage et Relations de dépendence chez les Touaregs Kel Gress', in: Meillassoux (ed.). *L'esclavage dans l'Afrique précoloniale*, Maspéro, Paris.
Bornemann, Ernest (1975) *Das Patriarchat*, Fischer, Frankfurt.
Boserup, Esther (1970) *Women's Role in Economic Development*, St. Martins Press, New York.
Briffault, Robert (1977) *The Mothers*, Atheneum, New York.
Brown, Judith (1970) 'Economic Organisation and the Position of Women among the Iroquois' in: *Ethnohistory*, No. 17, 1970.
Chattopadhyaya, Debiprasad (1973) *Lokayata, A Study in Ancient Indian Materialism*, Peoples Publishing House, New Delhi.
Childe, Gordon (1976) *What Happened in History*, Penguin, London.

Dross, Annemarie (1978) *Die erste Walpurgisnacht, Hexenverfolgung in Deutschland*, Hauser, Wuppertal.

Dube, Leela (1978) 'The Seed and the Field: Symbolism of Human Reproduction in India'. Paper read at the Xth International Conference of Anthropological Sciences, New Delhi.

Ehrenfels, O. R. (1941) *Mother-Right in India*, Hyderabad.

Elias, Norbert (1978) *Der Prozess der Zivilisation*, Suhrkamp, Frankfurt (English: *The Civilising Process*).

Engels, Frederic (1973) *Origin of the Family, Private Property and the State*, International Publishers, New York.

Fisher, Elisabeth (1979) *Women's Creation*, Anchor Press, Doubleday, Garden City, New York.

Fröbel, V., Kreye, J., Heinrichs, O. (1977) *Die neue internationale Arbeitsteilung, Strukturelle Arbeitslösigkeit in den Industrieländern und die Industrialisierung der Entwicklungsländer rororo aktuell*, Reinbek.

Goodale, Jane (1971) *Tiwi Wives*, University of Washington Press, Seattle and London.

Gough, Kathleen (1975) 'The Origin of the Family', in: *Toward an Anthropology of Women*, (ed.) R. Reiter.

Grossmann, Rachael (1979) 'Women's Place in the Integrated Circuit', in: *Southeast Asia Chronicle*, SRC, Issue No. 66.

Guillaumin, Colette (1978) 'Pratique du pouvoir et idée de Nature. I. L'appropriation des femmes, II. Le discours de la nature', in: *Questions Feministes*, 2 February, 3 May.

Hammes, Manfred (1977) *Hexenwahn und Hexenprozesse*, Fischer Taschenbuch, Frankfurt.

Heritier, Françoise (1975) 'Des cauris et des hommes: production d'esclaves et accumulation de cauris chez les samos', (Haute-Volta) in: Meillassoux: *L'esclavage dans l'Afrique precoloniale*.

Honegger, Claudia (ed.) (1978) *Die Hexen der Neuzeit*, e.s. Frankfurt.

Karve, Iravati (1965) *Kinship Organisation in India*, Asia Publishing House, Bombay.

Leacock, Eleanor (1978) 'Women's Status in Egalitarian Society: Implications for Social Evolution', in: *Current Anthropology* Vol. 19, No. 2.

Lee, Richard Borshay (1980) *The !Kung San: Men, Women and Work in a Foraging Society*, Cambridge University Press, London, New York, New Rochelle, Melbourne, Sydney.

Lenz, Ilse (1980) From the Farm to the Global Assembly Line: The Situation of Women Workers in the Free Production Zones in Malaysia, Paper read at I.S.S.

Leukert, Roswitha (1976) *Weibliche Sinnlichkeit*, unpublished thesis, University of Frankfurt.

Lorenz, Konrad (1963) *Das sogenannte Böse*, Wien. (English translation: *On Aggression*.)

Martin & Voorhies (1975) *Female of the Species*, Columbia University Press, New York & London.

Marx, Karl (1974) *Capital I*, Lawrence & Wishart, London.

Marx, Karl & Engels, Friedrich (1970) *The German Ideology*, (ed.) C. J. Arthur, New York.

Meillassoux, Claude (1974) *Femmes, Greniers et Capitaux*, Maspero, Paris.

Mies, Maria (1973) *Indische Frauen zwischen Patriarchat und Chancengleichheit*, Anton Hain, Meisenheim/Glan, 1980: (English version): *Indian Women and Patriarchy*. Concept Publishers, Delhi.

O'Faolain, J. L., Martines, L. (1973) *Not in God's Image: Women in History from the Greeks to the Victorians*, Harper Torch Books, New York.

Pearson, Ruth, Elson, Diana (1977) 'The Internationalisation of Capital and its implications for women in the Third World', Paper, Sussex.

Reed, Evelyn (1975) *Woman's Evolution, From Matriarchal Clan to Patriarchal Family*, New York.

—— (1978) *Sexism & Science*, Pathfinder Press, New York.

Reiter, Rayna (1977) 'The Search for Origins', in: *Critique of Anthropology*, Women's Issue, 9 & 10, vol. 3.

Rowbotham, Sheila (1974) *Hidden from History*, Pluto Press, London.

—— (1972) *Women, Resistance and Revolution*, Penguin, London.

Slocum, Sally (1975) 'Woman the Gatherer', in *Toward an Anthropology of Women*, (ed.) R. Reiter, Monthly Review Press, New York.

Sohn-Rethel, Alfred (1978) 'Zur kritischen Liquidierung des Apriorismus', in: Sohn-Rethel: *Warenform und Denkform*. e.s. Frankfurt.

—— (1970): *Geistige und körperliche Arbeit*, e.s. Frankfurt.

Tiger, Lionel and Fox, Robin (1971) *The Imperial Animal*, Holt, Rinehart and Winston, New York.

Thomson, George (1965) *Studies in Ancient Greek Society: The Prehistoric Aegean*, Citadel Press, New York.

Turnbull, Colin, M. (1961) *The Forest People: A Study of the Pygmies of the Congo*, Simon and Schuster, New York.

Wallerstein, Immanuel (1974) *The Modern World System: Capitalist Agriculture and the Origins of the European World Economy in the Sixteenth Century*, Academic Press, New York, San Francisco, London.

5.   On the Concept of Nature and Society in Capitalism*

Claudia von Werlhof

'Nature' and 'Society'

Why are women, as well as the largest, purportedly 'Third' part of the world regarded as 'nature' and treated as objects to be appropriated, exploited and destroyed? And why does such behaviour incur no penalty, as if it were merely a minor misdemeanour? Why does the smaller part of the world, the so-called 'First' World and these petty offenders, men in general and white men in particular, count as 'society', subjects, real 'people'? What does this seemingly natural – that is, biological or geographical – counterposition of 'black' and 'white', 'man' and 'woman', First World and Third World, mean?

Ideas about what make up 'nature' and 'society', or 'human' and 'non-human' have always differed everywhere. Consider first the location of the dividing line between 'nature' and 'non-nature'; where does 'nature' and 'non-nature' begin? Not only is there no universal agreement about the answer to this question, but views about the relationship between 'nature' and 'non-nature' also vary widely, and always have.

It was the emergence of a world economy, the 'capitalist world-system' (to use Wallerstein's term), which put the final seal on the victory of the Biblical injunction to 'subdue the Earth', and established it as the general intellectual foundation of 'civilized man'. The relationship between 'nature' and 'non-nature' first began to be seen as antithetical, and then beyond that as a hierarchy in which necessarily 'nature' was subject to 'non-nature' (Norbert Elias), in the 15th and 16th centuries, in association with the beginning of the age of discovery. Our present-day understanding of 'nature' is, therefore, far from natural. It is a historical and social creation. 'Nature' can be defined only if something exists that can be defined as its opposite. Our contemporary notions of nature and society should, then, be seen as having arisen simultaneously: they belong together like two sides of a coin. We cannot, in principle, talk about, reflect on and use the terms 'society' and 'humanity' without simultaneously employing a particular notion of 'nature' – an activity

* Revised version of 'Frauen und Dritte Welt als "Natur" des Kapitals oder: ökonomie auf die Füsse gestellt' in Dauber, H. and Simpfendörfer, W. (eds), *Eigener Haushalt und bewohnter Erdkreis. ökologisches and ökumenisches Lernen in der 'Einen Welt'*, Peter Hammer Verlag, Wuppertal, 1981: pp. 184–217.

which our fragmented and compartmentalized science, with its division of labour, has always tried strenuously to prevent. Science has clung to and defended precisely what it should have investigated: its own division of labour. The social sciences, supposedly, are not concerned with nature; and the natural sciences, again supposedly, are not concerned with society.

The concept of nature: people as 'nature'

The concept of nature has no connection with nature meaning the woods down the lane. It is not 'wild birds and bulrushes' (Murray Bookchin) and bears no relation to what we perhaps continue to think of as nature *per se*. The concept of nature is not determined by biology but by economics: it does not distinguish between people and animals but between people and people – and it varies.

From the standpoint of the rulers (be these 'whites', managers – public or private – or simply men and husbands) 'nature' is everything that they do not have to, or are not willing to pay for – everything that should be free (or as cheap as possible). This covers everything that can be appropriated through robbery (as opposed to exchange), and beyond that everything they can neither renew nor preserve. This 'everything' does indeed amount almost to *everything* – the entire globe, along with its products, commodities and peoples.

More specifically, at any given historical instant, 'nature' is what the economic process consumes as 'inputs'; this embraces the land and the soil, the products of the soil, mineral resources, the products of industry and handicrafts, services and – first and foremost – the people to work and produce them: without human labour power none of the other products would be available or valorisable – that is, convertible into 'value'. The 'what' of nature is, therefore, ultimately a *who*. Labour power above all is indispensable, both in the workplace and in the family.

Not only should these products and services, and especially workers, be available but they should be as cheap as possible. That is, their own production and reproduction, their genesis and their maintenance before, during and after their use, should incur either only minimum or no costs to whoever needs and uses them. Seen from the standpoint of the dominant logic, (the logic of the dominators) there is, then, a tendency to maximize the range of resources, products and people (as bearers or possessors of labour power) to be treated as if they were nature and available gratis, like air. The labour of these people is therefore pronounced to be non-labour, to be biology: their labour power – their ability to work – appears as a natural resource, and their products as akin to a natural deposit. (cf. Maria Mies, 1980a)

We are witnessing a progressive extension of the concept of nature to cover all people, their work and what they produce. This concerns not only women, blacks and the wageless, but in the final analysis, white male wage-workers. In contrast to the usual assumptions about advancing 'humanization' or 'socialization', with its implied limitation of what belongs to nature, the real process is heading in the opposite direction. An ideological and material process of 'naturization' or 'feminization' is taking place. Based on the ideal type of women's 'nature' – domestic labour and the housewife – the process might also be termed 'domestication' or 'housewifization'. (V. Bennholdt-Thomsen, 1979; M. Mies, 1980b)

The 'naturalness' of work

Being 'natural' initially means poverty despite work. According to UNO figures women perform two-thirds of all the hours worked – including housework – in the world. For this, they receive no more than one-tenth of world income and own one-hundredth of all private property. (*Frankfurter Rundschau*, 26 June 1980) The same applies to the Third World. To quote a resident of Soweto: 'I own nothing in this country simply because I'm black' (*Frankfurter Rundschau*, 20 June 1980).

What is available virtually free to the economic process and transformed into 'value' within it appears to have no cost simply because it costs its beneficiary nothing. Those people, products and institutions declared to be 'nature' appear, like manna, to have fallen from heaven. Placed by God in the 'lap' of the white man, the managers, pimps and husbands, they 'have always been there'.

There *are* costs – but for the other: for nature and those things and people defined as nature. These are the so-called 'social' costs, quasi-, non-, or 'extra-economic' costs, as if there were no economy prior to, after and alongside the factory. (cf. K. W. Kapp) It may already be becoming clear who gains from a definition of the economic which is so narrow as to exclude precisely what makes the 'economy' possible, and who certainly has no concern for its consequences. The 'social' costs of the destruction of the environment, for example, are treated as 'natural' costs – costs to be borne by nature or whatever is declared 'natural'. In any event, the damage is not paid for by its perpetrators. Natural resources are plundered like the air and water, land and soil.

'The world is seen as an exploitable mine.' (G. Anders) The 'only thing that capital leaves behind is . . . a hole in the ground' (J. Galtung); the world as a violated virgin or sexual slave, forcibly prostituted.

Wage-workers also are subject to 'social' costs. These fall into two types: 1) those too large to be covered by the wage; and 2) those which, in principle, cannot be met by money. They include the physical and psychological losses and erosions experienced at work and which have to be made good if those involved want to continue to work and live. Men without a wife or woman have to bear these costs alone – which is why most do have a wife/woman. Irrespective of exactly how much of these 'human' costs can be off-loaded on to women via housework, what is certain is that women, and the majority of similarly unpaid workers living in the Third World, are systematically and disproportionally drawn on to bear the consequences of this plundering of the entire world, and to produce and reproduce the preconditions for such plunder

– raw materials and labour power. The fact of this robbery and depredation is also systematically denied. It simply does not fit in with the image of our, supposedly, enormously liberal and democratic, complex and subtle 'exchange' society, capable, again supposedly, of such immense economic achievements 'out of its own resources'.

Bearing 'social' costs means either being overwhelmed by them, being destroyed by them, or finding a way to offset or at least mitigate them. After all, most people prefer to carry on living, even at the price of being someone's prize. The labour of making oneself available for exploitation by others is, of course, 'naturally' unrewarded. It is not voluntary, however: it is compulsory, it must be performed. But why should this mean that it has to be paid for? It is this that comprises the present-day form of forced labour.

For most of those who do not have to perform it – broadly, whites, capitalists and most wage-workers – this work remains 'invisible'. They either fail to see it or look away: 'work' which should not exist, cannot exist. Work in the dark, in the shadow (I. Illich) of 'real' wage labour, not only costs 'the economy' nothing, it also gives it something. For the shadow-workers who are not counted as part of this 'economy', it signifies a double exploitation. The 'economy' forces them to work twice over, virtually at no cost. Once to produce enormous volumes of cheap raw materials and fresh labour; secondly, to repair, gratis, the damage done by and to these by the 'economy'. They have no other option, if they want to continue to live. And this most basic of interests is precisely what is exploited. First, however, it has to be established in an exploitable form. This requires creating the appropriate conditions: people have to be divested of their former control over land, tools, knowledge and themselves so profoundly and for so long that they possess nothing other than their naked ability to work; this ability is the only means by which they can survive. They will, therefore, work, and in fact be forced to do any work, even if they are barely paid or not paid at all. In contrast to pre-capitalist forced labour, however, there is no need for someone to stand over them with a whip.

Labour that produces but costs nothing is subject to the same principle as labour that produces more than it costs. In this respect, wage labour is rather expensive for 'the economy', and generalized 'proletarianization' could never be afforded, which is why it has not taken place and – contrary to many expectations – will not be possible within our system.

Curiously, even critics of the system continue to identify what is, in fact, the upshot of the massive advance of capitalism across the globe and its transformation into a single 'natural resource' for itself as not yet, non- or even pre- capitalist backwardness. This is why, in global terms, 'proletarians' are so rare: it is not the product of tradition, but in fact of modernity.

Convincing us that the product of a centuries-long orgy of violence against nature is 'natural' is a brilliant ideological achievement. Its accomplishment is the forced exploitation of the majority of the world's population – women and blacks. Initially designated a danger, and then hunted and exterminated, finally brain-washed and broken in: tamed, civilized, evangelized and cultivated. Broken in from 'naturally' evil witches and savages to equally 'naturally' passive and phlegmatic maids of all work, they themselves are expected to believe 'that progress and civilization began with the arrival of the white man, that sexual and racial apartheid is ordained by God and that obedient submission is the 'natural' role of the black man [and all women].'

The limits of nature and the necessity of the monopoly over women and land

Economic, political or ideological factors may at different times greatly vary the boundaries between 'nature' and 'non-nature' as regards the extent to which wage-workers are also to be 'sent back to nature'. Although there is no necessary upper limit on what constitutes nature, however, nature itself (without the quotation marks) does impose a bottom line.

These truly natural limits are set by the fact that there can never be an infinite number of workers, an infinite area of land, or infinite quantities of mineral resources. Workers, land and minerals can only be discovered, conquered, valorised, appropriated, transformed and destroyed. Capital alone cannot even do that, let alone give birth, enlarge the area of land or conjure up minerals where none existed before. Nothing emerges from capital itself. It is quite dead; past, 'dead' labour. Paper money or machines, on their own, are simply scraps of paper and heaps of scrap. Capital begins to 'live' only through a relation, the capital relation, in which it is brought into contact with human life, living people (cf. the vampire motif in literature and horror films). Machines have no meaning or at least no value until someone switches them on. Production can, if necessary, take place without machines, but never without people.

Capital can also establish a relationship with non-human, external nature only via people. Even the most efficient and gleaming tractor cannot drive itself across a field: it needs a driver, a person. And the sole supplier of people are women and their wombs. But wombs cannot simply produce as many new human beings as might be demanded, even if they were to be transformed into child-producing machines. So far, men, and specifically capitalists, have been unable, to their great regret, to liberate themselves from their dependency on the uterus. (As compensation, they 'created' the 'creative' Spirit, God, the Entrepreneur, Man.) And since, so far, there has been no substitute for the uterus, women, as its 'bearer', became the first people over which men had to establish control – and will be the last over which men will relinquish control. Men in general and capitalists in particular could not, and cannot, abandon their control over procreation (either expanding or limiting), as the production process of the most important, because indispensable, 'means of production': human labour-power. In fact, the capacity to bear children has probably never played such a central role in history as under our present system. In contrast to its predecessors, control over this capacity is an indispensable precondition for this system. For, as much as it would like to replace living with dead labour, no other system has been as radically dependent on such massive depradation of nature and human labour-power. (Perhaps this is one of the most fundamental distinctions between the present and previous forms of patriarchy.)

Much the same applies to the land and soil, including minerals, on which all other forms of production, including industrial production, is and will continue to be dependent. No substitutes exist for this either. And again, because the supply of land and mineral resources is of necessity restricted – they are either available or not, a fact unalterable regardless of how much or how efficiently capital and labour are applied to them – control must be established over them too.

Under our system, anything subject to natural limitations appears as inherently scarce. Capital is insatiable. It needs more than nature has; it needs infinitely more. Hence, anything subject to natural limitations, 'scarce' in the system's terms and, moreover, anything which is an indispensable precondition as a means of production for further production, must – in an economic system such as ours – not only be under *some* kind of control but be brought under *monopolistic* control. In the case of women and land, this drive for control becomes a drive for monopoly because both *can* be monopolized. Anyone who controls the land, the riches within it, and women, can exercise a monopoly over their use – a monopoly to which all others become subject through force of need, or better, nature. The monopolist's monopoly is free, and its object is in abundance, as if there were no 'scarcity', as if as much as might be wanted is available. In contrast, he can create an artificial scarcity for all others and make a product or resource so impossibly expensive that no one else can afford it – and, as in the case of women and land – no one except the monopolist can produce at all. In a competitive system, therefore, each must strive to become a monopolist in order to forestall the other. Moreover, he must try to achieve a monopoly of everything – even of things which he cannot at present use – in order to deny access to a competitor. Beginning with the drive to establish an absolute monopoly over women and land, monopolization therefore extends to everything else, *as if they were women or land*, and the monopolist continues to appear as the 'life-giving creator'.

Monopoly as violence: the perpetuation of 'primitive accumulation'

Once this process reached capital itself, there was sudden concern about the hazards of monopoly and of 'monopoly capitalism', as if monopoly was something new in the history of this mode of production, a feature of its 'late phase'. Nonetheless, the fact that Europe was once characterized by a supposedly monopoly-free phase, so-called 'competitive capitalism', is no proof that, as liberals like to assure us, this is a 'typical' or 'authentic' property of capitalism. Firstly, this phase has been found nowhere in the Third World – and not because these areas have 'not yet' been 'integrated' into capitalism. And secondly, even competitive capitalism in Europe was not free of monopoly: there was merely no concentration of capital. This phase of so-called 'free and perfect competition' had been preceded by another process which established the conditions for the possibility of 'competition' – if only fleetingly and only in the First World: the process of 'primitive' or 'original accumulation'.

To anticipate one observation or criticism: the establishment of monopoly is nothing new, nor is 'primitive' accumulation solely a thing of the past. Pronounced dead since, at the latest, the 18th century, it has in fact lived on as our faithful companion throughout the world. I term this 'continuing primitive accumulation' – not 'non'-capitalist (Frank) but specifically and emphatically capitalist. Effort continues to be expended to persuade us that not only is this process long since complete, but it was essentially a product of a 'brutal display of vigour' of the Middle Ages, 'shrouded in darkness'. Certainly, blame cannot be laid at the door of the capitalist mode of production, which is held to have commenced with the onset of industry in the 18th century. The – continuing – fate of women and 'witches' and the colonies is not seen as intrinsic to this brutal form of the accumulation of capital, but rather as an expression of 'alien mentalities' or 'feudal traditions'. Embarrassingly for this view, however, they are neither alien nor feudal, but native and very modern. 'Primitive accumulation' should, therefore, be seen as a historical and a contemporary necessity of our mode of production, and one operating on a world scale.

The truth is very simple: the process of 'primitive' accumulation is primarily about the struggle to force women and the land, including mineral resources, under the monopoly power of capital.

Such a process is hardly likely to be a peace-march. The method of 'primitive accumulation' is overt violence, with the aim of robbery wherever, whenever, and against whomsoever this is 'economically' necessary, politically possible and technically feasible. And, as we have seen, this method was and is necessary against women and the land because the production of wealth hinges on controlling them. This meant, first and foremost, power over the former possessors of the land and controllers of procreation: peasants, women, and more broadly the populations of the colonies. The plundering, burning, violation, rape and murder have not ceased since then.

In addition to other forms of non-wage labour which have spread, especially within the colonies, the most important outcome of this process is contemporary domestic labour. (See Bock and Duden) The journey 'from witch to housewife' took several centuries. It began with the conjuring-up of the woman as 'vixen', with her supposed untrammelled 'Satanic nature'; this then justified any step taken against women to 'subdue nature'. The 'nature' which was to be combated, and hence dominated, thus first had to be *invented*. (G. Becker et al.; C. Honnegger et al.; A. Dross)

Women as absolute nature and the violence of their domination

The end-product of this process – the housewife – has, however, no claim to any 'consideration' for her domestication, for being readmitted to 'society'. On the contrary. She not only remains 'nature' but is also expected to be grateful for having found her 'true nature'; whether 'whore' or 'saint', tamed or not, woman remains woman: 'nature'.

In contrast to black and other people treated as 'nature', women are the only people on earth who *always under all circumstances* count as 'nature'. The natural foundation for this ideology is their procreative capacity – the ability to bear children. Women have, as it were, a natural monopoly of this capacity. This is sufficient to render them born mortal enemies of our system, irrespective of where she is on the globe, black or white, rich or poor, subservient or not. Our system will only tolerate monopoly when it is exercised by men and is under the control of capital.

Women have to be assigned to 'nature' precisely because they have been deprived of their nature, because, un-naturally, they are not to be permitted to control their natural capabilities. The universal drive to turn women into 'nature' is the absolute economic precondition of our present-day mode of production as distinct from its predecessors. The diverse forms of patriarchal control over women seen in preceding systems, such as exchange and theft of women, marriage regulations and kinship systems, never attained the intensity, extremes and absoluteness of those operating at present, leaving aside for a moment its global extension – a fact unaltered by any seeming 'emancipation'.

If 'primitive' accumulation means the rapacious appropriation of others' labour, products and capacity to work, the example of women shows precisely why it has not been possible to bring this process to a historical close, and why it must continue as long as the capitalist mode of production exists. Women are people, not land. One act of seizure and possession of land is sufficient, in principle, to secure it in perpetuity. Matters are not as simple with human beings. The ability to rob them of their labour, their products and their capacities must be constantly renewed, from generation to generation, and sometimes even from day to day. Control over people, the monopoly of force and robbery over them, has to be permanently established, maintained and imposed in the face of resistance. We are supposed to believe that immediate, direct, so-called 'extra-economic coercion' has now yielded, and is continuing to yield to indirect, 'structural', so-called 'economic coercion', with the implication that people now force themselves to work instead of having to be forced by others.

Although this new form of violence is quite evident, it is also clear that the old form continues as a complement to it, although perhaps in new guises. One only has to look: in the family, school, in the armed forces, in prisons, at confession, at the doctor's surgery – in short, direct force, both psychic and physical, is applied in all institutions of instruction and healing. Children have to be 'properly brought up', potential rebelliousness suppressed. Rebels can always be expected where people are to be robbed, especially in the Third World and amongst women. Non-violence is, therefore, instilled into them from the outset; they must recoil from any violence, both of others and possibly their own. No one has a more remarkable relationship to the direct use of violence than women (for the Third World, see Franz Fanon). They are deeply anxious about it – both that of others, and their own. But this almost 'inborn' fear of overt violence is not 'natural'. It is the result of centuries of continuing, unbroken *war against women*.

This war is waged because within our system women's own control of procreation constitutes an enormous threat, which is why most women are deprived of control over any other capacity, working activity and product. Having once exercised self-determination in one field, might they not acquire the taste or ability to exercise it in others? This is why, in every other way, all women, whether of child-bearing age or not, are treated, in essence, as if they were a uterus.

The artificial gender

No black or white man is confronted with such a degree of violence, or as radically and unconditionally assigned to 'nature'. Instead, each individual man, including black men – even when treated as 'nature' – is given a mini-monopoly over a woman. Like the great white man, even the small white man is permitted to dominate a piece of 'nature' as if it were 'natural' property or his 'colony'. Even black men receive the 'nature of their nature'. Even where land, implements, a house, let alone capital, have been denied, one thing has been guaranteed – a woman. Her place is to serve as substitute for the lost land, the lost security, the lost self-determination and the experience of exploitation. (See K. Theweleit)

No social order in history has extended, distorted and used the natural difference between the sexes as brutally and systematically as ours. This 'order' first transformed natural sex into a social, artificial gender, made 'men' out of men, and 'women' out of women – in fact, turned 'men' into 'the human race' and women into simply a sex as such. It has made the sexual question into the prime social problem, in fact, into *the* general class question. It has also transformed every other type of natural difference, skin, hair and eye colour, shape, size and build, into social problems. And finally, having created these differences, it declares them to be 'natural' again, in order to render them economically exploitable. Even such social differences as religion, nation and region, have become social problems by being rendered 'natural' differences. This biologism turns biology into a social question and society into a biological question.

By humiliating women and accepting the humiliation of women, men sign a blank cheque for their own humiliation.

They sat in this room in their best clothes, thinking this is where judges live, doctors, permanent secretaries, estate-owners . . . Two quiet men had sat there, two men who regarded themselves as indispensable, two men who thought themselves fair partners of the management, two men who believed they were completely free . . .

The icy cold which began to spread through his body as the foreman suddenly stood alongside him, the icy certainty, as he went up into the personnel office, as he was given his letter of dismissal. He suddenly realised that they could take everything from him: work, home, wife, children, even his life. (G. Fuchs, *Der Arbeitslose*)

The unemployed man is a non-wage-worker. His 'maleness', his 'humanity', his guaranteed right to 'the second sex', his 'nature', the housewife, disappear when he loses his wage. He himself becomes 'naturized', 'domesticated', a kind of 'black', the 'land' on which he once stood.

Exploitation of 'nature' as the extraction of a rent from women and the colonies

'Nature' is cheap, even free. It demands no wage for its labour and no price for its products. It has no needs and does not have to be renewed. It is 'forced nature', subject to forced exploitation, the 'landed property' of small and large monopolists.

With the monopoly over nature and 'nature', the *most valuable and irreplaceable things on earth*, living labour power, people and natural resources, simultaneously become the *most worthless*. Their 'scarcity', the wealth of nature, appears as a social abundance producible at will, as mere 'matter', consumable and destroyable at will. It has no 'value' because it costs no money. Money has a value; but not life. According to the macabre logic of our economy, 'the human producing by means of violence also treats his own kind as mere raw material.' (G. Anders)

The fact of violence leads from appearance to essence. The necessity of violence means that analysis has to be turned from its head on to its feet: raw materials are not found – people are robbed. Men rob them because they are very directly needed. Their use-value is so high that it could never be paid for; our system could not even manage the most limited experiment in this direction. At bottom, this use-value cannot be expressed in money. It is therefore treated as if it had no value, no exchange value: its use-value is not paid for because it counts as of 'extra-economic' nature. The stolen products and labour services are not, therefore, 'valueless' 'by their nature', but rather *are not socially valued, are treated with violence as being without exchange value* ('primitive' accumulation).

These 'non-values' become subject to exchange – at the highest possible value – principally in the First and Second World only after being accumulated and transformed into values ('valorisation') through wage labour.

The high social evaluation of commodities, their exchange-value or price, thus presupposes the lowest possible evaluation, the 'de-valuation', of the labour necessary for their production, and in particular of the labour which precedes or accompanies wage labour, and which is not, therefore, remunerated at all. Moreover, this labour, which is stolen, not exchanged, must be extracted forcibly, directly or indirectly; since it is not paid for, it would not otherwise be performed.

One method of putting value theory back on its feet is to draw on the almost forgotten theory of rent. We see then that what is involved is the extraction of an enormous capitalist rent based on the monopoly of women and the colonies as quasi-landed property.

In contrast, the few attempts to consider the process of the appropriation of non-remunerated labour as rent have been on the basis of the emergence of a pre-capitalist rent (for example, C. Meillassoux's labour rent). Although this labour is acknowledged as labour, its character is misapprehended. The essential property of such labour, the basis of its current existence, is the fact that it enters into the formation of capital and is not extraneous to it. This point is also overlooked by a number of feminists who view patriarchy as a 'non'-capitalist 'dual' system separate from the capital relation. For 'radical' feminists, for example, the economic process ends once the man has exploited his wife. Conversely, 'socialist' feminists have still not recognized that wage labour has a very relative significance in our system because it could not exist without unpaid labour (principally housework) (cf. the debates in PROKLA; in France in *Questions Feministes*; and in Great Britain in the Conference of Socialist Economics (CSE) journal *Capital and Class* and *Feminist Review*; see especially Datar). Economics does not take place only at home; nor does it only begin on leaving the household, as is commonly supposed. Wage-workers not only have to obtain their labour power, but also constantly expend it. They cannot simply hoard their ability to work, that is, the rent produced by their wives: the purpose of receiving it is to expend it in the process of wage labour – and if possible all of it.

The rent extracted from women and the colonies is transferred to the centre and enters the process of wage labour. In fact, it is the absolute precondition for this process. Both the products produced in the colonies which are used in the wage labour process there, and the paid labour power itself are available only because unpaid labour, in particular domestic labour, has been applied to them, and is contained in them as a kind of rent. (cf. Bennholdt-Thomsen/Werlhof)

The surplus value created by wage-workers must, therefore, contain this element of rent which is certainly worth more than the additional value added by the wage-worker. In other words, profit, too, essentially consists of this rent. Those who, by their nature, are the richest on the earth – women and the colonies – therefore 'naturally' and of necessity become the poorest.

The process of enforcing labour and the simultaneous robbery of the rent created by those who work constitutes contemporary capitalist 'primitive' accumulation.

The economy is 'naturized' and nature 'economized'. The inevitable result of omitting these connections and inversions is a never-ending shuttle backwards and forwards between economism and idealism.

Democracy, exchange, industry, wage labour, suddenly appear quite differently when we discover that their indispensable foundations are their exact opposite. Surplus-value, value, commodity, profit: who would have thought how they really arose? Who or what is our 'developed society' really?

The concept of society: things as 'society'

Under capitalism, the concept of society in the first instance has nothing to do with society in the sense of the universal human organizational form of all people. It has no relation with what we might understand as people 'as such'. Rather, it cuts right through human groups and it is not always the same; but first and foremost, it also designates things, non-people, and even nature as 'society'. From the standpoint of capital, anything which can yield a profit to capital – that is, anything which costs whatever is not-capital, the producers and consumers, a lot – is 'society', or at least, is treated as such. In other words, 'society' is anything which has an exchange value and can be exchanged on the market for the universal equivalent under capitalism: money. This 'anything' tends to be all 'outputs' of the process of production which appear on the market – be it the market for goods or for labour power: that is, commodities. This includes consumer goods, capital goods, money, and that portion of humanity which is regarded as labour power, that is, as a commodity; and that portion of nature which is regarded as a commodity, that is, is either saleable or has to be sold, whether transformed or awaiting transformation. Anything which has to be bought and sold, which has got or receives a price, is, therefore, endowed with a social character: and the higher the price, the more evident is this 'social' character. The most expensive things are unreservedly social, without further qualification: in the final analysis, only capital itself, either as money, physical means of production or a product made under capital-intensive methods. The human individual does not belong to 'society' simply by virtue of being human, but only because, and to the extent that, he/she wants to or is able to enter into a relation with capital – money – and commodities in general. The extent to which someone is defined as 'socially' useful or necessary and so on, as 'human', a person, an individual, citizen or subject – the degree of their social identity – is not determined by the simple fact of their existence, but through their relationship to capital, their control over the means of production and the scale of their property or ownership of goods. In the final instance, therefore, only the *capitalist* is truly and unqualifiedly *human* (cf. Schumpeter), and 'real' society is ultimately the assembly of entrepreneurs. Whether, and to what extent, a person is defined as 'human' at all within capitalism thus depends less on her/himself than on things, and on the 'social' things: capital, money and commodities. This means – and here the topsy-turvy state of affairs becomes particularly clear – that the initial question as to 'what' 'society' is, remains primarily 'what', and only secondarily, 'who'. In contrast to the concept of nature, society turns out to be 'some*thing*' and nature as 'some*body*'. This is what Bloch means when he refers to the 'cadaverous' quality of the commodity, to the necrophilia of a society whose highest expression – capital – comprises 'dead' labour extracted in the past from the living. Meanwhile, living labour becomes incorporated into the insatiable body of the cadaver, as if it were a non-human, as if it were animal, vegetable or mineral, 'natural' matter.

As we have seen, however, under capitalism 'nature' does not signify anything 'good'. Rather, it merely denotes whatever is waiting to be thrown into the process of valorisation as an input, and because it is 'nature', free of charge. In contrast, whereas the concept of society applies to only a very few people, it increasingly embraces all 'outputs'. Material goods become the only authentically 'social' and 'human' things, valuable and 'justifiably' expensive and hence legitimately glorified. The progressive extension of the concept of nature to embrace all humans and their labour, whilst the concept of society extends to everything which can become or be transformed into a commodity – a thing – including people and their relationships as well as nature, is the foundation for the contempt for nature and people which characterizes this system. This is a standpoint from which even the exploited cannot detach themselves; anyone wanting to be 'human' within this system must learn to despise nature and other humans, especially those exploited, those who have even less of 'society', of commodities and money. They must, therefore, come to despise the poor, women, blacks, the old, children, the 'a-social'. Their 'upward' solemn and fervent gaze contrasts with their constant striving 'downward' to kick themselves loose from and deny their own 'naturalness', their poverty, their wife, their body and their emotions. They are the cyclist, bent over double but pushing down below. They are racist, sexist, obsessively hygienic, love order, rationality, and their superiors, are authoritarian with subordinates and when pushed, Fascist. Like the capitalists, their astonishment at insurgent 'nature' inevitably turns into a fanatical hatred of it; for them it seems that nature – not capital – is the obstacle in the struggle to become or be a 'person'. The existence of women's, black's, unemployed's and Third World movements are, therefore, akin to 'natural disasters'. Not only do they prevent the 'human', the white man, reaching their objectives but threaten to propel him back to the time he believed long since past, the time before nature was conquered.

The 'humanity' of the machine

What, then, are the material relations which allow the one to cherish hopes of becoming 'human', and the other not, if, for capital, *all* humans tend to become 'nature', non-human. The main source of this illusion is the wage relation, and those who share the illusion are wage-workers. One interesting subject for study might be whether and to what extent the previous history of trade union and workers' movements has essentially been a struggle by male wage-workers for recognition by capitalists as 'people', as human beings. This struggle evidently had its successes in as much as 'human rights' became applied at least to white men, wage-workers, who thenceforward counted as 'free, equal and fraternal' (!): they were the first to obtain the vote and after a certain age were regarded as mature, responsible, enfranchised citizens, able to sign contracts and own property – unless they were criminals, lunatics or revolutionaries. Such rights have become available only to the majority of the world's population – women, even as wage-workers, blacks and non-wage workers and children – either after much delay, sporadically, and partially, or not at all: they were, and are, treated on a par with criminals, lunatics and revolutionaries. 'Human rights' were, however, always suspended where workers were to be dismissed. The struggle by wage-workers for recognition as 'human', like the capitalists, is, therefore, an illusionary one for several reasons. *Firstly*, it is confined to a minority – male wage-workers – and its prospects for success are accordingly equally limited. Trade unions generally continue to refuse to represent former wage-workers, the unemployed and non-wage-workers such as the members' wives, even when these demand it, as occurred, for example, in a factory in the small German town of Erwitte. *Secondly*, not only is the wage labour relationship not being universalized, but it has been on the retreat for some time, both quantitatively and qualitatively, and at an accelerating pace (most wage-workers do not have permanent employment): a push 'back into nature' – 'feminization', 'domestication', 'housewifization', 'marginalization' – is taking place. This is an illustration of how precarious and reversible previous achievements are. Finally, and probably most fundamentally, the wage relation itself has either totally prevented the possibility of, or obstructed the path to, becoming 'human' both in the capitalist and the utopian sense.

The illusion of belonging to 'society' is the wage illusion, 'money in the pocket'. (Selma James) What differentiates humans more clearly than anything else is ownership, or lack, of the 'queen of commodities'. (Marx) The wage is, however, given to workers only to buy as many commodities as are needed for their survival as wage-labour, including that of the next generation, and housewives who work for no wages. Wages are, therefore, chronically insufficient even to approach the 'human' quality of an entrepreneur. The appalling character of this relative 'humanization' in the capitalist sense stems from the fact that it is the exact opposite of what being a person is in any 'proper' or utopian sense of the term. Why, then, have wage-workers not only accepted their transmogrification into a commodity, but on occasions considered it something worth striving for? Why have they believed – and do still often continue to believe – that they can become the 'subject of history' by being, of all things, an object of capital accumulation? Was this object status really better than that which continued to be regarded as 'natural' simply because it was pronounced 'social'?

The 'social' object is still probably better off than the 'natural' because of the power of the wage: power not over capital, but over 'natural' objects, and in particular over women. One reason why wage-workers have been able to tolerate their alienation, their degradation to a commodity, to a thing, to an object – if a 'social' one – is possibly because non-wage workers were even worse off, and because wage-workers were placed over them in a hierarchy. Every wage-worker receives as compensation for his alienation and exploitation the right and the guarantee to a woman, that is the right to exploit her as a 'natural' object. So far, very few wage-workers have rejected this non-collectively bargained, life-long bonus, even though it might entail reducing the 'normal' wage; on the contrary. The prospect of losing his wife along with the loss of wage-labour is clearly cause for greater concern than the level of pay, exploitation and alienation combined. Ideological factors apart, might the reason be that male wage-workers are not in fact the 'main-producers' in capitalism? They are obliged to produce *dead* things, 'cadaverous' commodities, but their womenfolk produce *living* labour power? What is capital's interest in labour power? The fact that it *is* alive. It is what capital is not. Capital's most burning interest is not in the commodity, labour power, the objectified, unified, disciplined and hence in general underpaid object part of the worker. The fact that this is paid for leads workers to believe that their essence, their identity, consists in their commodity character, the 'social' character of their labour, their 'humanity'. But this is to fall prey to the deceptive surface appearance of this mode of 'production', or better, 'destruction'. They believe, must believe, that the more their labour power is transformed into a commodity, that is, the more permanent their employment, the higher the pay; in fact, the more *they themselves* become commodities, *machines*, the more 'human' they will be (cf. the ideals of labour discipline, morals, Puritanism, and the organizational forms of the workers movement).

The double character of labour power as domesticated nature

The twofold character of labour power, its character both as a standardized commodity as well as a living power, a human force of nature, is disguised by the capitalist concept of society and its underlying 'reality'. Only the domesticated element in living labour power is perceived: its naturalness in the human sense (Alfred Schmidt), the fact that it is living, is denied. Consequently, the wage-worker appears as a person divorced from their own nature, which is regarded as non-human, just as conversely non-wage workers (and in particular women) appear to be separated from their commodity character, their social quality which stamps them as human. This semblance and the 'reality' which underlies it, in the positivist sense, prevent us from seeing how little even the best-paid worker is remunerated – and for which they make over their life – not to mention non-wage workers, and specifically, women. Worse still, this state of schizophrenia – albeit a divided existence which remains confined within the system's boundaries – means that we can scarcely discern that the 'naturalness' and 'humanity' realizable within this system are, in fact, perversions of our truly natural and human potential.

The assertion that it is things, objectified relations, fragments of labour, reified labour power, bits of people and only small groups within humanity, who find the substance of their reality in these things, which count as 'social' and are treated as 'society', also applies to nature itself. Society counts as 'nature' and 'nature' as society. People are treated like 'nature' in order to be able to exploit them like – unpaid – animals.

'Liberation' from nature as the death of the capitalist mode of production

Just as the social character of humans and their labour is denied, so the dependence of society, humanity, commodities and capital on nature is also denied. *The commodity is regarded as producible in unlimited quantities at will.* It is precisely this 'property' which lifts it out of nature and distinguishes it from this limited and limiting entity. *Progress* consists not only in the domination, subjugation, appropriation of nature (or 'nature'), but, in the final analysis, in 'liberation' from nature and its constraints, in independence from nature and from women, and hence, above all, from the ability to bear children, and from the land and its mineral resources with their so-called 'scarcity'.

The recognition of the contradiction that capital can only valorise itself through destroying people and nature has so far been obscured by the belief in progress: that is, belief in the possibility that natural limitations can ultimately be overcome through the 'pure' capital relation. The journey there is seen as a kind of evolution towards the transformation of all labour into wage labour, of all products into commodities, of all theft into exchange, of all direct force into indirect, and of all people into 'free', equal, enfranchised citizens. Corresponding Utopias mainly concern themselves with the abolition of work *tout court*, an activity to be virtually wholly assigned to machines. The Utopian promise, therefore, consisted – put somewhat differently – in complete and universal socialization, and hence in *'emancipation' from nature*, that is, freedom from nature and its limitations.

The hunt for 'guilty parties' begins wherever this evolutionary path becomes blocked. Wars and crises seemed not to be caused by capitalists but by 'nature': women, foreigners, the 'other', the neighbour, the enemy, the Third World. The ideal of the pure capital relation as something unhindered by 'nature', elevated above it, untainted by it, soaring like a rocket, has been, and is likely to remain the ideal – an ideal constantly sought but, none the less, objectively impossible. Seen as movement and process, this *seeking but never finding* constitutes the true, impotent, addictive character of the capitalist mode of production.

Liberation from nature would be the end of this mode of production. Its 'accomplishment' would mean its death.

In fact, the process moves quite differently to the 'prescribed' ideal. What is being universalized is *not* wage-labour, but the ideal-type of housework and other forms of non-wage labour. Capital's hunger for profit, for valorisation, is so desperate that existing nature no longer suffices: in order to find anything living which can be fed into the insatiable corpse of capital, it must be *created artificially*, increasingly via robbery and direct force – methods characteristic of what is alleged to be the long-since superseded phase of 'primitive' accumulation. Dominating nature is becoming more, not less, of a problem, not because nature cannot be dominated but because it is being destroyed, torn out of its equilibrium. No longer there.

Sources

Anders. G., after E. R. Wuthenow. in *Frankfurter Rundschau* (FR) 12. 7.80.

Bataille, G. (1975) Die Aufhebung der Okonomie. Munich.

Becker, G. et al. (1978) Aus der Zeit der Verzweiflung, Frankfurt.

Bennholdt-Thomsen, V. (1979) Marginalität in Lateinamerika. Eine Theoriekritik, in: die u. a. (Hg.): Lateinamerika, Analysen und Berichte 3. Berlin, S. 45–85.

Bennholdt-Thomson, V., und Werlhof, C. v. (1978) Die Anwendung der Arbeitswertlehre auf die Arbeit der Frauen im Kapitalismus, Manuskr., Bielefeld.

Bloch, E. (1979) Das Prinzip Hoffnung, es, Frankfurt.

Bookchin, M. (1980) in: *Pflasterstrand* Nr. 71, 72.

Datar, Ch. (1981) 'In Search of Feminist Theory. A Critique of Marx's Theory of Society, with particular reference to the British feminist movement', thesis, ISS, The Hague.

Dross, A. (1978) Die erste Walpurgisnacht, Hexenverfolgung in Deutschland, Frankfurt.

Elias, N. (1978) Uber den Prozess der Zivilisation, Frankfurt.

Fanon, F. (1967) *The Wretched of the Earth*, Penguin, Harmondsworth.

Frank, A. G. (1977) On so-called primitive accumulation, in: *Dialectical Anthropology*, 2, S. 87–106.

Frankfurter Rundschau (FR), 20.6., 26.7., 18.8.

Fuchs, G., Der Arbeitslose, in: *Konkret* 6/78.

Honegger, C. (Hg.) (1978) Die Hexen der Neuzeit, Frankfurt.

Illich, I. (1980) Shadow-Work, Manuskr., Cuernavaca 'Schattenarbeit' in: ders.: Vom Recht auf Gemeinheit, Reinbeck 1982, S. 75–93.

James, S. (1980) Vortrag, Bielefeld.

Kapp, K. W. (1979) Soziale Kosten der Marktwirtschaft, Frankfurt.

Mass, B. (1975) *The Political Economy of Population Control in Latin America*, Montreal.

Marx, K., *Capital*, Vols. I and III.

Meillassoux, C. (1976) Die wilden Früchte der Frau, Frankfurt.

Mies, M. (1980a) Gesellschaftliche Ursprünge der geschlechtlichen Arbeitsteilung, in Beiträge zur feministischen Theorie und Praxis 3, München, S. 61–78.

Mies, M. (1980b and 1982) Housewives produce for the World Market, The Hague and London.

Mies, M., Chapter 5 of this book.

Prokla, 50 (1983) Feminismus–Marxismus–Debatte.

Schmidt, A. (1971) *A Concept of Nature in Marx*, London.

Theweleit, K. (1977) Männerphantasien, Frankfurt.

UN (1980) World Conference of the United Nations Decade for Women: Equality, Development and Peace: Programme of Action for the Second Half of the United Nations Decade for Women, Copenhagen. S. 38 ff.

Wallerstein, I. (1979) 'The Rise and Future Demise of the World Capitalist System: Concepts for Comparative Analysis' in *idem, The Capitalist World-Economy*, Cambridge.

Werlhof, C. v., Chapter 2 of this book.

6. The Future of Women's Work and Violence Against Women

Veronika Bennholdt-Thomsen

What does women's work have to do with violence against women? I argue here that the types of labour relations in which women in our society find themselves are repeatedly imposed on them by force. In so far as women are concerned, the social relations of compulsion are not simply the product of economic laws, but are produced by individuals: they emerge out of the direct, tangible acts of violence that women experience every day. My aim in this chapter is to demonstrate that this influences women's work and to show how it occurs.

The current situation: some general theses

Women are the first to be affected and are the hardest hit by the current crisis. This takes two main forms.

Firstly, unemployment: this affects women more rapidly and on a greater scale than it does men; a woman will lose her job before a man is made redundant. This, however, applies only to skilled or better paid work. The number of women in so-called 'unprotected' employment generally entailing dirty and often monotonous jobs is increasing. Parallel to this, more men are now employed in areas that formerly were considered to encompass typically women's work (nurses, nursery workers, specialist and supervisory positions in cleaning etc.). The view that the crisis is driving women back to the kitchen is, therefore, only half the story. Falling incomes and the increased insecurity of men's jobs are increasingly forcing women to look for paid employment on whatever conditions are on offer.

Secondly, women's subordinate position as housewives: the loss of relatively secure jobs, or more difficult access to them, has increasingly confined women to the status of housewives, but the crucial point is that women are accorded this status in order to make them work without pay as housewives *and* work in paid employment in unprotected and underpaid jobs.

Women's precarious position in paid employment forces a housewives' existence on to them; and in turn this role underpins their lack of power on the labour market. Housework and women's paid work therefore condition each other. It is precisely this mutual relationship that contains the moment of structural violence. Women earn less (even with the same skills as men), work under worse conditions (part-time work and fixed-term contracts, 'temping' etc.) and perform the dirtier and more monotonous jobs because they provide a 'second income', supplementing the men's 'family wage'. And because women are badly paid, and limited to intermittent work, they cannot live alone, economically independent of a man, particularly if they have children. Women are, therefore, forced into marriage or a similarly dependent relationship and this, in turn, fixes their position as secondary earners.

Where does the cause of this coercive relation lie? In the woman as housewife, or in women's paid employment? At what points is structural violence the product of overt violence? Why do women continue to become housewives – again now and on an even greater scale?

What does women's paid employment *mean*?

Women's work in Western society: two contrasting approaches

Two approaches have been suggested for understanding the question of women's work in Western society: 1) the 'women's labour capacity', approach; and 2) the 'women's labour as forced labour' approach (to which I subscribe) as developed by the Bielefeld Project Group 'The future of women's work' ('Zukunft der Frauenarbeit').

I propose to contrast these two approaches, and in the process hope to clarify and more precisely demarcate my own.

The 'women's labour capacity' approach was developed by Beck-Gernsheim (1981, 1976) and Ostner (1978) to answer the following questions: Why is women's participation in the labour force less than men's? Why are women concentrated in a few branches of the economy? Why do women occupy the lowest positions within the paid labour force in general; that is, the poorest paid and least valued within an occupational hierarchy? The Bielefeld Group also tackled these questions. Each approach produced very different answers.

This approach saw the key as lying in the content of women's work, in the actual *substance of their activities*. In contrast, the view that women's labour is forced labour saw the cause of poor women's lowly status in paid employment not in *what* they do, but in *how* they must do it: namely, that women have to be available as whole people. Not only is their labour power appropriated, but along with it their bodily character, their sensitivity and their sexuality. In wage work too, the whole woman is appropriated. The 'womens labour capacity' like men's approach proceeds, implicitly, from the assumption that women's labour power is a commodity, but equipped with special, female, capacities.

In contrast, we hold that, unlike men, women may not freely dispose of their labour power, like a commodity. Rather, their labour power is sold – or simply appropriated – far from freely, together with their bodies and their sexuality – that is, their distinctiveness as women – and hence includes themselves as bearers of that labour power. It is, therefore, women's position as 'subject', as 'unfree', and not the substance of women's work, which is crucial in analysing women's employment.

Both approaches attribute a central significance to *housework and/or the status as housewife* in determining women's work in contemporary capitalism, although with very different premisses. The 'women's labour-capacity' approach states that because of their socialization as housewives, women develop capacities which they use in their paid employment or which are demanded of them occupationally in the form of typical women's jobs: nurses, teachers or secretaries, involving the use of such domestic abilities as caring for and nurturing others.

In contrast, the 'Bielefeld approach' contends that in modern society there is only one typical form of female labour which puts its stamp on both paid employment and domestic labour in equal measure: it comprises the compulsion on women to be available to meet the needs of others. This quality might be compared to that of the joker in a pack of cards: women's special character is precisely that their activity is not fixed – they can be used for any function. Jokers, however, are relatively rare, whilst women's labour is provided on a massive scale. Women's work in the home, and outside it for a wage, mutually condition each other in so far as the position of women in paid employment facilitates their total availability in the home, and conversely their position as housewives and mothers forces them into subordinate positions in paid employment. Behind this structurally coercive relationship lurk relations of direct force, in particular those created through laws, religious ordinances, trade union support for male workers and medical control over the female body.

Below we expand on these approaches, first by considering the 'women's labour capacity' and then counterposing it to 'women's labour as forced labour'.

'Women's labour capacity'

This approach sees women's labour as determined by housework. For Beck-Gernsheim society is divided into two fundamental spheres: that of employment: male; and that of housework: female. Women's paid employment is, therefore, essentially a kind of incursion into alien territory, possible only because women possess special skills and knowledge which men do not have and which are needed for certain occupations. This specialist community of women arose as follows:

> Influenced by their assignment to the intimate sphere of the family . . . women develop . . . willingness to adapt and emotional dependence, the capacity to nurture and the virtues of sensibility. (Beck-Gernsheim, 1981, p. 9)

Or, elsewhere: 'Labour orientated towards reproduction calls for a heart and a mind for the other – it calls for a personal and person-related sensitivity, an ability both to feel and to feel for.' (p. 38)

Given that these capacities are supposed to be tied to specific activities they seem remarkably abstract features, rather, of a servile social status group. In fact, Beck-Gernsheim comes close to characterizing the position of women as that of a permanently available resource. She, however, does not analyse it in this way, together with the compulsion that underlies it, because she is concerned to extol the positive side of these 'human' qualities. In doing so she comes dangerously close to an ideology which distorts the truth of the subjugation of women. For example, she does not ask why, in contrast to the usual practice, women are neither appropriately rewarded nor highly remunerated in respect of their special abilities but rather seem to be penalized for those abilities, by being especially poorly paid and held in especially low esteem. To ask this question would, in fact lead on to the idea of the appropriation of women as whole persons, with all their 'feelings', 'heart' and 'thoughts' and 'sensitivity', and correspondingly enhanced labour power. For it is the total appropriation of women – like slaves or serfs – that explains why, far from being held in particular respect, they are particularly despised and plundered.

Beck-Gernsheim sketches out an image of the family, which evidently owes a great deal to bourgeois ideology, without questioning either its historical or current validity. The family consequently appears as a secure enclave, an intimate and eternal personal sphere suffused with positive feelings: there seems no suggestion of, for example, the violence in the family.

The same applies to her concept of 'socialization'. Instead of examining the origins and substance of socialization, both for the past and present, the idea is simply pressed into service as an answer to every question. Ultimately, the absence of a proper derivation leads to a new version of biologism – with socialization taking over the role which the gene plays for the socio-biologists.

Ilona Ostner sees a less exclusive determination of women's labour power by domestic labour, by identifying an interaction between employment and the home: 'Domestic labour is, therefore, labour which exists in a relation to industrial commodity production. It is determined by this form.' (Ostner, 1978, pp. 150–1) But the common factor in domestic and paid labour is not that both are performed by women; also, for her, 'employment' is something essentially male. Women's paid employment is regarded as something extraordinary because women's labour power is characterized by empathy, experiential knowledge, intuition, and a capacity for divergent thinking, which seems to have strayed, as it were, into the matter-of-fact, cold and rational world of paid employment.

One possible counter-argument might be that women have always worked in paid employment. Proof of this might be the hypothesis, raised by Ostner herself in a joint paper with Willms, that the participation rate of women in the workforce in Germany has remained constant over the last 100 years at around 36%. (1982, p. 216) Why not then allow housework to be determined by women's wage labour? In fact, A. Wolf-Graaf (1981), for instance, has tried to show that the first wage-workers were typically women; we know from the early phase of industrialization, in the textile industry for example, that women accounted for a higher proportion of the workforce than did men. There is no reason, except for the dominant ideology, why we should regard the material and emotional nature of domestic labour as the paradigm for women's labour. In my view, there is a third factor common to both, determining domestic labour *and* paid employment: this is the low, slave-like status of women; a status maintained through violence.

This view is diametrically opposed to the strongly subjectivist 'Women's labour-capacity approach' which argues that women's socialization adapts them for a particular role, and that women carry out the tasks assigned to them more or less voluntarily. There is constant reference to the choice of occupation exercised by girls and women, as if it makes a big difference in a woman's lifestyle whether she is a crane-driver or hairdresser. A simple glance at the German Democratic Republic or other Eastern European countries, where it is quite normal for women to be crane-drivers, should be sufficient to dispel this idea. The trial experiments carried out in the project 'Women in Male Trades' (*Frauen in Männerberufen*) point in the opposite direction. Women are more easily accepted in those male trades that offer fewer opportunities for future careers. (Glöss et al., 1981, p. 141) Moreover, women in such fields also get trapped at the lower levels of the occupational hierarchy. In my view, interpreting the low occupational status of women as a product of their personal behaviour seems more likely to generate feelings of guilt and prevent women from acting rather than explain anything. Ostner, however, considers that 'the identification of women . . . with housework is not without implications for women's labour capacity, and hence for their occupational behaviour.' (1978, p. 187) Furthermore, she sees 'a typical women's way of being subject to occupational demands.' (p. 15) 'Domestic labour is the primary orientation point for women's labour-power, and as a consequence employment is only rarely the key element in women's lives.' Beck-Gernsheim even claims that 'the jobs which women prefer' are located 'at the lower end of the occupational hierarchy.' (1981, p. 83) The reason for this is supposedly that women are oriented towards use-value, rather than exchange-value: their choice of occupation is guided by the nature of the job, not the level of pay. My response to this would be: why then do women become teachers rather than professors? Both involve dealing with people, teaching, and both call for empathy and understanding. Alternatively, why do women work as assembly-line operatives in the electrical engineering industry instead of becoming car mechanics? It is difficult to see why one should be regarded as more use-value orientated than the other. Why are women nurses and not consultants? And finally, why are women, who invariably do the cooking, rarely head cooks?

In my view, the subjectivist 'women's labour-capacity' approach, with its fixation on the content (significance) of activities, together with its obligatory interpretation of women's paid employment as housework activities, has its roots in a repression of the violence in everyday life. One thing is certain: women are not free to choose. They do not volunteer to work in badly paid and low-status jobs simply because they set great store on use-values. Either these occupations become low-status because women work in them, and/or women are assigned to them because they are low-status. In other words, women may be perfectly free to choose their occupation, but, wherever they succeed in exercising this freedom, these occupations then become low-paid and low-status in proportion to the increase in the number of women working in them. Or again: women have the freedom to choose poorly-paid and low-status occupations because they will, in fact, be able to work in them. Any attempt to analyse women's employment must eventually turn to those mechanisms which act to lower women socially such that all their actions, and especially their work, come close to count as low in esteem. The issue is, therefore, that of women as social beings and whole persons, not of one aspect of women's lives.

The women's labour-capacity approach, on the contrary, deliberately focuses on one specific and partial aspect: women's labour power is defined as a socially acquired *role*. The general criticism of role theory, that it entails a fragmentation, individualization and de-historicization of complex social facts is particularly appropriate here. Women's 'role' is hardly the appropriate term to denote an entire sex which is accorded a low status because of its very sexual identity. Nor can the mechanisms for this process be deemed 'socialization'. This is really making a molehill out of a mountain. There is little sense in characterizing women as bearers of a social role – alterable by a different socialization! – when the main issue is to understand why and how women are kept available for low-valued activities precisely by virtue of their bodies, their female-ness, sensitivity and sexuality. Why do Beck-Gernsheim and Ostner leave out those universally demanded specifically female, occupational capacities which relate to the female body or sexual aspects? Verena Fiegl's study of one week's job advertisements from the daily newspapers *Frankfurter Rundschau* 3–10 January 1981, led her to conclude:

> What are 'Wanted' are 'Secretaries, typists, administrators [all carrying the female suffix in German] who are 'young', 'charming', 'loveable', 'empathetic', 'pretty', 'attractive', 'well-groomed' and 'always smiling', from whom 'her fellow-workers and boss can expect a smile on Monday morning' and who are also naturally 'chic' and 'enjoy meeting people'.

The all-embracing character of women's subjugation corresponds to the all-embracing nature of their appropriation: they are inseparable, especially as regards women's paid employment. Women are not respected as people. Rather, 'the personal boundaries of women are constantly violated: spatially, verbally and physically.' (Fiegl, (1983) p. 7) Of 172 women working in the UN Headquarters interviewed, for example, 152 felt sexually harrassed and discriminated against. In the US Marines the figure was 82% and in the American magazine *Redbook*, 89%. (Bernhard, 1980, Fiegl, p. 3) Within the general separation of personality and sexuality – the norm in this society – women embody sexuality. The woman *is* the sexual aspect of the factory or office – bought in along with the office equipment. Advertisements for office equipment and work-clothing regularly feature secretaries and female office staff sitting around naked. And according to the image chosen for a *Stern* magazine front cover, secretaries accused of spying in Bonn also work naked, but without faces. Women are interchangeable and women always sell 'their sexuality along with themselves.' (Fiegl, p. 5)

Women's labour as forced labour

The purpose of characterizing women's labour as forced labour is to make clear that the jobs which women do in this society are neither freely chosen nor are they specifically female and even less so particularly meaningful. Both domestic and paid labour are equally imprinted with this coercive character. Women are made into housewives from birth: the characteristic hallmark of women – a natural resource equally as good for any type of activity free of charge or for the lowest possible pay – dictated to women because of their sex: it is not acquired as a specific type of skill or qualification. This allocation is reproduced in every individual instance and every historical phase of capitalist development as the tangible breaking-in of women through social, and especially state, control mechanisms, and where women refuse to submit, through direct, brute force. In Western society, to be a housewife is to belong to a low social status reserved for and forcibly imposed on women. It is a capitalist work relation of production much more all-encompassing than wage labour. Rather it is contained within the position of housewife in a form of the specific female housewife – like wage labour. It simultaneously signifies an extreme restriction in the choice of occupation, in mobility, and women's freedom of movement generally. In other words, our society consists of men – manual workers, white-collar workers, civil servants, the self-employed and entrepreneurs – and a slave or serf caste: the housewives who do exactly the same jobs as men, considered in terms of their content, but from a position of quasi-slavery. Women have to do more work than men, and are allocated the dirtier, more disagreeable and more exhausting tasks.

A comparison with the slaves transported to Rome from the conquered territories might serve to illuminate the position of housewives. Slaves' main task was to undertake the fundamental everyday jobs in the home and on the fields; a few of them were teachers, but they taught under conditions of slavery, and could always be transferred to other tasks and subjected to violence. Elsewhere we have compared the position of women with that of the colonies. Like colonized peoples, women do not belong to the society of the ruling White Man (to which even the poorest White Man belongs); they are subject to other rules: those of subordination. (Bennholdt-Thomsen, Mies, Werlhof, 1983)

Within actual sexual division of labour are mechanisms operating to reinforce subordination, but the division in itself is not the cause. All societies exhibit a sexual division of labour. Inasmuch as this is the case it would be wrong to characterize the status of housewife as an exacerbation or deepening of the sexual division of labour. Rather, we should analyse how the structures of the sexual division of labour have changed historically and identify what has been responsible for these changes.

This fact equally makes it somewhat pointless to search for the male original sin that brought this about. A sexual division of labour, in itself, does not necessarily imply hierarchy and inequality, rather, these are the product of particular forms of sexual division of labour. It is, therefore, important for us to understand which components and combinations of the sexual division of labour render it hierarchical and unequal.

In all pre-capitalist societies, the sexual division of labour takes place via an allocation of activities with a particular content. Only with the development of capitalism and the category of abstract labour did a sexual division of labour based on the allocation of particular forms of work – work relations – become possible. In other words, although pre-capitalist work relations encompass a sexual division of labour (for example, slavery, with male and female slaves or serfs) no particular work relation was characterized as specifically male or female on the basis of sex itself. The implication was not of a division according to types of work relation but according to the content of activities. In contemporary society, however, there exists a sexual division of labour relations which also means that there are qualitatively different male and female types of wage labour. The issue is to specify the particular character of this women's 'wage-house-work'. Accordingly, the sex-specific segmentation of the labour market should be studied not in terms of the criterion of different occupational contents but abstracting from the content, in terms of differing contracts and conditions of employment, different forms of organization of the work process and different mechanisms of coercion. Here, we are concerned with a different relationship to time and to violence and different relations of dependence. This hypothesis is developed below.

The criterion 'abstract labour' applies equally to men's and women's work: that is, the situation is not that men's work (wage labour) is abstract labour whilst women's work is concrete labour. Housework is also abstract labour. Just as anyone can undertake any type of wage labour, anyone can undertake housework. It has its abstract rules and standards and is hence subject to a yardstick. Just as the wage-worker is subject to the contract of employment, so housewives are subject to a general yardstick in housework through the marriage contract. Furthermore, women's labour in the sphere of paid employment is equally as abstract labour as is men's. Despite these common properties we can, nonetheless, distinguish two types of abstract labour – male and female. What distinguishes the one from the other is also abstract. It lies in the different use to which labour power is put and hence, as I argue below, the different utilization of men's and women's labour time.

For a male worker it is possible to draw a reasonably clear line between the man as an individual and the labour power which he is compelled to sell. For women this separation is not possible: the use of woman's labour power, as we have noted, includes her female bodily character, sensitivity and sexuality. Depending on what is centrally at issue, these can be more or less wrested away from her. Thus 'sexual bargaining' will certainly increase in the future. Women are wearing miniskirts again, are wiggling their hips, smiling and offering maternal warmth and comfort in order to obtain a scarce job. This does not involve concrete individual qualities which the individual woman brings with her, but rather abstract characteristics which belong to 'women as labour power'. How much of them is necessary is a function of the different phases of capitalism. What is stolen from women, or has to be bought at a high price during a boom, may be available cheaply or free of charge during a downturn. This is the meeting place of general social relations of coercion – which, as I show below, force women into particular straits in contrast to men – and the concrete exercise of force. Structural and direct force also reinforce each other.

Fiegl characterizes the difference between women's and men's labour within capitalism even more pointedly. In the case of men, labour power becomes a commodity; in the case of women, the whole person becomes a commodity. (See too Irigary 1976, p. 7) But as the characterization as a commodity already implies, this does not involve the appropriation of a specific woman, but rather general abstract qualities of the female body and female capacities: women are not unique, but interchangeable. We can now see that there is no real contradiction between characterizing women's work within capitalism as abstract labour and the fact that women have to be available in a very concrete form as whole persons. What is demanded of 'woman' in the form of 'womanliness' is indeed abstract. This abstract quality is best understood if we look at advertising 'which presents its products merely using fragments of entirely interchangeable women's bodies, or where men prefer blondes, pretty "dolls" and pick them up like a bar of chocolate'. (Fiegl, p. 1.) Thewelweit describes how this process of abstraction from the concrete woman, the reduction of the woman, her body and sexuality to a few symbolic objects has taken place, and how this abstract pattern has been forced on real women like a corset. Using her as the 'abstract commodity labour-power "woman"' is then just a short step.

Five central social mechanisms make contemporary women's labour into forced labour. They are:

1) the sole responsibility of the mother for the organization of work with children;

2) the specific structuring of time in women's employment;

3) the reduced access of women to social insurance;

4) the assignment of women to repetitive, monotonous and hence stressful production processes; and

5) low wages based on women's status as a 'second-income'.

Although here the crucial role is played by the isolation of the mother in the patriarchal nuclear family combined with her sole responsibility for child-care, the other mechanisms cited combine to prevent women freeing themselves from this situation and autonomously developing alternative forms of living. Child-care, therefore, occupies first place, although the other points cannot simply be derived from it.

Contemporary and crisis mechanisms of coercion

One crucial, sex-specific principle in current forms of employment is that men tend to be assigned to indefinite or long-term employment, implying a job for life or a career, whilst women work periodically on short-term contracts. The reason lies in the assignment of *sole* responsibility for all work involving children, especially small children, to mothers in their role as housewives.

Typical manifestations of this are the breaks which women insert into their working lives to cope with child-care; or part-time work, where women use a reduced daily or weekly working time to combine both spheres of labour. If we look at the structure of women's paid employment over recent decades, there is a visible trend from full-time work interrupted by breaks to part-time work. Part-time work, 90% of which is carried out by women, is a typically female form of employment. In 1960 women working part-time accounted for 19% of women in paid employment, by 1980 the share had risen to 30%: almost 60% of women part-timers have children to care for. (Guttstadt, et al.) Recent figures compiled by Petra Müller show an increasing trend towards part-time work. The steady rise in the participation rate of married women in the workforce is also an indicator of a fall-off in interruptions to employment. Women are entering the labour market in larger numbers, a fact expressed in the growth in the share of women in employment in all women of working age, as well as the numbers of unemployed women. Given that responsibility for child-care has remained constant (the number of children has decreased, even dramatically in West Germany, but the particular care has immensely increased) this is possible only through increased part-time work.

Annemarie Tröger has shown how, in the Third Reich, the ideology of motherhood and the forced obligation of women to assume sole responsibility for child-care was deliberately used to structure working hours in paid employment. The express aim was to obtain workers for Taylorized jobs who would occupy these jobs for only a few particular years of their life, since it was assumed that no one would be able to tolerate that type of work, physically and mentally, for their whole working life. The Fascist government was not, in principle, therefore, hostile to women working in paid employment, but only to their permanent and long-term employment. The Nazis had no objection to women working on assembly lines and certainly did not oppose unpaid labour both in the home on a massive scale and as auxiliary labour on family farms. (Trüger, 1982)

Whereas the issue in the Third Reich was that of obtaining assembly line workers for a few years, the focus has now changed to that of obtaining workers for a few hours per day and per week, workers who do not resist such forms of employment and in fact enter them 'voluntarily' because of other coercive relations. 'Capacity orientated variable working time' (KAPOVAZ), a recent form of unprotected employment, makes the relationship between the status of housewife and typical women's employment particularly clear. This form of employment presupposes that women live in the vicinity of the firm, that, as housewives, they are at home and can be called upon when, for example, a suddenly-crowded shop makes it necessary, and that they rely on this income as a second income. In other words, 'KAPOVAZ' presupposes the housewife.

Just as Taylorism marked one crucial technological upheaval, so too now with the micro-processor. Its increasing application will almost inevitably lead to a substantial increase in the demand for fragmented working times. Work on VDUs, for example, is already limited to six hours a day, and there is no reason why companies should want to pay an extra two hours if they can make use of a supply of part-time workers. In fact, it appears that this form of work is now to be massively promoted with state support, using the same mechanisms as did the Third Reich.

The mechanism of force against women simply consists in control over their fertility: it includes not only rape and sexual violence but also the coercive administration of the uterus by the state and medical profession. Current discussions about a tightening-up of the provisions of Paragraph 218 – the West German legal provision on pregnancy termination – against women's interests, for example, the refusal by sickness insurance funds to meet the costs of abortion on social grounds, and cuts in provision for counselling (Pro-Familia and similar organizations) have less to do with population policy than with mechanisms for disciplining women as workers. These moves are augmented by the wave of propaganda pushing a maternalist ideology, which has not only reared its head through the Conservative Parties (CDU/CSU) but began during the preceding Social Democratic Party (SDP) government's office with the slogan 'Women can do more', aimed at mobilizing women's labour power on an unpaid and private basis for what were otherwise public and paid social services. The new Nurseries Act, the aim of which is to extend privatization of child-care, also constitutes a continuation of previous policies which never seriously considered the provision of public funds for non-private care of small children up to three years of age. Women are, therefore, forced by husbands, fathers and the state to take on sole responsibility for child-care: a supply of labour is thereby created, whose time is already structured to fit the needs of particular branches and departments of industry.

The state's interests in this structuring of the supply of labour focus on the problems of social insurance within the model of the welfare state. The mass unemployment and underemployment caused by the economic crisis and introduction of new technologies can be dealt with only within the social insurance system at extraordinarily high cost. One mechanism of control for cutting costs consists in reducing access to social insurance for women. Annemarie Tröger has shown how this mechanism also played an important role in the Third Reich. It was evident that workers would soon be exhausted and prematurely invalided by constant assembly-line work. One possible answer – the abolition of the Bismarckian social insurance system – was not politically feasible. The response was to resort to a 'social technical solution'. Low pay and periods of unemployment meant that women, foreign and forced labourers would acquire either no, or only low, entitlement to social insurance. This could be justified by arguing that the needs of these social groups could be met in other ways. Women were not authentic wage-workers: their true biological vocation was a housewife and mother. Analogously, foreign and forced labourers were regarded as biologically inferior, and not genuine German workers: their social security was also not to be borne by the 'body of the German people'. (Tröger, 1982, pp. 265/6)

Today, women's access to social security is obstructed by temporary and part-time contracts of employment. Carola Möller, therefore, refers to:

> legally, materially and socially undermined, insecure and self-terminating 'unprotected forms of employment' which contrast with the employment of so-called 'core workers', protected by collective and works agreements: that is, temping, part-time work, temporary help, occasional work, fixed-term contracts, 'free' help, home and illegal work. (Möller, 1982, pp. 183/4.)

One important area in which such forms are unprotected is the exclusion of employees from unemployment insurance (below 19.9 hours per week) and sickness and pensions insurance (below 15 hours). (1982, p. 187) In addition, sporadic employment also encourages illegal employment, with no protection on offer even where legally required.

Women are driven into unprotected forms of employment by the alliance of interests between employers, the state administration and (married) men. (Married) men have a very basic interest in the unpaid labour of women, in her person, in the home, in the care of the old and sick, and in child-care. They have the power to impose these tasks on women using the mechanisms of both structural and direct force:

● Women are treated basically as second earners on the labour market. That is, they are granted access only to low-paid work on short-term contracts. This makes it virtually impossible for women to live alone – especially with children – without being dependent on a man.

● The fact that women need a protector in this society means that husbands and fathers have the power to force women to perform unpaid labour, thus overburdening them, so that they are unable to undertake a full-time paid job. A woman alone is treated like a piece of ownerless property and can be dealt with by force. The unpaid labour performed for (married) men is, as it were, a tribute demanded of her by her protector.

● This protector role also has a dual face as women are especially exposed to direct violence in marriage, as Murray Straus ironically observed, calling the marriage certificate a licence to beat. (1976)

It is almost taken for granted that the protectors will also be violent. If this equation is felt to be too drastic, remember that figures show that in Federal Germany, one woman is raped every five to seven minutes and that most rapes are planned (Brownmiller, 1975), that women are permanently subjected to a nightly curfew, and that women's bodies are forced into procreation under the provisions of Paragraph 218. This situation is comparable with a permanent state of war in which organized gangs terrorize peasants, handicraft workers, and business people, with one gang ultimately claiming to be protectors and demanding tribute for their services.

The state equips men to keep women away from full-time work with the bonus that, through the husband, family insurance schemes provide some protection against sickness and old age for women and children. In turn, this benefits companies by providing a prop for their demand for a cheap, short-term, occasional and temporary labour force which does not incur additional insurance costs. They therefore lend their weight to the coalition of interests by offering women only those jobs which prevent them from establishing an independent economic existence.

One acknowledged mechanism in this is invoking the so-called labour-protective legislation for women. Also well-known are the arguments which contend that women's potential motherhood makes them more expensive and less intensive workers, supposedly unable to guarantee reliable and continuous attendance. These hidden mechanisms of force are accompanied by direct forms of sexist violence against women exercised by employers and potential colleagues and workmates in denying them better paid and long-term secure employment. (cf. Benard, 1980; MacKinnon, 1979) Sabine Klenke has shown how the introduction of new technology in the context of the economic crisis leads men to initiate a direct distributional struggle at work to obtain the more interesting and less stressful tasks and offload the monotonous work, often destined to be hived off to temporary workers, on to women. This is not the result of some housewifely empathy for VDU work, but the outcome of sexist coercion. (Klenke, 1983)

The status of women's work as second-income earning and as housework is justified by the supposed fact that men's demanding and responsible work makes them the main bread-winner; this was always a dubious argument. And current circumstances are making the idea of the male 'family wage' even more questionable. With the possible exception of the family insurance bonus offered by husbands and fathers, the current crisis has seriously undermined men's ability to 'provide'. Mass unemployment, short time and reduced earnings place a very basic question mark over whether men can provide a 'family wage' throughout their lives. What remains, at best, is a common family infrastructure (home, food, psychological needs) cheaper than for individuals and single parents, but no longer of indisputable economic benefit for the woman. In the final analysis it is women who create and maintain this infrastructure through their unpaid labour. In other words: women are forced to take up paid employment to ensure their own, and their children's, survival. That this is so is evidenced by the rising participation rates of married women in the labour market. This has two consequences. In the first place, women are forced to accept whatever employment is offered to them. In the second, women have to reckon with increasing direct violence with the erosion of the economic basis of the hegemony of the majority of husbands and fathers. The fact that the 110 women's refuges in West Germany are now full to overflowing bears testimony here. (See *Frankfurter Rundschau*, 27 December 1982) Crime statistics also show an increase in rape. *(Frankfurter Rundschau*, 23 April 1983; Fiegl, p. 10)

Any specifically female type of labour capacity which might be fostered by the forms of employment to which women are assigned would be characterized not by a capacity for empathy but a combination of temporal flexibility and a tolerance for monotonous stress. During the Third Reich it was argued that women's ability to mother and their inborn lack of logic made them particularly suitable for assembly-line work.

> The swiftly learnt tasks . . . do not establish close ties between women and their work, and more particularly to the import of their work . . . When at work they take pleasure in the images conjured up by their imaginations – the joy in the eyes of the children for whom they are working so hard. (*Jahrbuch der Deutschen Arbeitsfront 1937*, p. 339, quoted in Tröger, 1982)

Women's jobs now are also characterized by the worst and most inhuman working conditions. Sabine Gensior and Lothar Lappe have shown a particularly extreme division of labour in women's industrial work, with the labour process fragmented into elemental sub-routines. The same applies in the non-industrial sectors wherever electronic data processing is involved, especially in insurance, finance and public and private sector administration. Very few of these jobs call for skills. But, 'What is central in the scale of the division of labour, the stripping away of content, the deskilling and the stress are the methods used to organise work itself.' (Gensior and Lappe, 1982, pp. 93/94) The part-time work almost exclusively carried out by women is not only poorly paid, but – as is the norm in our system – also entails the worst working conditions. If a low income is taken as one indicator of monotonous and meaningless work, typically under strenuous piece-work systems, then the figures suggest that these conditions are almost wholly confined to women. In 1981 7.3% of men but 20% of women had a monthly net income of less than DM 600; 1.1% of men but 11% of women earned between DM 600 and DM 800; 1.6% of men and 13% of women received between DM 800 and DM 1,000, and 4.1% of men and 14.3% of women received between DM 1,000 and DM 1,200. (*Statistiches Jahrbuch 1982*, p. 97)

Nevertheless, in addition to tolerating monotony, women are also expected to be flexible with their time; for example, to switch from one activity to another at very short notice as in work on-call (KAPOVAZ). And housework regarded as abstract labour and a particular type of employment relation – not 'work for love' – is also evidently characterized both by monotony and the fragmentation of the work process caused by the constant repetition of tasks such as washing, cleaning, shopping etc. and the dependence of housework on the rhythms of both men's and women's paid employment and children's school hours. Finally, the installation of computer terminals in the home provides a striking demonstration both of the abstract, monotonous character of housework and the need to see women's labour in capitalism as a unity 'wage-house-work'. Such home-working combines the rhythm and stress of both forms: work at the terminal is an extension of housework and vice versa.

In fact, women's labour under capitalism (both paid and unpaid) has steadily shifted away from tasks with a definite content to abstract processes devoid of any apparent useful meaning. This is a process which has now come to a head as a result of the crisis, the dismantling and restructuring of the welfare state and the introduction of new technologies. Meaningful tasks for women and an apportionment of social labour between the sexes based on the material content of tasks is increasingly becoming a thing of the past. Contrary to the common assumption, the current development seems to be for men to be assigned all the integrated and meaningful tasks, while women receive the fragmented and meaningless work. (cf. Gensior and Lappe, 1982) Even what might otherwise be meaningful work with children is increasingly being undermined. A more mechanized and polluted environment is forcing women to exercise absolute control and discipline over children in order to protect them from hazards in their everyday surroundings. Nowhere can children move freely either at home (electricity, machines, cleaning agents, medicines) or still less on the street. They have to be constantly supervized by someone they know, not least because strangers show neither responsibility nor concern. Any pleasure and tranquillity in the mother–child relationship is being driven out by the pressure to take up paid employment, with its destructive rhythms, combined with sole responsibility for child-care and inadequate alternatives, forcing women constantly to make do with hectically rearranged provisional solutions.

If women's labour is understood as the inseparable unity of housework and paid employment, women have no other solution but to defend themselves at every level against the coercion which forces them into this relation of forced labour. Looking on housework as meaningful activity, retreating into the meaningful experience of motherhood and learning to survive as an individual within male institutions are essentially flights into a non-existent fantasy world. Housewives will not escape the pressure to take up paid employment, or monotony and sexual violence; motherhood is at best a victory in a struggle to conquer time, quiet and money, in a world which precisely and forcibly aims to make this impossible. Simply surviving together is a sign of strength and resistance. The woman who makes her own peace with male institutions at best will do so at the cost of being treated like a silly little girl: not only will she not be respected as a person but certainly will not escape from violence.

The future of women's work: summary

Women are especially hard hit by the economic crisis. This is why it is especially important to understand the direction of economic development and the place women will have within it. One thing is certain: the current trend is not to pull women out of paid work and pack them off back to the home. Rather, by exploiting the obligations imposed on women as wives, housewives and sole child-carers, increased efforts will be made to create a disposable unit of labour, hireable and fireable at short notice, forced to work anywhere for low pay and under appalling conditions and without adequate legal and welfare protection, with its lower social insurance costs, and on hand to meet cyclically or seasonally fluctuating demands for labour. What is diminishing is not women's access to employment in itself, (the economic crisis has seen an increase in women's work, both paid and unpaid) but to better paid, secure employment. On the unpaid front, they are forced to substitute with their own work what is no longer available because of cuts in welfare services and lower earnings. Not least, this situation forces them – more so than previously – to look even harder for paid work for which they receive less and which they have to perform under worse conditions.

In the present days, however, special measures are required to keep women away from better paid, so-called skilled jobs as well as massive interventions in the existing structures of care for small children, which are meagre in any case. The ideology of motherhood and the family is evidently not sufficient here because women do resist, setting up their own self-administered nurseries, pushing through a different division of labour with fathers and husbands with regards to housework and child-care, and acquiring higher skills. (Müller, Handl, Willms, 1983, p. 17)

One task for our future will be to regard these forms of women's resistance more seriously and build on them: they are practised on a massive scale, especially where women survive together and not in poverty, on their own and with their *own* children (and not children as the property of the father as is automatic under the patriarchal laws of marriage and the marriage contract itself). However, we can also expect such forms of women's survival to be subjected increasingly to attacks in the form of individual and collective force. This is particularly acute at present as the economic crisis means that it is the political coalition of male interests, rather than any real economic dependence on the male as bread-winner, that forces women into dependence on men. For men, too, have increasingly less access to money based solely on their existence as men.

In the future women will have to develop their own politics: men's idea of politics is of precious little use to us; it is valid only within the world of men from which we are excluded. It confines itself to organizations that confront each other in isolation from real life, and is played according to the regulations and rituals of male bonding: duels, parliament, collective bargaining, even war. In contrast, women are the targets of unregulated violence. A politics which rests on structures, rules and social circumstances in which there are neither perpetrators nor victims is simply invalid for women: it renders us immobile. Women are constantly forced into submission – on the street, at work and at home – by acts of *violence*. We must be able to respond directly. We can do this only when we overcome fear, including fear of the knowledge that how we work in this society is also a product of violence.

Sources

Beck-Gernsheim, Elisabeth: Der geschlechtsspezifische Arbeitsmarkt, Frankfurt a.M./New York 1981

Benhard, Cheryl: Immer nur lächeln? Sexuelle Belästigung am Arbeitsplatz in: Emma, 12, 1980

Bennholdt-Thomsen, Veronika; Mies, Maria; von Werlhof, Claudia: Frauen und Kolonien: die 'Natur' des Kapitals, Reinbeck b. Hamburg 1983

Brownmiller, Susan: Against Our Will

Fiegl, Verena: Gewalt gegen Frauen, unveröff. Manuskript, Bielefeld 1983

Gensior, Sabine und Lappe, Lothar: Zukunft der Frauenerwerbsarbeit, in: Sektion Frauenforschung in den Sozialwissenschaften in der DGS, Beiträge zur Frauenforschung am 21. Deutschen Soziologentag, Bamberg 1982, S. 91–115

Guttstadt, Gabriele; Hentschel, Helga; Lüdtke-Cosmann, Barbara; Gomell, Elfi M.: Frauen als industrielle Reservearmee, in: Kongress Zukunft der Arbeit, Materialienband, o. O. o. J., S. 282–293

Irigaray, Luce: Waren, Körper, Sprache. Des ver-rückte Diskurs der Frauen, Berlin-West 1976

Klenke, Sabine: Zukunft welcher Arbeit? in: Moderne Zeiten, 12, 1982, S. 18–22

Mackinnon, Catherine: Sexual Harassment of Working Women. A Case of Sex Discrimination. New Haven and London 1979

Möller, Carola: Ungeschützte Beschäftigungsverhältnisse — verstärkte Spaltung der abhängig Arbeitenden, Konsequenzen für die Frauenforschung und die Frauenbewegung, in: Sektion Frauenforschung in den Sozialwissenschaften in der DGS, Beiträge zur Frauenforschung am 21. Deutschen Soziologentag, Bamberg 1982, S. 183–200

Müller, Walter; Handl, Johann und Willms, Angelika: Strukturwandel der Frauenarbeit 1880–1980, Frankfurt 1983

Ostner, Ilona: Beruf und Hausarbeit. Die Arbeit der Frau in unserer Gesellschaft. Frankfurt a.M./New York 1978

Ostner, Ilona and Willms, Angelika: Strukturelle Veränderungen der Frauenarbeit in Haushalt und Beruf? in: Sektion Frauenforschung in den Sozialwissenschaften in der DGS, Beiträge zur Frauenforschung am 21. Deutschen Soziologentag, Bamberg 1982, S. 205–231

Schorsch, Eberhard: Beitrag in: Sexualpädagogik und Familienplanung, in: Zeitschrift der Pro-Familia, Schwerpunktthema: Sexuelle Gewalt, 2, 1983

Statistisches Jahrbuch 1982 für die Bundesrepublik Deutschland, Statistisches Bundesamt (Hrsg.), Wiesbaden 1982

Straus, Murray A.: Sexuelle Ungleichheit, kulturelle Normen und Frauenmißhandlung, in: Haffner, Sarah (Hrsg.), Gewalt in der Ehe, Berlin 1978

Theweleit, Klaus: Männerphantasien, 2 Bände, Berlin 1977

Tröger, Annemarie: Die Planung des Rationalisierungsproletariats. Zur Entwicklung der geschlechtsspezifischen Arbeitsteilung un des weiblichen Arbeitsmarktes im National-sozialismus, in: Anette Kuhn und Jörn Rosen (Hrsg.), Frauen in der Geschichte II, Düsseldorf 1982, S. 245–316

Part 3:
Politics Against Women and Women's Struggles

7.   Class Struggles and Women's Struggles in Rural India

Maria Mies

He who owns the land owns the women of the land

Class struggle from above

The picture of the rural masses in India painted by the Western media is that of millions of half-starved, analphabetical, apathetic peasants, who 'peacefully' accept their misery, because their religion and their karma have so ordained it. Bored and disgusted, the well-fed Western citizen turns off his TV when it brings this exotic misery into his drawing-room. All that bothers him are the reports that these pauperized masses produce millions more of such poor creatures.

As a new variant of this caricature of India's rural people there is the myth of the 'happy poor', who, although they lack all the comforts of Western civilization, are able to maintain their 'peace of mind' – and to live in harmony with themselves and nature. The spreading of this myth is particularly due to the interest in Eastern spiritual beliefs that accompanies the New Age movement.

Nothing is further removed from reality than these images of the rural poor in India. What is this reality today? Perhaps there is now no other country where the rural scene is characterized by so much every-day violence – a violence which, particularly in the last 15 years has increased and intensified. When news about the situation in the villages reaches the cities – or even the Western media – the violent clashes between rich peasants and landlords on the one side and poor peasants and landless people on the other are usually interpreted as communal clashes, based on differences of caste and religion. This view is made easy because the majority of the landless agricultural labourers are untouchables, whom Gandhi called 'Harijans', members of non-Hinduized tribes called 'Adivasis' or members of other low castes. The majority of the land-owning classes are upper-caste Hindus.

If, however, one troubles to collect and analyse the stray reports in the printed media about so-called 'atrocities against weaker sections' it becomes evident that the violence of the rich peasants or landlords and the police against tribals, poor peasants and women (because these are meant by the official terminology 'weaker sections') is part of a regular class struggle, a class struggle from above.

This war of the rich against the poor, the powerful against the weak, cannot be separated from the development strategies by which the rural areas in India – as elsewhere in the Third World – are compulsorily integrated into the capitalist market system. This development policy, thought out and propagated throughout the Third World mainly by the World Bank, was in the interest of US capital. As Vandana Shiva writes, this development war, in the three decades that the World Bank has shaped the destiny of many Third World countries, has left behind more human victims that the military wars, not to speak of the environmental destruction it caused.[1] A main objective of this development policy was/is to 'draw peasants away from subsistence' and replace traditional agriculture by commercial agriculture, and treat the countryside as a hinterland only, for the benefit of the industrial cities and the West. As in most countries where this development policy was implemented, the various programmes, beginning with big dam projects, but also the various 'revolutions' – the Green Revolution, the White Revolution (called Operation Flood in India) the Social Forestry projects, the Integrated Rural Development Programme and so on – have invariably led to greater class polarization in the rural areas and hence more conflicts among the rural people. These conflicts and violent clashes, however, are attributed not to the policy of capitalist agricultural development but to differences in ethnicity, caste, and religion. Thus for instance, the conflict between Sikhs and Hindus in Punjab is seen not as a consequence of the Green Revolution, but as a religious war.

In the following pages I shall present a few examples of 'atrocities against weaker sections' in the Indian countryside to illustrate the point that modern capitalist development leads to class struggle from above. In this war of the powerful against the weak the violence against women plays a crucial role.

1. In January 1969, in the village of Kilvenmani in Tamilnad, 42 Harijans, old men, women and children, were driven into one hut and there burnt to death. The Madras High Court, four years later, acquitted all the 25 landlords who had been accused of this massacre, for want of evidence. The judges were of the opinion that such rich and high caste gentlemen would not 'walk bodily to the scene to set fire to the houses, unaided by any of their servants . . .' What is the background of this mass murder of Harijans? In 1966 the paddy-growing landlords of the Nagapattinam taluk had founded a 'Paddy Producers' Association' for the protection of their interests against the union of the landless labourers, the Red Flag Union. Most of the agricultural labourers are untouchables, Harijans. Whenever their union called for a strike, the Paddy Producers' Association sent labourers from other villages to break the strike. This had also happened in 1969. Under the leadership of the communist Red Flag Union the labourers had gone on strike for higher wages. When the landlords imported labour from outside, a clash followed between the two groups, and the landlords refused to give any work in future to the strikers unless they would pay a fine of Rupees 250 each and become members of the PPA. The labourers rejected these conditions. During the negotiations about this issue an agent of the landlords was killed. Thereupon the landlords organized a regular

expedition of revenge. They came in police trucks with guns, sticks and axes, and set fire to the labourers' huts. Eight of the Harijans who were involved in the killing of the landlord's agent were sentenced to long and rigorous imprisonment, but all the landlords were acquitted.

The pattern of the Kilvenmani incident is typical of innumerable similar cases of landlords' terrorism against Harijan and Adivasi agricultural labourers in other parts of the country.

2. On 4 July 1974, in Ramanapalle in the Cudappah district in Andhra Pradesh, 500 caste Hindus, mostly landlords belonging to the Reddy caste, attacked a Harijan village with axes, swords and guns. They wounded 30 Harijans, including old people and pregnant women, and burnt 118 huts to ashes with all the belongings of the Harijans. As in Kilvenmani, these atrocities were the landlords' answer to the Harijan labourers' demands for higher wages. The Harijans also demanded the right to cultivate a plot of fallow land which the government had allotted them for distribution. Yet, when they had tried to occupy the land, they were driven away by the landlords. The government officials and the police said that they were helpless against the Reddy landlords' contempt of the law. They were not able to protect the Harijans against the brutality of the Reddys. It must be added that the Harijans, as in Kilvenmani, had been organized under communist leadership.

3. Another instance of the Reddy landlords' 'class struggle from above' was reported in July 1974. Three hundred Reddy landlords tried to forcibly appropriate the land of the Sugalis, a hill tribe in eastern Andhra Pradesh. The Reddys claimed that they had been allotted the ownership of the land in an ex parte court judgement. The Adivasis, however, had cultivated the land for many years. The Reddys appeared in buses with sticks and other weapons, but the Sugalis were prepared and retaliated. In the clash 40 Sugalis, including women, and 27 Reddys were wounded. As in the Ramanapalle incident the police came too late, although they had been asked to protect the Adivasis. They claimed to be unable to prevent the Reddy's violence.

4. On 12 September 1974, four landless labourers were killed by the Jat landlords in Devbaath in the Punjab. The Jats are the dominant landowning caste in the Punjab, as the Reddys and the Kammas are in Andhra Pradesh. They control the economic and political power in the state. Out of all Indian states, the Punjab has profited most by the 'Green Revolution', and the Jats have become powerful rural capitalists.

The Harijan labourers of Devbaath had been organised by CPI activists. When they went on strike for higher wages, the landlords declared a social boycott against them. On 12 September the Harijans had assembled under a tree to discuss how to react against this social boycott. All of a sudden a group of landlords arrived with guns. They asked one of the leaders to raise his arms, and shot him on the spot. The others tried to flee but three more persons were killed, among them one woman and a young boy. The police arrived on the scene after the shooting had gone on for 15 minutes. The leaders of the labourers' union had informed the police beforehand of the landlords' plans and had asked them to confiscate the firearms of the Jats, but nothing had happened.

All these clashes took place between high caste Hindus and Adivasis or Harijans. Yet, it is evident that they were not sparked off by caste issues, but by economic and political issues. The landless labourers demand higher wages and land, and they have begun to organise themselves to fight for these interests. The dominant rural class, however, uses its political, economic and cultural power, including direct violence, to keep the rural proletariat 'in its place', as they say. In this class struggle the ruling class very skilfully uses caste discrimination, caste feelings and the dependence of the untouchable labourers on the landlord as weapons.

The fact that, according to a report of the Home Ministry, every year about 200 Harijans are killed by caste Hindus, shows that the cases I have reported are not stray incidents. The same report admits that the number of such cases has increased significantly in recent years, and that atrocities against Harijans are now exceeding the traditional communal troubles between Hindus and Muslims.[2]

As a rule these 'atrocities' follow a stereotype pattern. The rich peasants and landlords have guns and either come themselves in big gangs to raid the villages of the poor or they send their hired *gundas* (thugs) to burn down the huts, beat up the men and rape the women.

While at the beginning of the 1970s the police played a rather passive role in these incidents – either arriving too late, or not interfering because they had been bribed – in the late 1970s and early 1980s they actively participated in these atrocities. One of the most gruesome cases was that of at least 34 members of the poor peasant class, mainly low caste and untouchable people, being deliberately blinded by the Bihar police. The victims were each dragged to the police station where one policeman pierced their eyes with a needle, then acid was poured into the wounds, so that the man was totally blinded. According to a report in the *Indian Express* the action was supervised by a doctor. When news of this case reached Delhi, the late Prime Minister, Indira Gandhi, ordered an enquiry and the punishment of the guilty. But the police demonstrated against the firing of their colleagues, and none of those guilty of the atrocity, even those directly responsible for this torture, were dismissed. The explanation given for this leniency was, according to the newspaper, that the then Chief Minister of the State of Bihar, Jagannath Mishra, had given as an election promise, that he would 'eradicate criminality by all possible means'.[3]

In this context, however, 'criminality' means every effort of the poor to defend their rights to subsistence, to their due wages or the land that had been allotted to them, or to defend their women's dignity. As stated above, this war of the rich against the poor invariably involves special violence, against the poor women, mainly in the form of rape. During and after the Emergency (1975–77) group rapes, many of them carried out by policemen, were frequent occurrences. For example, the press reported that on 23 April 1982, 21 women were raped by 12 policemen and a mob of 50 men in a village in the Basti district in Uttar Pradesh. The police justified these mass rapes as being to punish the villagers who were accused of having beaten up two policemen.[4] Similar cases were reported from many of the tribal areas in Bihar, Maharashtra, Madhya Pradesh and Andhra Pradesh.

One of these cases, the gang rape by several policemen of the fifteen-year-old girl, Mathura, sparked off the nationwide campaign of the new Indian women's movement against rape and other forms of male violence.[5] Only after small feminist groups in Bombay, and later in Delhi, had raised the issue of rape, not only in the countryside but also in the cities, did the extent of this violence against women become known to the middle class public. The government had to admit that the number of rapes reported to the police had risen from 2,562 cases in 1972 to 37,817 cases in 1978. The number of raped Harijan women in particular had greatly increased between 1981 and 1982.[6]

Other forms of violence against women are wife-battering and – commoner in the cities than in the countryside – the killing of young brides who fail to bring enough dowry.

Capitalist development and violence

The Indian Left used to interpret such cases of terrorism of the rich against the poor, especially the sexist violence against women, as remnants of 'feudal' or 'semi-feudal' production relations in the Indian countryside. Since, however, the increase of violence, particularly of sexual violence – not only in the rural areas but also in the cities – can no longer be denied, the thesis of feudal backwardness loses much of its plausibility. The most brutal forms of violence and of sexist terror are to be found in areas where agriculture has been rapidly 'developed' in recent years, where new forms of wealth appeared, where cinemas, alcohol, television and other new consumer goods were introduced as indicators of 'modernization'. Capitalist development or 'modernization' has not liberated the rural poor, the landless and downtrodden from feudal bondage and transformed them into 'free' wage labourers. On the contrary, the progress and the new wealth of the rural landlords and rich peasants is based on a number of non-wage relations, including a kind of slave labour (called bonded labour in India) which is often the result of indebtedness. Such labour relations are not survivals of a feudal past but genuine capitalist inventions. As a landlord from Bihar put it: 'There are two means to keep agricultural labourers in their place: (1) to make them dependent through credits (2) sexual exploitation of their women'. The ruling classes deliberately employ both these means as the cheapest and most efficient method of labour control. If the poor are made to forego their rightful claims to a minimum wage or to land that was allotted to them, then this new capitalist agriculture can achieve a 'growth rate' that would otherwise be impossible.

Whenever capitalist development has taken place in rural India in recent years we find direct violence and coercion. These are the secrets of 'modernization' and not, as is mostly said, a miraculous increase in productivity due to technological innovation. This point is illustrated, for example, by the increased violence against women in the wake of the Operation Flood. Formerly, poor women were allowed to cut grass on the edges of the landlords' fields but they are now beaten up if they do so, because this grass has become a commodity which is claimed by the owner of the field, who sells it to dairy farms.[7]

The increase of sexual violence proper, however, can be explained only by the fact that agriculture is increasingly industrialized and capitalized. As we saw above, sexual exploitation mainly in the form of rape, is a means used by the ruling classes to discipline the exploited classes. In order to punish rebellious poor peasants and landless labourers, landlords and police are not satisfied with beating up the men and burning their huts; in many cases they also rape the women of these men. Why? Obviously, these rapes are not, as is often believed, a kind of safety valve for the repressed sexual urges of the rapists. In fact, these acts have nothing to do with sexuality as such, neither are the targets the women as such, but rather the men of the poor classes. Women are seen as the only property that the pauperized men still possess. The rape of their women teaches poor men the lesson that their status is one of absolute powerlessness and propertylessness. This sexual aggression on the part of the landlords and the police against poor women is a weapon with which to beat the men of the propertyless classes and to stabilize the existing or newly emerging power relations in the countryside. Class rule and the oppression of women are here closely interwoven. *He who owns the land, owns the women of the land.* That the poor men in Bihar started a movement: 'Rape against rape' in order to avenge the rape of their women, only confirms their recognition of the close relationship between class rule and sexual dominance.

The sexual violence that affects poor, rural women in India today has an international or imperialist dimension, as well as the class dimension. In India, as in many other Third World countries, it can be observed *that today the traditional control of a repressive patriarchal morality is breaking down.* But this breaking down is not due to a liberalization in sexual mores, but rather because those classes who in recent years have become rich quickly can now afford to buy modern consumer goods, which also imply a certain consumer image of women. It is mainly the young, 'progressive' men of these classes, who are the first to discard the old sexual norms. They imitate the White Man, he is their model of modernity and progress. They wear his clothes, see his films, including porno-films, accept his way of life. For them 'development' means participation in the 'international' – Western, male and sexist – culture. But they expect their women to remain keepers and preservers of their own national culture. Women must wear the national/local dress. Sexual freedom is not for them, they must go on playing their 'traditional' role of mother and self-sacrificing wife. The recent renaissance of Sati (suttee) in Rajasthan, promoted by young men, is a clear indication of their repressive attitude towards women.[8]

I call this the 'Little Man–Big Man' syndrome. The little men imitate the big men, at first in their own country, but the same relationship exists between the 'little' brown and black men and the 'big' white men – today's supermen; but they do not want their women to imitate the 'big men's' women. This contradiction is clearly manifested in Indian films: the hero is usually a Westernized young man but the 'good woman' must represent 'traditional India' as it is understood by these Westernized men. For the screen hero and the heroine to kiss is not allowed, but many films have rape scenes. I see a clear connection between the profit interests of the newly rising classes and the violence against women in India, both in the films and in reality. It is the 'little men', often without a job or property, who provide the main audience for the films, bringing money to this industry. Unable to go to the West or participate in the international male culture, they are offered a rape scene in the films to compensate for their frustrations and so that they can identify with the 'big men', can feel that they are 'real men', because there is still a woman who can be attacked.

Peasant women organize

In the above accounts the poor peasants and the poor peasant women appear mainly as victims of landlord and police repression. We rarely hear anything about how they have reacted to this situation. In some reports the dominant classes' repression of the poor is seen as their answer to a new consciousness and increasing organization of the poor. But even in reports about peasants' movements we hear little about the role women have played in them.

As a result of the women's movement and its renewed interest in women's history, however, some peasant movements have been studied again, with a special focus on the role of women.[9] As a contribution to this process of documenting women's history I shall present here an account of a poor peasant women's organization that grew up in the context of a movement in the state of Andhra Pradesh aimed at organizing landless and poor peasants. I learned from these women that their struggle against the landlords, and against their own men, was absolutely essential to their movement. They showed how, in the course of their movement, the artificial subordination of the 'gender' to the 'class' question – which is mostly upheld by the Left – is a trick to uphold and stabilize, or create new capitalist–patriachal relationship of exploitation and dominance. The study of this women's organization took place in the context of a research project on rural women in the subsistence sector.[10] The analysis of this poor peasant women's organization raises a number of questions regarding the organizational potential of women. I was first confronted with such questions in 1973–75 when I studied the tribal women in the Shahada Movement.[11] The present case study confirms some of my earlier observations, but it also throws more light on rural women's potential for mobilization and organization around their own sex and class interests.

The women I am concerned with here are 'Harijans' or 'untouchables'. All were illiterate, poor, and earned their living mainly by coolie work (daily wage labour) in the fields of landlords and rich peasants; some had a small fraction of land. Their men were also mostly agricultural labourers and poor peasants, but many had lost their traditional employment due to 'modernization' of agriculture. The women, however, had lost little of their earlier employment, in fact, they performed approximately 80% of all agricultural labour in the fields.

This fact, and that they performed this work collectively (transplanting, weeding, harvesting and so on) had influenced their consciousness and behaviour. They showed an astonishing degree of assertiveness and militancy and a great capacity for clear-headed analysis of their problems and working out solutions.

This assertiveness was not an inborn quality of the Harijan women, but was the outcome of their work, their awareness of their importance for the survival of the family, and of the fact that they had to live by the work of their own hands. In contrast to the urban middle-class women, those women saw themselves not as housewives but as workers; most of their life was spent not within the confines of their poor huts but outside. They were too poor to have their private life separated from public life. Although their men are socially defined as bread-winners, as is the case with the upper-caste and upper-class men, these women knew that they would never 'rise' to the status of housewife, 'kept and fed' by the husband. In fact, they talked with a certain contempt of such women who could not do the hard work to which they were accustomed.

Work organization and women's consciousness

A major factor which contributed to the boldness and self-confidence of these women was the collective nature of their work in the fields. They always worked in groups of 10–30 women made up of smaller teams of neighbours, relatives and friends. These teams had developed a spirit of solidarity and mutual help which transcended the egoism of the individual family. Even the mother-in-law/daughter-in-law enmity, typical of caste-Hindu families, did not divide these women to the same degree as is the case in the upper castes. The collective spirit among the women was also strengthened by the fact that the landlords had to bargain with them collectively about the wage. They cannot recruit these women individually but must negotiate with their spokeswoman who, in turn is controlled by the other women labourers. The necessity to recruit large numbers of women for agricultural operations during certain periods of the year provided the objective basis for the development of women's collective spirit and organizational skill. Communal feelings, the discrimination of caste-Hindus against Harijans, also helped strengthen the solidarity among Harijan coolie women.

The agricultural work process itself, for example, in rice transplantation and weeding, its regular, rhythmic body movements by many women together also strengthened their feelings of solidarity. It was the physical basis for cultural activities which accompanied this process. The songs sung during rice transplanting and weeding not only set the work rhythm but also relieved the women of fatigue and emotional stress. The themes of the songs were often the key aspects of a woman's life: marriage, man–woman relations, relations between mother and daughter, mother-in-law, daughter-in-law. The songs maintained the unity between the 'private' and the work sphere. They also contained the hopes, aspirations and dreams of a better life, even though these ballads of landlords, princes, gods and goddesses fixed the consciousness on the patriarchal values of their oppressors. But the work process itself, the fact that they worked for a wage, prevented them from taking these dreams too literally and losing their sense of reality.

The songs were a mechanism in themselves to generate a feeling of collectivity, to prevent the atomization of individuals, the compartmentalization of life and sense of alienation, common in modern work processes. Thus, the women preserved a sense of human identity and dignity, and of cultural creativity.

This sense of pride in their songs and dances found its clearest expression after work and in their festivals. Women who knew the long ballads were famous in the area. In spite of their fatigue and the burden of their work, almost every evening after the evening meal, the women came out and sang and danced in the light of the moon or the petromax. They said they then felt more refreshed than when they went to sleep, which strongly indicates that the women's cultural production was necessary if they were to endure the otherwise crushing routine of work life.

The collective spirit generated by their work organization, the organizational forms they developed spontaneously, and the cultural expressions accompanying these processes, were already prevalent among these women before any effort was made towards their formal organization. They formed the basis upon which a formal organization could be built. Had the women been isolated and atomized housewives, dependent on the man's income, formal organization into women's movements would have been more difficult as is shown by the example of the lacemakers of Narsapur.[12]

Women's *sangams:* a formal organization of agricultural labourer women

This area was selected for the field work because, since 1977, the agricultural labourer women had been organized in women's associations or *sangams* by a voluntary organization: The Comprehensive Rural Operations Service Society (CROSS). In the period 1976–77 CROSS had begun to organize poor peasants and agricultural labourers – mostly Harijans – in the villages of Bhongir *taluk* (sub-division of a district), Nalgonda district, in the state of Andhra Pradesh. The creation of women's associations had not been in the minds of the CROSS organizers when they started their work among the poor peasants and agricultural labourers in Bhongir *taluk*. They had formed poor peasants *sangams* which theoretically included men and women. But women were not among the office bearers, nor did they come to the meetings or attend the night schools, which were among the principal activities of the village associations.

In summer 1977, the organizers discussed this lack of participation by the women, and concluded that no persuasion would bring the women to the meetings, not because they were not accustomed to speak up in the presence of the men, but because they had to do their cooking and housework in the evening while the men held their meetings. The organizers decided to form separate women's associations with their own office bearers and special programmes, and a woman activist took over the responsibility of organizing the women. The office bearers of the new women's associations were elected by the Harijan and other low-caste women in the village from among their own group.

Other caste women were not officially excluded from these women's *sangams*, but they did not want to join because of their feelings of caste superiority. Thus, for the first time, the Harijan and other poor peasant women had their own organization which was not dominated by the men of their community or by the women of the dominant high-caste Hindu landlords.

The women responded enthusiastically to the prospect of forming their own association. Between July 1977, when the first association was set up in Sikandernagar, and December 1978, 20 women's associations were formed with a total membership of 705 women. By December 1980 the number of village-based women's associations had increased to 84.

The formal structure was introduced because it was felt necessary for the achievement of one objective of the organization, namely to get access to funds and credits for the economic programmes for small and marginal farmers. But the organizers used the existing system of the community fund, the chit-fund system,[13] to introduce the idea of the women's associations.

The objectives of the women's associations were based on the same strategic principles as were the men's: the organization should give the small and marginal peasants and agricultural labourers the necessary collective bargaining power to gain access to the funds made available by the government for the economic development of the weaker sections.

These economic programmes were seen as a necessary precondition for organizing the poor peasants, because it was felt that they could not resist the despotism of the landlords unless their own economic base was strengthened. Even a struggle for higher wages or land would inevitably fail if they had nothing of their own to fall back upon. These economic programmes were accompanied by a programme of conscientization and education through night-schools, which combined alphabetization with political and social education.

Following this double strategy of combining programmes for the economic betterment with conscientization and education, the women's associations started to use the local chit-fund system to raise initial common funds. The interest collected through the chit-fund was common property, and was saved for common projects such as the building of a night-school. At the same time, regular weekly meetings were held in the villages, at which women discussed a variety of subjects related to their lives. The women responded with enthusiasm to these meetings which combined singing, and discussions of their problems, of possible solutions, and of strategies at the village and block level. The meetings helped to broaden the solidarity among the women and gave them an action orientation. In contrast to other such discussions, which often remain on a purely rhetorical level, members of the women's *sangams* often started to act immediately after having identified their common problem and discussed a strategy.

Economic programmes

But the women were not only motivated by the prospect of more education and cultural action. CROSS was known as an intermediary institution which helped to get funds for buffaloes, wells, general stores, vegetable vending and other such small income-generating projects; the women, therefore, expected individual economic benefits, and saw their *sangam* activities also as a means to this end.

Meetings of the women's *sangams* were used to identify the beneficiaries for these economic schemes. The criteria for their selection and the procedure were the same as in the men's *sangams*, that is, only individual women could benefit, not the whole *sangam*. Whereas in some villages the men's *sangams* had been able to get funds for such community projects as a well, the women's associations had been unable to do so. For example, they wanted money for the construction of a night-school, because they had to hold their meetings on the road under a tree; and they demanded that electricity should also be brought to the Harijan colony. But since all funds were based on the credit system, the banks and the government authorities who provided subsidies and margin money were not interested in projects which were not 'productive', that is, which were not of a surplus-generating nature but only helped the poor to improve their collective conditions of life.

The economic programmes for women were accompanied by educational activities, mainly in the form of night-schools which provided a forum where women could discuss their problems, but also where they could acquire the necessary knowledge and training for their socio-economic uplift such as literacy and knowledge about health, child-care, food, and so on.

These programmes were based on a double strategy, namely, that of combining the effort to raise women's economic status with that to raise their social, political and cultural status in society and to enable them to fight against their oppression through their own organization. Although this double strategy seemed the only possible one in the given situation, it was not free of contradictions in its implementation. These contradictions are part and parcel of all economic programmes aiming at income generation based on the individual family or the individual women. By granting loans to individual women for one of these schemes, for example, for a buffalo, the general aims of the educational programme, namely, to strengthen women's solidarity and unity and increase their bargaining power, were partly jeopardized. Some women were selected as beneficiaries of these schemes and others not, therefore divisions among the women were bound to arise.

The woman who had started the *sangams* realized the problem, and tried to avoid such divisions by appealing to the solidarity of the women, assuming that it would take time for all to benefit from these schemes, and by asking the women to select the poorest and most deserving who needed help most urgently. This appeal to their spirit of self-sacrifice rather than to their common interest, appears to overlook the political side-effects of these schemes, namely, to further competition among individuals and to introduce capitalist values to the poor. They do not aim at benefiting the rural poor as a class. The economic gains from these programmes to the individual family were quite negligible, and in the long run they even contributed to pauperization.[14] But the prospect of individual betterment and the lack of alternatives still had the effect that women opted for the schemes, although they did not expect much from them.

Despite these contradictions and difficulties, the women were keen to join the *sangams*, and women from many villages wanted to have a sangam. It seems that the divisive tendencies inherent in the economic programmes were neutralized by the sense of collective power that the women derived from their organization. The actual success of the associations was due to the fact that they gave the women a feeling of organized collective strength and could be used as an instrument for struggle. The issues taken up by the women's association in Kunur and Sikandernagar in 1978 show that they were able to use it for issues that were more relevant and crucial to all of them than individual economic schemes. In fact, as soon as the first *sangam* meetings took place in these villages, the women began to discuss the issue of wages and the organization of a strike. They also discussed other issues, such as the differences between men's and women's wages, and land.

Their collective experience and their common interest as workers helped them to use their organization for more general objectives. In our group discussions with the women in Kunur it became evident that their aspirations went beyond the limited aims set by the economic programmes. They first told us how the *sangam* had started, about the problems they had in attending night-school during the transplanting and weeding season, and about their efforts to persuade other caste women to support them in their strike. When we asked what problems they discussed during their meetings they first enumerated their various demands: 'We want a general store, buffaloes, electricity, a flour mill.' When we asked whether they also wanted better houses, one woman said 'Houses are not going to feed us. We want land, our plots are all on bad land and are too small. We want land, all the rest is humbug.'

They then went on to say that all their difficulties, the fact that despite all their work they could not fill their stomachs, that the landlords abused and harassed them, that they were not allowed to cut grass, and so on, were all related to the fact that the others had land and they had not, or only very poor plots. 'Now we want LAND. Then we will feel that they have done something for us. We are scared of them for every small thing. We do not want to be like that.'

These discussions revealed that the women did not need conscientization to make them aware of their exploitation. They were also able to analyse correctly the root cause of all their problems: their lack of control over the main means of production: land. They were not against asking for buffaloes, goats, a general store, better houses, and so on, but they did not take these things too seriously since these would not change the basic production relations in their area and hence would not solve the problem of how 'to fill their stomachs'.

In contrast to the philosophy that the programmes of the Small Farmers Development Agency (SFDA) would solve the problem of poverty of the rural poor, the Kunur women realistically assessed these programmes as palliatives. Neither did they distinguish between economic exploitation and social and cultural oppression – a distinction usually made by outside activists. They saw clearly the connection between the landlords' contemptuous and highhanded behaviour and their own lack of bargaining power. Their enthusiasm for the *sangam* was, therefore, not the result of individual self-interest but rather due to the prospect of having an instrument which would give them more power.

Methods of mobilization

The role of songs

We had observed the important role songs played in the organization of work in the fields and as a means of collective expression after work. We showed interest in their songs, recorded them, played them back to them, asked for translations; as a result, the women themselves felt inspired by our interest and came together to sing and dance more often than they would without our presence. Singing was already an established feature of the night-school programmes, but the women did not respond with equal enthusiasm to all songs. These were of two types: their own traditional ones, which they sang during their work and on festive occasions, and those introduced by the organizers, which were expressions of social criticism and of the aspirations of the poor. They asked us to join in their dancing and singing when they met informally after their day's work, and began to teach us their songs; they also wanted to learn some songs from us. As one of my research assistants was a very good singer and knew a number of new and inspiring songs, she became very popular among the women. The young girls began to learn her songs. As they could neither read nor write, their night-school teacher, a young man from the caste village, wrote down the texts of these songs and taught them to the teenage girls. At the weekend camp, which was held two months after we had left the village, we discovered that all the women of the village had learned these songs and had presented them to the assembly of all the other women as one of their cultural contributions. These songs so impressed the women assembled there that they, too, wanted to learn them. It was suggested that a group of good singers should be formed which would teach such songs to the women of other villages.

The response to the new songs introduced by my research assistant shows not only the importance of songs as a powerful means of communication, mobilization and organization of illiterate peasant women generally, but also that the people were clearly able to differentiate between songs with an abstract or superficial analysis of their situation, and those which expressed it in concrete terms. About one such song, which became very popular afterwards, one man said: 'This is *our* song.' In other words, they recognized their own lives, worries and hopes in the words of the poet and made this song 'their own'. In short, the women did not blindly accept or reject everything offered to them from outside, but made their own choice among the new cultural items introduced to them.

The women's response, the initiative they showed in acquiring new insights, inspiration and knowledge, made it clear that their objective and subjective condition was such that they needed very little stimulation and encouragement to start going ahead on their own. The methodology used during the field work[15] also contributed to realizing the women's own dynamics, their intrinsic learning motivation and creative spontaneity. Had there not been an organizational framework, however, and some activities which guaranteed the continuity of the process, the stimulation generated during the few weeks of the research team's stay in the villages would not have lasted and would have been of little consequence for the future development of the women's associations.

Weekend camps
The women's militancy, their ability to make a clear analysis of their situation, and to use their organization for their own emancipatory goals, became evident during the periodical weekend camps which were organized for their education.

Whereas the night-school programmes in the individual villages met with a number of practical difficulties, these weekend camps were successful and have since become a regular feature of the women's *sangams*. The following account of the development of these camps gives some insight into the development of women's collective consciousness in the course of two years.

The first camp for the women of several village *sangams* was organized after a year's organizational work. Fifty women from ten villages attended this camp in the *taluk* town Bhongir. The woman activist had invited representatives of various government departments, for example, the person in charge of the women's welfare department, and a professor from the Home Science College in Hyderabad, to speak to the women. The lectures were on 'Sanitation and Health and the Role of Women', and 'Malnutrition and Food Values'. These lectures were followed by discussions on the Minimum Wages Act, the difference between men's and women's wages, and the cost of living. The women reported on the situation in their respective villages and discussed strategies with which to fight the landlords for an increase of their daily wages. This weekend camp was a great success and encouraged the organizers and the women to continue their efforts.

The second women's camp, held in a college in Bhongir, organized on 28 and 29 October 1978 had a different focus. It was planned jointly by the *sangam* organizers and our project team. We felt that it would be good to bring the women from the villages where we had worked together in order to share and discuss past experiences with the *sangams* and their struggles to feed-back some of our findings to them and to widen their horizon which is usually limited by the boundaries of their villages.

About 70 women from 15 villages attended this camp. The village groups had prepared songs, role plays and sketches which they presented to the audience. One of them also talked about their previous months' experience and their problems and successes. The women participated actively and enthusiastically in the programme. In the role plays which they had prepared themselves, they gave very sharp and witty descriptions of some of their main problems. The themes of these plays were: men's drinking and wife-beating, dowry, negotiating about wages with a landlady. In particular the audience participated enthusiastically in the role play about wages, suggesting to the actors what they should do to get a better wage from the landlady.

After this cultural programme the women continued to sing and dance until late in the night. It was obvious that they thoroughly enjoyed being away for two days from their daily drudgery and from their responsiblity for husbands and children.

On the second day we talked about peasant women and their problems and organizations in other parts of the country. The aim was to show how other poor peasant women in India are also struggling successfully against their exploitation as women and workers. This also helped to give the illiterate women some idea of their country, their geographical knowledge being usually restricted to their own village, some neighbouring villages, and the next *taluk* town.

On evaluating this camp, it can be said that its main significance was the fact that it provided a forum for women from various villages to come together, to exchange their experiences, and to enjoy their own cultural productions. The women seized this opportunity for recreation and inspiration with gusto, and enthusiastically demanded more such camps.

The experience also taught us that poor peasant women are by no means satisfied with an improvement in their economic situation alone, but that they also struggle for their human emancipation, for the restoration of their human dignity and creativity. They do not want to be mere objects of development and teaching.

Some of the organizers felt that the second camp had focused too much on cultural activities, on 'fun' and not enough on giving the women some practical knowledge (for example, lectures on health, nutrition and such like). The third camp, on 19 November 1978, therefore, tried to combine functional education, for example on the rice zones in the country and on education, with the usual cultural programme of role plays, songs, sketches and dances. Ninety women came from 19 villages, having prepared some more dramas and songs and learned the new songs.

The enthusiasm these weekend camps generated was so great that the women decided to have a camp at least once a month. They also decided that on these occasions all the women should discuss particular problems of a single village, dealing with the most urgent problems first.

These two decisions show that the women understood the necessity to expand their organization beyond the boundaries of their villages, and to learn from each other's experiences. They also felt that their actions could be successful only if they had a strategy which encompassed more villages. The decision to have such camps every month was also an expression of the need for time for reflection and recreation. The women usually have no time in their villages to attend meetings and longer study sessions. Either their husbands demand their services, simply oppose their going out, or their children bother them.

An analysis of their working day shows that the main problem of these women is lack of time.[16] The demand for more weekend camps was thus the women's tactics to find time for themselves, for recreation, as well as for reflection and education. The CROSS organizers felt that one camp a month would antagonize the men who might protest against the frequent absence of their women, but the women insisted.

The fourth, and last weekend camp in which we participated, was organized on 17 February 1979 in the village, Veeravalli. This camp brought into clear focus the major contradictions with which the agricultural labourer women in the women's *sangams* have to struggle: sex, caste and class.

It marked the end and culmination of a certain process of organization and mobilization, based more on the initiative of the organizers, and the beginning of a new phase in which the *sangam* members came to the forefront as leaders. Because of its importance for the further development of the women's associations, a detailed account, given below, was written immediately after the camp.

Weekend Camp in Veeravalli

The women's *sangam* in Veeravalli had prepared and organized the meeting to which the women from seven other villages had been invited. The reason for selecting a village for the venue of the camp was that the women wanted to be hosts to other women, and also to root these meetings more in village life generally.

The president was a very dynamic woman. She and her secretary and the other women had organized the meeting in the open shed of the night-school; they had also managed to get a loudspeaker and a microphone.

A provisional kitchen had been installed at the side of the school shed where some men and women were already preparing the rice and vegetables for about 100 people. (The common meal had become a regular feature of these meetings and the women thoroughly enjoyed being served food without having to bother about the cooking.) Around 11 a.m. the shed was filled with women, some of whom had also brought their children. When all had properly settled down, the programme started. It had been planned that the president should welcome all the guests and introduce the programme. Before she could start, however, a small group of elderly caste women arrived and came into the shed and sat in the centre next to the microphone. We were told that this was the president of the old Mahila Mandal (Women's Club) dominated by high-caste women, with her friends. Nobody had invited her. As the women's *sangams* are mainly all-Harijan organizations, the caste women kept away from them.

It was an awkward situation. It was obvious that the old president wanted to speak and to inaugurate the meeting. She wanted to show that she was in charge of the women of this village. The *sangam* president asked the Mahila Mandal President to say something. She addressed the meeting and spoke about the Mahila Mandal and its activities. It was surprising that she, a high-caste woman. had dared to come to a Harijan women's meeting. But she and her friends made a special effort not to touch any of the Harijan women or to be touched by them. She spoke for around five to seven minutes, then she sat down. Then the *sangam* president addressed the meeting and explained the programme. Then a high-caste woman talked about hygiene, about the necessity to look after the children, to send them to school, about cleanliness, about food preparation, and so on. It was obvious that this kind of lecture about things beyond the economic reach of the Harijan women made no sense to the *sangam* women, but they listened patiently. Finally, someone suggested the microphone should be given to women in the audience who wanted to reply. After an initial shyness, due to the fact that they had never used a microphone, the Harijan women discovered its use and power. They told the woman that they would very much like to send their children to school but where would they get the money for the clothes and school uniforms? 'When I send my eldest boy to school, the other one has to stay at home, because he has no clothes. Will you give us clothes?' one woman asked. They countered all suggestions by reminding her of their basic economic problems, their low wages, lack of work and land. The woman who had spoken earlier sat down and kept quiet because she had no answer to these questions.

The *sangam* women, however, had captured the microphone and began to talk about their main problems: wages, lack of land, men's insufficient contribution to the family income. The main theme was the low agricultural wage. Many women participated in the discussion and felt inspired to speak out about their grievances. The caste women all sat in one corner. It was obvious that they did not like the Harijan women speaking about their exploitation by the rich people in the village, but they did not dare to say anything because they were only a few amongst almost 200 women.

But then an old Goud woman, who was standing outside the shed, began to criticize the *sangam* women. She spoke in favour of the rich people and said that the Harijan women had no right to speak like that about them, and that they should be satisfied with their wage, and so on. This angered the *sangam* women, who countered: 'Who are you to talk on behalf of these people?' The exchange of words between them became increasingly aggressive. The Goud woman was challenged as to how she had made her money – namely by selling liquor to the men of the village. 'Even to your men,' was the retort, 'tomorrow they will come and take Kallu [local country liquor] from me; even if they cannot pay they take it on credit. Today you speak about exploitation. Tomorrow you beg for money.'

The discussion had turned into an aggressive exchange of arguments between the *sangam* women on the one side and the Goud woman, the speaker for the rich, on the other. (Although the Gouds do not belong to the upper castes, it seemed this woman identified with the upper caste and class people in the village rather than with the Harijans.) Finally, the Harijan women asked her why she had come at all: 'Who invited you to our meeting? Why did you come to start quarrelling here? We did not invite you.' The meeting then closed for the lunch break and all the caste women and the Goud woman left. They did not return in the afternoon.

Many children and men had gathered around the open shed and constantly disturbed the women. In the afternoon, the programme continued with role plays and discussions. One of the role plays made by the women themselves was about wife-beating. A woman from Chandupatla played a drunken husband. she wore a turban and shouted at the wife. As a special item this drunken husband wanted to kiss his wife – to the great merriment of the audience. When she scolded him for his drinking and squandering the money, he beat her with a stick.

The discussion which followed was not very excited; but some good suggestions were made. One woman suggested: 'The men should pay for the rice out of their wages and we would pay for the rest, the vegetables, sugar, out of our wages. If they would do that, then they would at least regularly contribute to the household. If they then drink afterwards we would not have to starve with our children.' The men who had gathered in front of the shed were asked whether they would agree to such an arrangement, but none replied.

However, they created a lot of disturbance, several of them going about with a stick, beating children and pushing the women around who were not in the shed. Some of them obviously felt they had to give orders and directions. A meeting of women in which they had no function was something they could not accept.

Until this time the women's associations had not met with serious opposition. The men organized in their village *sangams* had regarded the women's *sangams* with benevolence or indifference. The issues the women had taken up, such as the wage issue, were to their benefit also, as were the economic programmes. The men did not take the cultural activities, the role plays on drinking, wife-beating, dowry, and suchlike too seriously, particularly as these performances had taken place far way from the villages, in the sheltered atmosphere of all-women camps. The Veeravalli camp, however, was held in the midst of a village, on an open space, amongst crowds of men and children, under the eyes and ears of the upper castes. The new quality of this camp was that it acquired the character of an open public meeting, using a loudspeaker and a microphone. Maybe it was this emphasis on publicity and the more elaborate preparation of the camp by the Veeravalli women that attracted both men and upper-caste women.

The active participation of the men – they cooked the common meal for 100–200 women, and were supposed to look after the children was in itself a great achievement and can be seen as a sign that the women's *sangams* had grown in importance. Similarly, the fact that upper-caste women dared to come out of the caste village to a meeting of Harijan women and even sat with them under the same roof, close enough to be touched by these untouchables, shows the impact of this organization of the poor women.

However, the increased visibility and organizational strength and self-confidence of the Harijan women, their fearlessness in speaking openly about exploitation and about oppression by their men in the presence of the upper-caste women and their men, accentuated the existing contradictions. Because the women exposed the men and the exploiting landlords *publicly*, those attacked reacted for the first time, and the women's struggle assumed a much more serious and more explosive character. The Veeravalli camp was followed by a series of repercussions and events which showed that for these poor women emancipation can lead to violent confrontations with their oppressors and exploiters.

Aftermath of Veeravalli

As our field work was completed in February 1979, the following account of events after the Veeravalli camp is not based on our own observations. It seems that the fact that so many women spoke openly about their exploitation by the landlords, that they used a microphone to do so, and that they exposed drinking and wife-beating in front of their men, enraged both the landlords and some of their men. The consequence was an increase in wife-beating. One woman in particular, who had spoken at the meeting, was very badly beaten by her drunken husband afterwards. Moreover, the landlords spread rumours about illicit relations between the daughter of the president of the women's association and a man. This led to a grave crisis in the village *sangam*.[17]

The aftermath of the Veeravalli camp showed that the poor women have to reckon with serious consequences when they begin to speak openly of their oppression. It also shows how that oppression is used to maintain caste and class dominance. The women were not discouraged, however, by these negative reactions. On the contrary, they maintained their organization; they understood more clearly the male complicity in the oppressive system of the village; and they worked out a strategy which did not aim at glossing over the contradictions between men and women, but at giving themselves more autonomy and organizational strength. Their militancy was enhanced, not broken, by the events of Veeravalli. In fact, these events were discussed by many *sangams* in the surrounding villages; and the next weekend camps in Motakundur and Aler on 24 April 1979 focused on the issue of wife-beating, on the practice of dispute settlement by village elders, and the payment of fines by the 'guilty' to the community leaders. The Veeravalli events were concrete points of reference for these discussions. The report on these camps says:

As a result of the day-long liberations, the women decided to set up an area committee consisting of women leaders to look into various cases, to visit the villages, to conduct meetings about women's problems, and to put an end to the practice of referring cases of women to the village elders, who make money out of the disputes from both the parties without doing justice to either of them. This will also help the women to break the barriers to which they are confined for ages.[18]

A further outcome of this camp was that teenage girls from three villages formed a separate group as part of the women's *sangams*. They wanted to play a more active part in the songs and other cultural activities for the mobilization of poor women.

Since the camp in April 1979, women's associations have continued to increase in number. But more importantly the women, in spite of opposition and difficulties, are making the associations more and more their own autonomous organization, which they can use as an instrument for education as well as for the generalization of their struggle against exploitation and oppression.

Shortly after the Veeravalli camp a reorganization of the men's and women's *sangams* took place. Cluster Committees were set up which met every fortnight. They consist of the representatives of the men's and women's *sangams* from six or seven villages, hence of a man and a woman from each of these villages. In these meetings all important issues are discussed, as well as such women's issues as wife-beating. When the women want to discuss such a problem, they first discuss it in their village *sangam* and with the women representatives and form an opinion on it. The women representatives then bring the problem to the meeting where it is discussed by all, including the men. In these meetings, women confront men not as individuals, but as an organization. A women's committee is often set up to implement the solution. These cluster meetings now take up the question of settling marital disputes. If they are unable to find a solution the matter is taken up by the steering committee which consists of representatives of women's and men's *sangams* and some of the organizers.

The following account of how the issue of wife-beating was dealt with shows the effectiveness of this organization, particularly with regard to so-called women's issues.

One woman, Rukamma, who, right from the beginning, had been very active in the women's *sangams* became the cluster representative of her village. She was also a very good actress and had participated in a role play where she had played a drunken husband. Her husband, who was a drunkard himself, began to resent his wife going to the fortnightly cluster meetings. He also felt insulted by his wife's play about a drunken husband, so he began to quarrel with her and beat her every time she went to her meeting.

Rukamma first told her village *sangam* about this, which meant she talked publicly about this 'private' affair. The women of the village *sangam* discussed the matter and came to the conclusion that Rukamma should separate from her husband and that he should vacate the house. They decided to punish him by not giving him food or water and they were supported in this decision by the other women's *sangams*. The man had to go to his mother's house for food.

At the next cluster meeting the women's decision was discussed but it was decided also to discuss the matter at steering committee level with some of the organizers present.Some of the men attending felt that the man's punishment was too harsh, others felt something should be done to help him overcome his inferiority complex which was due to his wife's political activities. Still others, men and women, felt they should not discuss this matter at all since it was a private affair between husband and wife. But most of the women insisted that it was a public (political) matter since it affected their organization. The man's resentment was mainly due to the fact that his wife attended the fortnightly meetings. He felt she neglected the household, and accused her of having illicit relations with another man at these meetings and of not wanting to look after the buffalo. He also complained that his wife now had more importance than he had himself. The women, therefore, almost unanimously agreed that the man should leave the house. 'A woman should never leave her house. The house belongs to her. The man should get out.' The decision of the women at the village level was thus endorsed by the other women representatives. The organizers decided to send a team of two to talk to the husband.

The women, however, insisted that the man should apologize to his wife as well as to their women's *sangam*, and promise to mend his ways. They also demanded that such a man, if he refused to change, should be expelled from the men's *sangams*. Hence, they used the mechanisms of social boycott as sanctions against such men. None of the organizers had proposed this strategy to the women. In fact, the organizers were not very happy about the radical way the women dealt with the issue of wife-beating and tended to play it down as a common and negligible problem. But the women refused to accept this 'normal' state of affairs any longer.

The way the women handled this matter shows that their action was not simply a spontaneous outbreak, but was well-planned, based on a realistic assessment of their own organizational strength, and their situation.

What is striking about this case seems to me the following:

(a) The women refuse to consider wife-beating (man's drinking) as a private affair, they see that the personal is political.

(b) Their decision to throw the man out of the house – instead of the wife vacating the house – shows their clear understanding of their need to maintain their material and organizational base – a house in their village where they have their work and their organization. The men can find work elsewhere. This decision seems to me more 'revolutionary' than the strategy adopted by Western women to establish shelters for battered women.

(c) The women do not believe in simply talking to the man and trying to convert him. They use collective pressure tactics to make him change his ways. These tactics are effective because the women are organized.

(d) They do not treat this issue as an isolated case but discuss it widely among themselves in all villages. Thus it becomes a generalized – that is a political – issue.

The camps and meetings have become important instruments for women's mobilization, education and organization. Particularly the all-women's camps or conferences have become a regular feature where all women meet. In December 1980 they had already had 13 such camps.

The women attribute so much importance to these meetings that they are ready to forego one day's work for them, and that means one day's wages and food. They use the money from their chit-fund to finance their organizational and educational activities.

This demonstrates how the women have advanced in their consciousness and organizational strength in the course of two years. Their gain in human autonomy and dignity is due mainly to the fact that there was an organizational effort which brought them together. Because of this and their double exploitation as women and workers, they moved ahead faster than their men.

The militancy and the organizational strength of the women also had an effect on their men in the general village associations. The men, who formerly had protested when their women wanted to attend meetings and weekend camps, realized that in their own dealings with the landlords and other dominant groups, they received more support from their organized women than they had formerly from their oppressed individualized wives. They began to understand that the ruling classes could easily break the unity of their movement by stressing the patriarchal authority of a man over his wife. They realized, contrary to common opinion, that separate women's organizations strengthened rather than weakened their own movement.

Perhaps the most encouraging success of this movement was that the women's *sangams* were able to produce their own village-based leadership and night-school teachers. Seventy-five girls from the villages who had some primary education, were in 1982, working in the night-schools of the *sangams*. Although they still lack administrative and co-ordinative skills they were very active and enthusiastic organizers and teachers. The emergence of local organizers and leaders was an important step in overcoming the problem of paternalism and élitism so often encountered when middle-class leaders try to organize poor peasants. This development was a step towards a truly autonomous poor peasant women's organization. Another factor which seems to have contributed to the success of the women's associations was that the woman activist who had initiated the formal organization of the poor village women acted as a co-ordinator rather than as a leader who provided a particular orientation or ideology. She did not interfere with the decision-making processes at the village level or during the periodical weekend camps or cluster meetings, but stayed in the background. This lack of 'strong leadership' and of the imposition of a 'line' from outside, seems to have provided the Harijan women with the necessary milieu within which they could discover and develop their own ideas and strategies, based on a rational assessment of their collective experiences.

Conclusions

The development of the peasant women's organizations and their consciousness in the course of two years, in the area where the study was carried out, is evidence of the fact that these poor, illiterate women did not react to the new trends of their integration into a capitalist market economy as helpless victims. The account of the women's organization given above shows that the poor peasant and agricultural labourer women need very little encouragement and help to become mobilized and organized. In fact, it seems they are just waiting for someone to help them overcome the initial hurdles. The reasons for the rapid advance of their organization and consciousness seem to be the following:

(1) The problems they face in their day-to-day existence as women and workers are such that they welcome *any* initiative to end their double oppression and exploitation.

(2) The nature of their collective work has provided them with an informal organizational infrastructure, a spirit of solidarity and a tradition of cultural expression which provide the basis and the actual qualitative sense of belonging together for the formation of a formal organization.

(3) The combination of economic with educational programmes, in spite of inherent strategic contradictions, proved to be a realistic base from which to start the organization.

(4) The formal organization, though initiated from outside, put most decision-making power into the hands of the women. Equal participation of all was more important than hierarchy and centralized leadership. But the formal structure preserved the continuity of the *sangams* and avoided individualism, looseness and arbitrariness, the characteristics of middle-class feminist women's groups.

(5) This organizational structure was a necessity for the poor peasant and agricultural labourer women, because even the beginnings of their speaking out about their grievances met with direct violent reaction by the men and the landlords. Because of such consequences, their movement had to consolidate itself organizationally and acquire a much more serious and urgent character. Speaking out was not only an exercise in asserting themselves individually, it could also have serious consequences.

(6) But the women were not cowed and intimidated when they met with opposition and repression. They used it for their own conscientization and the strengthening of their organization. It was the experience of their own organized power which contributed most to their conscientization, and not the 'inputs' from outsiders.

The experience of the women's *sangams* in the area around Bhongir also leads to several conclusions regarding the strategy for women's emancipation, the most important of which seems to be the following.

(1) The agricultural labourer women have shown that the separation of their

struggle into 'women's' struggle and 'workers' struggle is wrong. The argument that women first need economic independence and that they should restrict their movements to economic aims does not take into account their social reality. It has often been argued that poor women need 'bread' first, only then can they think of 'emancipation'. This view ignores the fact that these poor women will not have even bread if they do not fight for their emancipation. The Bhongir women have shown that their struggle for better economic conditions is linked *inseparably to their struggle for human dignity and self-respect.*

(2) The women have also shown that it is wrong to suppress their struggle against male oppression and exploitation in the name of class unity of all the poor. *Through* waging a struggle with their own men, they began to be taken seriously by them and to be relied upon for their support.

(3) It is a myth that the poor women need teachers from outside to make them aware of their situation and help them to analyse it. What they need are prior initiatives, the provision of platforms and of an organizational framework which guarantees continuity. They also need, at least in the initial phases, co-ordinators who help them to transcend the limited horizons of their village existence and put them in contact with each other and the wider network of social relations.

(4) The leadership of the organization has been largely collective. No single leader has emerged who assumed authority over the other women. Yet there are many strong women, who were selected as cluster representatives and who collectively decide on important issues.

(5) The camps are the main general forum for discussion and decision-making. They ensure the democratic participation of all women and prevent the usual appearance of bureaucratic centralism.

(6) The women have also shown that it is correct to encourage *separate* and *autonomous* women's organizations based on class. These organizations provide women with a power base from which they can fight class exploitation as well as sexual oppression and exploitation. They double the strength of the class and do not weaken it. This was recognized even by the men.

(7) The material base for this organization is the fact that these women work and bargain collectively and that *they are not housewives*. They form the bulk of the rural working class; their women's organization is, therefore, a class organization.

(8) The fact that the women made their *sangams* increasingly their *own* does not mean that 'outsiders' are not needed to start a process of the type already described. Without some initiative from somewhere, no movement gets off the ground. But the 'ousider' may also be an 'insider' at the same time, as was the case with the woman activist who initiated the *sangams*, who as a woman was an 'insider', as an educated middle-class woman an 'outsider'. The same was true for our research team. If such 'insider–outsiders' remain conscious of their contradictory reality they can help to initiate and stimulate this process of politicization and self-organization without imposing their own views on the people.

The difference between 'outsiders' from a party and 'insider–outsiders' from small voluntary action groups seem to be that: the party outsiders will try to organize people along the political line laid down by the party. The outsiders are 'leaders' in the sense that they are the bearers of the party's ideology. They bring this ideology *to the people* and the struggle is organized according to the strategic goals of the party. This strategic line is based on the assumption that the party has the correct overall analysis of the situation. The people's consciousness has to be 'brought up' to the level of this analysis. The party outsider therefore plays the role of a traditional teacher.

The 'insider–outsider' in our case, however, considered herself as part of the whole process of making an analysis and getting organized; no 'line' was imposed from outside, but methodological help was given to the women to deal with their own contradictions. The 'insider–outsider' in our case was a 'weak leader', without a clear political line. Because of this she was able to stimulate a process of politicization and organization 'from within' and the formation of an organization *of* the women not *for* the women. Politicization 'from within' means that people become *subjects* of their politics (of making their history) by recognizing their contradictory reality and by getting organized to solve these contradictions.

(9) It is often argued that only a national party can protect the people effectively against repression and that organizations based on self-organizing cannot withstand the pressure. Though it is not possible to generalize from the limited experience presented above we can say that an organization of the people based on politicization 'from within' may have a better chance to resist repression than a centralized bureaucratic party which fights *for* the people. This became evident when the landlords began their repression against the peasants' organizations. The women proved to be more militant and loyal to their organization than did the men.

Notes

1. See Vandana Shiva, 'The Politics of Aid', in *The Illustrated Weekly of India*, 20 September 1987.

2. See Maria Mies, 'The Shahada Movement: A Peasants Movement in Maharashtra', in *Journal of Peasant Studies*, Vol. III, no 4, July 1976.

3. See Arun Shourie, 'The Bhagalpur Blindings', The Evidence so Far, in *Indian Express* 10 and 11 December 1980.

4. See *Maitreyi* June–July 1982. *Maitreyi* is a newsletter, issued by the Feminist Resource Centre in Bombay, which systematically collects and documents reports about atrocities against women.

5. See also Maria Mies, *Patriarchy and Accumulation on a World Scale; Women in the International Division of Labour*, Zed Books, London 1986, pp. 145–74.

6. See *Sunday*, 27 July 1980.

7. See Maria Mies, 'Indian Women in Subsistence and Agricultural Labour', ILO, Geneva 1986.

8. Madhu Kishwar and Ruth Vanita discovered that the revived *Sati* cult, around Roop Kanwar, who was burnt to death on her husband's funeral pyre on 4 September 1987, is

promoted by young urban- educated and based men, not by 'backward' peasants. Madhu Kishwar and Ruth Vanita: 'The Burning of Roop Kanwar', *Manushi*, 42–43, 1987.

9. See among others: Peter Kusters, 'Women in the Tebhaga Movement', Naya Prokash, Calcutta 1987. Also the Telengana Peasants' Uprising has been studied again by the women's organization Stri Shakti Sanghatana of Hyderabad, with a focus on women's role in this struggle, an account of which is to be published shortly (jointly, by Kali of Delhi and Zed Books of London).

10. This study was sponsored by the ILO. The fieldwork was carried out by me and two Indian women, Lalita K. and Krishna Kumari in the years 1978–79. The results of this study were published by the ILO under the title: 'Indian Women in Subsistence and Agricultural Labour', Geneva 1986.

11. See Maria Mies 'The Shahada Movement', op. cit.

12. Maria Mies, *The Lacemakers of Narsapur: Indian Housewives Produce for the World Market*, Zed Press, London 1982.

13. A 'chit' is a piece of paper on which the regular contribution of the member is written. The chit-fund is a kind of village savings system. Each member contributes a small amount regularly. When she or he (men also have this system) is badly in need of money, she/he can take a loan from this fund which has to be repaid with interest. Amounts taken from the chit-fund are usually small.

14. See Maria Mies, 'Indian Women in Subsistence and Agricultural Labour', op. cit.

15. See Maria Mies, 'Towards a Methodology of Women's Studies', Occasional Paper, No. 77, Institute of Social Studies, November 1979.

16. See Maria Mies, 'Indian Women in Subsistence Agriculture', op. cit.

17. The village elders, all belonging to the upper-caste landlords, were asked to settle the matter of this rumour. They imposed a fine to punish the 'guilty' young man and then went to drink away that money.

18. Baby Kanakassery: 'A Report on Women's Organization Activities at CROSS', Bhongir 1979, unpublished.

8.   Why do Housewives continue to be Created in the Third World too?

Veronika Bennholdt-Thomsen

Women do two-thirds of all the world's work. In exchange they receive 10% of all income and own a mere 1% of all the world's means of production.

These figures, produced by the UN for International Women's Year, should be kept in mind whenever we talk about women and their work, especially when considering women's work in the Third World, as these figures are particularly expressive of the current situation in developing countries. I begin with them here as the start of a search for an explanation of the glaring inequality between women and men – since, by implication, men perform one-third of the world's work and are rewarded with 90% of the income and 99% of the means of production.

My initial hypothesis is that: the appalling situation of the majority of Third World women is not a remnant of archaic systems of patriarchy, or a sign of backwardness and underdevelopment; on the contrary, it is a sign and product of modern development. The positions of women in the developing and industrialized countries are drawing closer all the time: but for women in the developing countries, this means absolute impoverishment. The concept of the 'housewife' is central for any understanding of this process.

The housewife, as we know her today, emerged in the First World during the 19th century. She is the result of a protracted historical process comparable with and closely related to that of proletarianization: we, therefore, term this process 'domestication' or 'housewifization' in this context (*Hausfrauisierung*). In other words: housework as performed by housewives does not represent a set of tasks which women have always carried out because of some natural predisposition, but is the product of a particular history. Nor did the housewife emerge, as it were, spontaneously, in response to the dictates of an economic system. She was created – by the church, through legislation, medicine and the organization of the workforce (protective legislation, the 'family wage'). And since the world is now spanned by a gigantic centralized apparatus of planning and administration in the form of a development policy and its various authorities, we can reasonably suppose that the present-day emergence of the housewife in the developing countries is aimed at even more deliberately than before in history.

Who or what is the housewife?

A sketch of what housewives at present do throughout the world would include the following: They look after and provide for children (ranging from carrying a small child tied to their backs while working in the fields to chauffeuring them to nursery and piano lessons); they wash, clean, cook, fetch firewood and water over distances of miles. They make jam and prepare oil from nuts they have collected (karite in West Africa and salseeds in India); they sell small amounts of food and engage in retail trade (the informal sector worldwide); they work at home in outwork (from basket-weaving to administrative tasks on home computer terminals in the living-room); they work on short-term contracts in the lowest 'women's grades', and first and foremost as part-timers (in West Germany 99% of all part-time workers are women); they sell their labour power in the 'offshore plants' of Export Processing Zones, where 80% of the workforce are women.

Two things emerge from this. Firstly, the concrete activities which housewives carry out are very diverse, varying between different regions and continents – but with a common structural property which marks them out as housewives. Secondly, the work and status of housewives clearly embraces much more than child-care and the daily maintenance of the household. Women's paid employment in particular – precarious, sporadic, poorly paid and unprotected – is neither possible nor explicable without the existence of the woman as housewife.

The central structural feature of the social category of 'housewife', over and above its specific regionally varying forms, consists in a specific relation of employment or relation of production. The housewife is not characterized by *what* she does, but by the conditions and the *relations* under which she does it. In contrast, ideologies which represent housework as naturally female, always give precedence to the 'what', that is the nature of housewives' activities as the crucial link.

Given the historical change that has occurred, even with domestic labour in the narrow sense, and given the broad spectrum of activities which housework currently covers across the world, any categorization by activities is empirically odd to say the least. Conversely, the same ideology sees no problem in putting steel-workers in Europe and agricultural day-labourers in India into the same category based on a common relation of production, that is their dependence on a wage.

The structural principle which makes different women's tasks worldwide into 'women's-house-work' is a function of the sexual division of labour under which men tend to be allocated paid, and women unpaid, work. As soon as the modern money and commodity economy gains a hold, women find themselves relegated to the unpaid or lowest paid spheres of work. In part, this can involve the same activities as before money intruded: but the existence of paid labour and its concentration in the hands of men gives these spheres a quite new quality. In particular, women cease to be able to live autonomously with their children in a world which runs on the money to which they have such restricted access. Growing propertylessness forces them to submit to dependence on men. This is coercion inasmuch as relations between men and women stop being co-operative and, based on these objective circumstances, necessarily become hierarchical. Although the often-quoted objection that 'housewives' existed prior to a money and commodity economy is correct, what was meant then by housewife was something qualitatively different. The peasant housewife in what Brunner terms the 'the whole household' – a 'unity of production, consumption and generative reproduction' – did not perform tasks subordinate to those of men, but work which was equally necessary and valuable. Although women carried out sex-specific tasks, their special knowledge and abilities meant that, in contrast to the present day, women's work was just as valuable as men's. Without women there would have been no hens, eggs, milk and cheese, for example. Men and women co-operated; both were necessary for the functioning of the unit as a whole. And the man's contribution was just as much housework as the woman's: there was still no distinction between private and public, between work in the home without money and work outside the home for money.

The definition of the housewife and the sexual division of labour

All societies have a sexual division of labour. Understanding the modern housewife does not therefore hinge on the existence or non-existence of a sexual division of labour to which she is subject. What is new is that – first in Europe, and then in the developing countries – compared to all previous forms the sexual division of labour is no longer based on specific activities, but rather on more or less access to money. And since in modern society money and social esteem are closely related, those whose access to money is severely limited are also denied esteem. Given this state of affairs, it seems especially curious that reference is still made to pre-capitalist relations when discussing housework in the First World and the housewife's existence in the Third World. Finally, within generalized commodity production money is directly tied to the question of the accumulation of capital. We cannot, therefore, avoid seeing this form of the sexual division of labour as an authentic feature of the capitalist mode of production.

The fact that women are now branded housewives by virtue of their sex does not primarily mean that they have to perform housework but rather that they have a low social status. From birth onwards they constitute a unit of labour power which is either unpaid or poorly paid – and hence inferior. It is not housework *per se* but this inferior status which constitutes, as it were, a tertiary sexual characteristic of women in Western society. This can be seen in the Third World too if, for example, we look how, compared with men, survival rates of women in India have worsened over recent decades. The cause is neglect of the female, lesser-valued, child. Or in China, where the imposition of the 'one-child family' has led to the most harrowing dramas in women's lives. Women are rejected, treated with contempt and even murdered because the only child they have borne is a girl – an inferior being. And what conclusion does a senior official of GTZ (the German Society for Technical Co-operation) draw from this, guided by his male chauvinist ideology? That it might be a good idea to develop a pill to prevent girls being born in order to spare mother and child the anticipated suffering! I can already hear the plea that killing girl children has existed in many ethnic groups, and cannot, therefore, be seen as a phenomenon of the present-day capitalist formation. My response to such a monolithic and one-dimensional understanding of human history and of patriarchy would be to propose a *concrete* historical approach: the issue is not why women were regarded as inferior in some individual social contexts but why they are so today. Which elements of our present day economy, politics and culture perpetuate the characterization of women as inferior beings or, what is more frequent, create them as such?

There is not the space here to provide the history and background to this phenomenon, but I would like to outline those stages which have made the subordination of and contempt for women into the most prominent element of our present-day society. Firstly, women lost control over birthing and fertility – that is, control over their own bodies. Women were forcibly deprived of this control both in Europe and in the colonies by: the persecution and murder of millions of them as witches; patriarchal marriage laws; the banning of abortion; the rule of modern medicine; and, in the present-day, forced sterilization. The colonies, in particular, exemplify how private property denied to women their former access to land – which had previously been mediated through common property in land and in some regions accompanied by control of the product of the soil – and imposed systems of patrilineal inheritance. In many colonial areas the forced introduction of money via poll taxes or taxes on products led to the spread of the sex-specific rationality of money, and consequent devaluation of women's labour. Finally, the forced migration of the men led to the contemporary sexual division of labour which assigns women to unpaid work and imposes on them the enormous labour of ensuring the existence of their children, the aged and themselves.

I now want to turn to the contemporary mechanisms which create and recreate cheap, low-status female labour power. They are the same the world over: housewives, that is primarily mothers with sole responsibility for child-care, who are so constrained in terms of working hours and spatial mobility – not only while caring for small children but throughout their working lives – that they are forced to make themselves available as the cheapest wage labour power both in the factory and as home-workers. In particular, the more highly qualified occupations are usually built around the idea of a two-person career – with the woman standing behind the man. Women are therefore marked out as second-earners on the labour market – so they can become mothers – and are accordingly offered a variety of low-paid temporary contracts which are often outside the scope of social insurance or protective legislation.

The high numbers of women in export processing zones and 'offshore manufacturing' has less to do with actual than potential motherhood. Workers in such zones are generally aged between 16 and 24; in many cases they are dismissed if they have a child. The reason is that most offshore manufacturing work is full-time, and also so stressful as to be physically and psychologically unsustainable over a period of many years. It is assumed, not incorrectly, that young women are more likely to accept these conditions because of the coercive social mechanisms to which they are exposed: eventually they will be mothers or wives. This work is, therefore, merely an interlude when set against their real function. Clearly, this is merely a matter of ideology as women as mothers are also reliant on a cash income. None the less, it is an efficient rationale and one which makes this type of labour power particularly cheap. In contrast, the longer term supervisory jobs go to the men. State legislation also operates to subordinate women to the conditions of offshore manufacturing. EPZs (Export Production Zones) are created by Third World states which provide the infrastructure and set a regime of minimal taxes and controls on profit transfers, guaranteeing 'industrial peace' by banning trade unions. Given that work in EPZs is almost wholly carried out by women, the state takes on the appearance of a kind of pimp. But indeed, in a non-figurative sense, either to supplement their meagre wages or to survive after their employment has been terminated, many women workers in EPZs are forced to earn their living as prostitutes for First World male tourists. Women's bodies are used without inhibition, especially by Asian states, to tout for investment, market their airlines and encourage tourism. Women are offered and sold like a freely available natural resource. The definition of women as nature which can be exploited without recompense is a world phenomenon of the process of the 'housewifization' of women.

A further mechanism which creates and constantly reproduces the housewife is the separation of male commodity production and female subsistence production, a process becoming increasingly widespread, especially in the rural areas of the Third World. Men are engaged in cash-crop production – as farmers and/or wage labourers: women produce for the immediate consumption of the family and must also hire themselves out as homeworkers and occasional day labourers for a meagre money income. This process of the making of the peasant housewife is very similar to the fragmentation of the once 'whole household' into 'private' and public spheres in Europe.

Responsibility for children, propertylessness and poverty force the majority of women in the Third World (and increasingly in the First) to take any kind of work for cash. Life as 'just a housewife' is inconceivable; men are poor too. Such a situation makes the notion of a family wage an anachronism. In fact, probably in the overall history of capitalism the family wage was less common than we generally think. Under capitalism the vast majority of women always were and still are forced to do paid work; disregard of this fact is one product of a narrow, male-orientated concept of paid work. The ideal-type, which itself applies only to a minority of male workers, is seen as an occupation performed for a lifetime, located outside the home, and preferably in the form of wage labour in large-scale industrial production. Women's paid labour, however, is characteristically unskilled and sporadic, petty commodity production and home-based paid work. In other words, not only is women's domestic labour invisible (as now universally claimed in all publications on development policy) but also their paid work. The underlying separation of the world of work into a domestic sphere, identified as female, and a waged occupation and career sphere, identified as male, is wrong because it does not correspond with reality.

Domestic labour and women's paid employment in the Third World: examples

Maria Mies's study *The Lacemakers of Narsapur (Housewives Produce for the World Market)*, (1981/82: 1982) examines how women from a former peasant caste in the West Godavari district of the Indian state of Andhra Pradesh crochet lace at home, for sale at low prices, in Western department stores. Mies' title itself evokes the apparent paradox – that being a peasant housewife and producing for the world market would not be contradictory; in fact they complement and condition each other.

> The extraction of surplus-value from the lacemakers by exporters (and their anonymous international partners, the lace importers) necessitates that the ideology of the isolation of the 'woman indoors' is retained. Even where the domestication of women might perhaps be justified by older forms of isolation, it has clearly changed its character. The Kapu women are simultaneously domesticated housewives and workers producing for the world market. In the case of the lacemakers this ideology has almost acquired the character of material force. The entire system is based on the mystification that these women cannot work outside the home (1981/82: 76)

> The work of the lacemakers and the labour time which it costs are not only 'invisible' for the exporters or the world outside but also for the husbands in front of whose noses the work is done. Even they define it as non-work. The money earned by the women appears as a miracle or as something natural. (Ibid. p. 82)

Women are not simply 'left behind' when men monopolize the new and lucrative spheres of the economy: they are in reality 'defined back' into the role of housewife. For only when women remain outside the formal sector and are defined as housewives can the double exploitation of their labour continue: (Ibid. p. 86)

For the African and Asian examples so graphically portrayed by Boserup, in which women carried out and controlled all agricultural work, it is also difficult to define whether the housewife in the narrow sense (that is, confined to real domestic labour) was created first, or whether or not this process was accompanied by typical 'women's-house-paid-work'. (Boserup, 1970) As far as the influence of development projects within this process is concerned, Rogers has shown how, instead of being taught new agricultural skills, women have been taught embroidery, knitting and cakemaking, in precisely those regions where they were the cultivators, and that improved agricultural techniques, especially the growing of cash-crops using credit finance, have allowed the control of agricultural production to pass into the hands of men. (Rogers, 1980) Parallel to this, development planners have also contrived so-called 'income generating activities' in which, in addition to the burden of unpaid labour, women are allowed to produce in a socially relevant (paid) economic sphere in order to earn at least a small cash income. These 'income generating activities' bear all the hallmarks of the housewife's paid employment: they provide a 'second income', the work is very poorly paid, there is no career perspective, they are dependent on market fluctuations, they have no statutory protection etc. They are an instance of the typical double burden which is the norm for women's work worldwide.

A further example of how women's status as housewives establishes a strong position of dependency, despite seemingly favourable circumstances, is illustrated in Birgit Menne's study of the market women in West Africa (Cameroon). (Menne, 1983) She shows how the significance of the long-distance trade between the coast and interior, orginally controlled by particular groups of women, has steadily been reduced to a point at which it is now no more than the customary retailing trade carried out by women in most other parts of the Third World within the so-called informal sector. Long-distance trade, transport and wholesaleing are in the hands of men, along with the title to agricultural property and other forms of skilled paid work. The mass of women, including the market women, are housewives: that is, they carry out the unpaid labour of child-care and maintaining the home, and the lowest paid work in retailing, home-working and agricultural production and other occasional wage labour.

The intimate connection between the position of the housewife and the lowest paid women's employment applies not only in Asia and Africa but also in Latin America. An example from rural Mexico, with which I am acquainted, is cited here. In one poor region of the southern state of Chiapas, domestic labour programmes (cooking, sewing, kitchen gardens), women's home-working and generalized cash-crop production suddenly came together as a result of development projects. In the village of Rio Grande, which I studied, agricultural production for the reproduction of the peasant household has, for decades, consisted of the cash-crop coffee and the subsistence crops maize and beans. Although women already lacked agricultural property and rights, development of hierarchical inequality was impeded by co-operation in unpaid subsistence production. Maize cultivation for household consumption was for the most part carried out by men. The World Bank's new development policies for the poor rural sector (explicitly since 1973) have led to a commercialization of these maize parcels, using credits. Unpaid labour (including agriculture) is now almost exclusively carried out by women; men work for cash. The package of measures for commercializing maize production includes social work-style activities which aim at raising the skill level of the implementation of domestic labour proper, along with a programme of commercialized poultry-breeding by women at home, and sewing on a putting-out basis for a large national clothing undertaking. The consequence of this development project has been a substantial worsening of families' nutritional standards: the poultry is intended exclusively for sale, and maize has to be bought from the receipts derived from other products. The volume of work performed by women has increased enormously.

Why do housewives continue to be created in the Third World too?

'Housewife' means far more than mothers and wives whose natural feminine propensity to serve leads them to assume responsibility for bringing up the next generation and maintaining the family home, with the necessary money and raw materials provided by a male 'bread-winner'. As we have noted, such an ideal hardly exists in reality. It is an exception particularly in the Third World, as the majority of the population lives in poverty and women have to look to their own survival under whatever conditions they can; and that means working for a cash income. It is also an exception in the North where, as the current crisis has shown, the era of the ideal-typical housewife was confined to a short phase (the postwar boom years) and even during this phase it applied only to a minority of married women.

The housewife *is* female labour power in capitalism: in a world in which money is the measure of all, she can be paid the least and need not be paid at all for the bulk of her work.

The structure of women's labour in capitalism has spread throughout the world because it is profitable. Low paid and unpaid labour is the foundation of the modern economy and society. The unpaid labour of the classical wage-worker, so-called surplus labour, is certainly one central mechanism, but quantitatively speaking may be of minor importance. Worldwide, both in the history of capitalism and now, capital accumulation takes place through so-called 'extra-economic coercion' more than through purely economic mechanisms of coercion: the plundering of entire continents under colonialism, direct force and the so-called structural violence of racism, and today, increasingly under sexism. The end of colonialism and the era of national liberation, or the abolition of the most evil and direct forms of racism are no grounds for self-congratulation. One 'solution' proposed by Fray Bartolome de las Casas, Bishop of Chiapas, in the early colonial period provides, perhaps, a useful parallel to illustrate this transformation. In order to save the indigenous population from extermination because·of the burden of forced labour for the Spanish conquistadores, he proposed the introduction of Black slaves from Africa into the colony. And if these lines remind the reader of the UNO figures on women's work and women's poverty quoted at the beginning, they will find my equation appropriate.

Sources

Bennholdt-Thomsen, V., Bauern in Mexiko. Zwischen Subsistenz-und Warenproduktion. Frankfurt a.M. 1982.

Boserup, E. (1970) *Women's Role in Economic Development*. St. Martin's Press, New York.

Brunner, Otto (1968) 'Das "ganze Haus" und die alteuropäische "ökonomik"' (1950) in Brunner, *Neue Wege der Verfassungs-und Sozialgeschichte*, Göttingen, 2nd ed.

Menne, B. (1983) Der Handel mit Grundnahrungsmitteln in Westafrika. Frauenarbeit und Subsistenzsektor im Akkumulationsprozess. Diplomarbeit an der Fakultät für Soziologie, Universität Bielefeld, unveröff. Manuskript.

Mies, M. (1982) *Indian Housewives Produce for the World Market: The Lacemakers of Narsapur*. Zed Press, London.

Rogers, B. (1980) *The Domestication of Women, Discrimination in Developing Societies*, London and New York.

Werlhof, C. v., M. Mies, V. Bennholdt-Thomsen (1983) 'Frauen, die letzte Kolonie'. *Reihe Technologie und Politik 20*, Reinbek bei Hamburg.

9. The Proletarian is Dead: Long Live the Housewife!

Claudia von Werlhof

If we have understood housework, then we have understood the economy

Housework is a most difficult phenomenon to understand. If we have understood housework, then we have understood everything. But that presupposes – and a great deficiency still exists here – that housework is not viewed too narrowly, or in a restricted sense, but that we relate it to, indeed, apply it to nothing less than the whole economy, in fact to world economy. Only then will the explosive character, the significance of the so-called women's question, become recognizable in its generality. The women's question is the most general – not the most specific – of all social questions, because it contains all the others and, in contrast to all other questions, it leaves no one out. This is neither feminist conceit nor arrogance, but is inherent in the functioning of our society itself. For, historically, our society has to date created a unique situation, namely one in which the women are always 'the ones below'. But only from below – at the bottom – can the whole be seen as the whole. Nothing is more important, or more vitally necessary than to support this tendency to analyse 'from below'.

The connection between the world economic crisis and war danger: war economy

The simple reason why a general theory of society and a corresponding policy is necessary is the world economic crisis that is beginning and the danger of war with which we are threatened. Why has no connection been seen between economic crisis and war? This question has not been asked up to now, not even in the rather broad peace movement in the Federal Republic of Germany (FRG). That is strange, for previously this connection has always been the subject matter of discussion. But today people are concerned only with moral or military–technological arguments. Why don't people simply ask: 'Why is there suddenly a danger of war now? The East–West conflict is not new!' Or: 'Why must we tighten our belts? What has happened to the economic miracle for which we sweated a whole life long?' But such simple fundamental questions on war and crisis are absent, at least in public discussion. Why?

The answer is clear: if there is a world-wide economic crisis, then it means that economic changes will take place everywhere. But can these changes be implemented without violence?

Recently, a German politician used the term 'war economy'; it is a kind of war economy towards which we are moving. I am not sure what he meant by that, but I think there must be some objective background for his statement. It appears to me that the world economy is changing very fast and this is becoming increasingly clear, even in the Western industrial nations. What is involved is not merely a cyclical crisis or a moderate structural change, but the beginning of a totally new phase of capitalist development, and no one knows the outcome. This new phase is characterized by the crucially important fact that it more or less signals the end of 'free' wage labour. Simultaneously, this development also questions democracy, human rights, equality, freedom and brotherhood, not to mention emancipation. In those countries which were among the first and the quickest to set this change in motion we hear daily of the brutal consequences: first Chile, then Britain, then the USA, Pinochet, Thatcher and Reagan are administrating the new medicine, the drastic treatment of the Chicago-Boys of Milton Friedman. The goal of this economic policy is to accelerate the process of adapting national economies to the world economy. The Third World is already deeply involved in this process, because production costs can be decreased by relocating parts of industrial production from the First to the Third World. Relocating industry as a strategy for cheaper production costs is also practised in Western countries, but in the Third World, minimizing production costs is achieved above all by using the cheapest, so-called unqualified, young and mostly female labour, which those countries offer in 'abundance'. The use of this labour power by the multinationals (that is by 'our' capital) does not, however, take place in the form of free wage labour, but exactly the opposite. What is involved here is an unfree, 'femalized' form of wage labour, which means: no job permanency, the lowest wages, longest working hours, most monotonous work, no trade unions, no opportunity to obtain higher qualifications, no promotion, no rights and no social security. It is plainly an example of militarily organized labour in the barracks of the so-called world-market factories and free production zones. (Fröbel et al.) The first to introduce such conditions in the West would be the first to become competitive again and make a profit, for crisis means only a fall in the profits of enterprises. Free wage labour is too costly and as far as possible must be eliminated. There will be dismissals, bankruptcies, industries will be 'rationalized', firms wound up and free wage labourers will either be sent back to the industrial reserve army or accept the same conditions of work that are prevalent in the world-market factories.

The 'pillar' of capitalist production, the proletariat, is disappearing

I think we are witnessing the historical moment in which the 'pillar' of capitalist production, the free wage labourer or the proletarian, is about to disappear for ever. Here, we mean that worker who, since the 19th century, has furnished the 'classical' figure of the exploited victim of capital and is, therefore, subjectively called upon to revolutionize society, at least in the opinion of the leftists. But the non-leftists also mean essentially this worker, although they did not call him proletarian, but the 'working class', 'the man in the street', 'the silent majority' and similar euphemisms. The proletarian or free wage labourer is not only the factory worker, but virtually everybody who earns their livelihood mainly through a wage (or salary), including the white-collar worker and the government officer. This type of wage labourer constituted a majority in the West; he (for this was invariably men) was the base of society, of democracy, the voter, the 'free, equal and brotherly' citizen: for him were meant the civil and human rights, he was the allegedly equal and adult contract partner of the entrepreneur, protected by law against arbitrary action and violence, enjoyed social security, was a permanent employee in a factory or office, freely organized in a trade union, and received a wage which was sufficient for him and his family to maintain an average standard of living: the citizen, the 'human being', the member of society, the free individual.

The 'vision of the future' is vanishing, this leads to general perplexity

All theories of progress and modernization, left, right and centre, subscribed to the belief that this type of *homo faber* should be spread and would spread: the free wage labourer represents the 'vision of the future' for all those who are not yet wage labourers and for most of mankind. That is the so-called proletarianization thesis, the favourite of the leftists. Others call it the expansion of the working class, but mean the same thing. The so-called women's emancipation is also related to the expectation that women, too, will become equal, quasi sex-neutral wage labourers; and the socialist countries claim to have emancipated women, because many more women are wage labourers than in the non-socialist countries. The Third World is said to have fared badly, has not 'yet' progressed, is underdeveloped, precisely because it has so few wage labourers. And is this wage labourer now to disappear?

Many people still cling to the belief that the present state of affairs will turn out to be a merely temporary phase of cyclical unemployment, and that eventually . . . etc. But slowly, I think they are also realizing that is not the case. As Oskar Vetter (trade union chief in the FDR) speaking about the restrictions imposed on continued payment of wages during sickness put it, the continuous erosion of the social achievements of the working-class movement is now reaching directly to the core, 'the substance'. The result is total helplessness. Nobody can imagine a society and economy without the free wage labourer, especially not in capitalism. But it is the capitalists themselves who are responsible for the situation! And what of the capture of power, the age-old dream of the leftists, the 'dictatorship of the proletariat' or government by the working class?

It cannot have been a mere illusion! Indeed it can: Marx had discovered already that equality and freedom (in their positive sense) can be only an illusion, and one from which those to whom these 'equal rights' with capital have been suggested formally especially suffer. So it will not be surprising if the equal and free proletarian, the hero of world history, is one day mercilessly banished to the dustbin of history.

The proletarian as minority phenomenon and the discovery of the 'informal sector'

The time has come when some of those few who until now did not consider the proletarian as a kind of non-plus-ultra of human development can rub their hands and say with malicious pleasure: 'Well, didn't we always say . . . ?' if it were not to stick in their throats. For the 'farewell to the proletarian', as André Gorz calls it, does not mean a welcome to those who are non-proletarians. Quite the contrary, and I do not share Mr. Gorz's unfounded optimism nor that of some other sections of the so-called Alternative Movement who think that, with the abolition of wage slavery, slavery itself will be abolished. It is wage that will be abolished. Nevertheless, some importance should be attached to the experiences and thoughts of those who are not free wage labourers but know something about them – an importance that is also becoming relevant for those who ignored these workers. For the proletarian wage labourer is a minority phenomenon during a particular phase of capitalism and is limited to a few areas of the earth. Today only a small percentage of the world population belongs to this category and it has never been more. The 'prototype' of the free wage labourer – male, white and over 21 years-old urban industrial worker – is even rarer.

Eighty to ninety per cent of the world population consists essentially of women, peasants, craftsmen, petty traders and such wage labourers whom one can call neither 'free' nor proletarian. A fact that should have received the attention that is only now beginning to be afforded to it: in the debate on women's work, Third World discussions, and the revived discussion on agriculture and peasants, that is, in discussions on those who, in principle, are not free wage labourers. What is promising to become the latest 'hit' in the debate is the so-called 'informal sector'. This sector, of course, also employs wage labour, but in contrast to that in the so-called 'formal sector', it is not a 'normal' one. It is exactly into that sector that the former proletarians are pushed: into part-time work, contract work, seasonal and migrant work, illegal work, 'borrowed' work,[1] as well as unpaid work like the so-called 'work for one's own' (v. Weizsäcker), 'shadow work' (Illich), subsistence work and, mostly 'forgotten', housework; in short, generally speaking (wage) labour that is not 'free'. So far, in the debate on this sector, the fact that there is nothing new about it is deliberately ignored. 'New' is only that now it is becoming the 'alternative' for the ex-proletarians, which is why it is of interest. That interest is, as always, one-sided (Werlhof a.); the problem has been approached from the wrong end.

What sort of a mode of production is capitalism? Conquest, 'the guilt question' and 'integration'

In view of the regression (or progress?) in the area of free wage labour, the question must be asked – and women have long been asking it – what sort of a mode of production is capitalism? This question sounds naïve, because there was, and still is, agreement between the protagonists in the debate and among those who characterize capitalism as an industrial system or the industrial society. But this kind of tacit agreement begins at a non-scientific level. They all say: capitalism has originated in and spread out of Europe through the achievements of Europeans, it is a progressive mode of production, and it functions through the interplay of or contradiction between wage labour, that is, free wage labour and capital. The economic results are progress, growth, incomes, profits and accumulation; the political results are the purported ideals of equality, freedom, brotherhood, in short, of democracy. This economic system with its political form of the democratic state is paraded as the 'vision of the future' for the rest of the world.

For me, this interpretation of capitalism is simply a glorification of the 'white man' as the creator of culture, civilization, and humanity. The white man as the human being par excellence (Werlhof b.). It is now time to abandon this conception. It has nothing to do with reality, but is ahistorical, racist, Eurocentric, imperialistic or colonialistic and, of course, sexist.

Not without reason did this concept begin to take shape exactly when the conquest of the world began – the first conquerors were the Crusaders and the seafarers. This world, today called the Third World, has up to now always been subjected to totally undemocratic and uncultivated methods of robbery, plunder, rape and mutilation. Simultaneously with the subjugation of the world was the subjugation of women, known in Europe as the witch-hunt, which went on for centuries and 'claimed' – as is euphemistically expressed – millions of victims. Only on this foundation, which we have blotted out of our consciousness, did the Western world 'rise' to the position of the First World and seek its justification by creating humanism and enlightenment.

That is not all. If 'violence as the precondition of freedom' had been only that solitary act – even if it had lasted for centuries – namely the phase of 'primitive accumulation', as Marx called it – then we could perhaps continue to believe in at least the non-violent nature of modern society.

But it was not so, and today we disregard even that, asserting that our ideals would spread everywhere and finally encompass the whole world. Today, as ever, our freedom rests on the unfreedom of others, our equality on the inequality of others, our non-violence on the violence against others, our wealth on their poverty, our democracy on dictatorships elsewhere; and that to an ever increasing extent.

For evidently our mode of production is not capable of producing anything new, it can only acquire already existing and produced things and 'transform' them, that is destroy them. For not only has the economic miracle failed, but, it may be asked: what is the result of hundreds of years of plundering the world?

Where has all the wealth gone? All that remains is 'a hole in the ground'. (Galtung) Our interest in suppressing this fact applies in the field of science as it does in politics.

The thesis that capitalism has actually been realized only in Europe and the USA, that what exists elsewhere are pre-, post- or non-capitalist modes of production, or peripheral capitalist or deformed capitalist modes of production is upheld by ever-new variations with astonishing tenacity. In this way the blame is laid at the victims' door. For the concomitant conditions of such modes of production are correspondingly characterized as traditional, backward, primitive, archaic, undeveloped and so on. The people who live under such conditions are considered – in contrast to those in the Western world – stupid, lazy, apathetic, obstructive, conservative, narrow-minded, ignorant, passive; also emotional, dangerous, impertinent, bestial, violent, insidious, unbridled and so forth. To we women these clichés are well-known. They are applied to us exactly as they are to the Third World.

Whether admired or hated it is believed that only by the so-called 'integration' of these people and these conditions into the capitalist system can they develop, to a certain extent, from animal to man and be promoted out of 'nature' into society. Whether priest, development expert, entrepreneur, minister or husband, none of them would like to be reminded that he is just that: priest etc. only *because* his 'partners' – as they are called today – are heathens, underdeveloped, exploited and subjugated people and women.

So they must also remain what they are and never become priests etc., themselves. (In Britain today, for example, there are three classes of passports.) Hence there is nothing to integrate. That, and nothing else, is what integration really means. Can one be made into a human being? Is the state essential in order to have that certified? I think people do not *become* human beings, that is what they are.

The Third World and the housewife as the 'pillar' of accumulation, the 'vision of the future'

But to return to the economy in its narrow sense, women must have noticed already that it all leads towards the significance of housework and all that is connected with it. What I mean is that the work of women is comparable to the work in the Third World.

In the previous section I tried to describe what we generally mean by capitalism, accumulation, growth and all that, and to determine the 10% to 20% of the world population – the free, white, male wage labourer in the West – that excludes the other 80% to 90%, the unfree, coloured, female non-wage labourer in the Third World, the old and the children – who are not part of it. Now I ask: is capitalism so inept that so far it has failed to integrate these masses in its system? Is it even in the process of abolishing itself by abolishing free wage labour? That seems unlikely. The solution of the puzzle is very simple: everything is the opposite to what it appears. Not the 10% free wage labourers, but the 90% unfree non-wage labourers are the foundation of accumulation and growth, are the truly exploited, are the real 'producers', the 'norm', the general condition in which human beings find themselves under capitalism. And this state of affairs is now also threatening the proletarian. For, against all protestations to the contrary, the human being under capitalism finds himself unfree, unequal, unfraternal, surrounded by violence, misery and oppression, without rights or powers, unorganized, without wage or property, insecure, starving and cold – but working. It is not really true that the 'unemployed' do not work; without a wage or income they must work much more than the 'employed' in order to just survive. They do everything possible to get a minimum income. Since one activity yields too little, they must perform several: they are simultaneously small peasants and seasonal agricultural labourers, petty traders and service people, producers and sellers of self-produced commodities, prostitutes and part-time wage labourers, contract- and home-workers,[2] and this state of affairs will gradually become the norm in the Western countries, too. The Third World is coming to us. It reveals to us the 'vision of the future' and the real character of our mode of production. More explicitly: the West's economy will become 'femalized', 'marginalized' 'naturalized' or 'housewifized' – but never proletarianized.

The housewife as the opposite of the proletarian and the continuum between housework as the model of work

My thesis is that the principles of the organization of housework will determine our future and it will not, as so far assumed, be determined by the principles of organization of proletarian wage labour. The housewife is the exact opposite of the proletarian. Let us first take this in the sense of contrast between white and black. In principle, you can include every woman, for under capitalism all women are housewives. I am not concerned with the glorification of the housewife or of the proletarian. Theoretically, it could be very pleasant to be a housewife, for nobody else has the opportunity to perform so manifold and different activities; look at the biographies of women and you will be astonished. What I am asking is that housewives be perceived from a different perspective. First let us consider the contrast between the proletarian and the 'pure' housewife, both rare, but nevertheless proto-typical inventions of capitalism. (Bock/Duden; Kittler) This economic couple is a rarity, not only elsewhere in the world, but also in Western countries, at least in so far as a life-long union is implied; but this is in the process of becoming extinct. Despite this, it has become the ideal type to which all people of the world are enjoined to strive for. It is the white, Western, middle-class nuclear family, the virtue of which is, today, the subject of a huge propaganda campaign – even in the slums of Calcutta where nobody has any chance of realizing this allegedly noble ideal.

The woman corresponding to the proletarian or free wage labourer, is the life-long full-time housewife. The word 'life-long' suggests that she is virtually imprisoned; the cage may be gilded a little, but that does not change its character. And neither the wife nor the husband can change this situation voluntarily. Both may be quite satisfied, for perhaps they know of no alternative, or there is none. Moreover, their relative economic security depends on them living together; they are, as it were, the Siamese twins of our economy.

The proletarian is apparently free, equal, fraternal and so on; the housewife is not. In reality she is doubly fettered since, first of all, she may not choose or change the place, type of work or her particular job freely, she is bound: to the house/apartment, the husband and the children; secondly, neither is she free from all means of production, so it cannot be said that she merely possesses her labour power, as, in a certain sense, does the proletarian. What she does have, and no man has, and which is treated as a means of production is her child-bearing capacity; also she 'has' the husband as 'bread-winner'.

In addition, her status is not one of equality although formally, of course, there is now sexual equality of rights, but even where these rights are honoured their effects are rarely beneficial for women (for example, in divorce law), because as long as they are housewives, women are unequal. Equality of rights for women, is analogous to the pretence of equality between proletarians and capitalists, that is, only an illusion of alleged sex-neutrality in capitalism. Women, of course, are no longer considered as minors, they have been granted voting rights and so on, but the specific areas of law have clearly been split according to sex, as in the marriage law for example. Thus rape in marriage is not a punishable offence; toleration of rape is included in a wife's one-sided marital obligations.

In addition, women's inequality is primarily a social inequality, based on the fact that the husband has 'the queen of the commodities' (Marx) money, in his pocket, but the wife is not paid for her work. The husband must give her only 'board and lodging', as he would also have to do for a slave. Neither are the housewife's working hours, conditions of work, holidays, leisure, settled by contract; the marriage contract is not comparable to the employment contract. There is no right to strike, no sisterly organization of housewives; they are instead, individualized and atomized. They enjoy no social security on the basis of their work as housewife, nor are they protected by law from the despotism and violence of their husbands (cf. houses for battered women). In the home nobody ensures the observance of human rights, here they are a 'private affair', which allegedly do not concern the public, even when there is no guarantee of physical safety.

The wife must serve, and above all, obey the husband; he can demand this in a court of law. In short, the housewife is an unpaid worker, at the disposal of the husband, round the clock all her life; even more, her whole person is at his disposal, including her sexuality and child-bearing capacity, her psyche and feelings, she is at the same time slave and serf who is compelled to do all the work that the husband and the children 'need', including demonstrating love even when she does not feel any. Here one works out of love and love becomes work. (Bock/Duden) The situation may not always be intolerable, but it is impossible to predict that it will not become so. Therefore, it is not necessary to look at the Third World in order to find an absence of human rights and of overall 'free' conditions of work and life.

I believe that the contrasting conditions of work between the free wage labourer and the housewife constitute the two poles of a continuum of capitalist conditions of work and relations of production – reality lies somewhere in between – leaning sometimes more towards unfree, unpaid housework. All kinds of conditions of work worldwide lie between these two poles, including those which are usually labelled pre- or non-capitalist. Today slave-work, unfree forms of wage labour, home-industry, and peasant production among others, all lie on this continuum of capitalist production, which increasingly is sliding towards the conditions of housework. For all have one thing in common: market-dependence and generally dependence on money, more exactly, on a wage. In principle, everyone is dependent on a wage, because generally, they no longer possess or control any worthwhile means of production such as land, tools, skills, and so on, upon which to survive.

That is why all work can be understood only from the point of view of housework – from below – and not from the point of view of wage labour. Basically housework, not wage labour, is the 'model' of work in capitalism. All people in the capitalist system are, of course, potentially wage labourers, but in reality they are rather 'housewives', an industrial reserve army, relative surplus population, relative, that is, in relation to the existing wage labour.

Only very few housewives are 'pure' housewives, as we have already noted. Almost everyone – women and men – are at some time in their lives, or from time to time, also wage labourers or they sell products made in and sold from the home (especially in the Third World). But never does the female wage labourer or the unfree male wage labourer resemble the free wage labourer. All conditions of femalized or directly female wage labour are of a housework-like character, so that it can be better understood as paid housework rather than as free wage labour (understood in this sense, wages for housework is nothing new and also not a 'revolutionary' demand). Women's wage labour is organized and seen as an extension of their housework, and for this reason correspondingly badly paid. Women working outside the home are, therefore, also unequal to men – as they are at home, which is why all women are housewives and always treated as such. This sexism also provides the model for racism: a coloured wage labourer is never a free wage labourer, and even if he becomes one is not treated as one. That is why there is no race-neutrality in capitalism.

Sexual division, hierarchization and devaluation of labour: the model of the international division of labour

What we have here is a 'sexual' division of all labour, and not simply the 'normal' sexual division between housework and wage labour. This sexual division that exists world-wide within wage labour extends far beyond what is determined by biology, and produces a hierarchization between the sexes comparable to that between the races and 'classes'. As I. Illich says, it means an unprecedented 'degradation' of work on the basis of a 'degradation of women'. This devaluation of women's work and, with it, of women's life and the female sex, this rigid subordination of women, operative throughout the world and effective in all spheres of life, initiated and maintained by men, was unknown in pre-capitalist forms of sexual division of labour, including the exploitative ones. This is important, because in the West both women and men believe that they are now better off than in earlier times, just as many people in the Third World still believe that the 'progress' the white man has allegedly brought them is beneficial.

They believe this because they are also victims of the suppression of history. Three-hundred years of witch-hunting, running parallel with the colonization of the world, were necessary to snatch from the women – as from Third World people – their power, their economy and their knowledge, and to 'socialize' them into becoming what they are today: housewives and 'the underdeveloped'. The housewife – and with her the 'underdeveloped' – is the artificial product, resulting from unimaginably violent development, upon which our whole economy, law, state, science, art and politics, the family, private property and all modern institutions have been built.

This 'model' is a world-wide export 'hit', not only today. The treatment of the colonies, the enforcement of an international division of labour following the pattern of the sexual division – that is, the division into white wage labourers here and coloured, 'femalized' non-wage labourers there – was also initiated, perpetrated and forced through by violent means. The Third World is the 'witch' of witch-hunting days and is the 'general-housewife', 'the world-housewife' today, including Third World men. The relation between husband and wife is repeated in the relation between the First and the Third World.

The 'Why' of the division: child-bearing capacity and female versus male capacity for work

The dissimilarity of the conditions of work and the division and hierarchization between working people leaves the main question open, namely, that concerning the content of the divided activities. And here the black–white contrast does not suffice for our analysis, nor does the simple below–above view.

The question about the content of the work is tantamount to the question about the 'Why' of the division, about its economic significance for the system.

We know that women's work is – corresponding to its payment – considered to be worthless, unproductive, even parasitic, socially unnecessary, viewed as a 'natural process' and not even as work. The proof of this treatment lies in the following figures: taking the world as a whole women perform two-thirds of the total work, but receive only one-tenth of the world income and control only one-hundredth of the means of production in the world. Obviously, opinion about the Third World's contribution to the total work worldwide in relation to that of the First World (like that of agriculture in relation to that of industry) is similar to that expressed on women's work.

The work of the housewife consists in executing, producing, preparing what should be free of charge for 'the society', what is excluded from the responsibility of the enterprises. That is expressed in what the husband does not do and/or what cannot be purchased by a wage, because it is too lowly or because money cannot buy it: that is, 'genuine' emotional care. According to feminists the wife looks after the physical, psychological and social production and reproduction of the husband as wage labour force and of the next generation of wage labourers and housewives. In addition, she performs some extra out-of-home duties – the housewife has a double work-load.

The all-round duties of the housewife have as purpose the production of human labour power, production of living human beings; that is, production of human beings in contrast to the production of things. The housewife is 'specialized' in human beings, the wage labourer in things. That is the 'secret', why housework as a 'model' of organized work will not disappear along with (free) wage labour, and that is the decisive qualitative difference between the two. Woman is in the truest sense of the word the soil on which the wage labourer stands. He is defined as human being, she as 'nature'.

The 'true essence', so to speak, of this division and its starting point is nothing more than women's natural monopoly: their child-bearing capacity. In no mode of production throughout history is the child-bearing capacity, the prerequisite of production of human beings, so central as in the present. The reason is that the surplus value, the sole purpose of capitalist production, can be extracted only from living human beings. In principle, the more human beings, the more surplus value is possible. It is no accident that capitalism's so-called 'Population Law' is considered to be nothing less than the 'general law of capitalist accumulation'. (Marx) It is this law which turns women into child-bearing machines and is responsible for the so-called population 'explosion'.

Machines cannot produce surplus, they can only imitate human labour. For the purpose of capital accumulation and profit human beings are irreplaceable, simply because they are living. Capital alone is dead. Only its vampire-like sucking of fresh blood makes it appear living, which is also why, for the entrepreneurs,the producers of human beings are basically much more important than the producers of things, they are the prerequisites of the latter, without them nothing will work. (That is why everybody becomes nervous when women do not want to bear children, refuse to do housework or serve men, do not marry, do not 'obey' and so on.)

The more labour power is pushed aside or made redundant by technology, the more the system has to put human labour to use in other spheres, and if possible on a mass scale. This question is never discussed by those who believe in capital 'being alive' and/or those who can identify only wage work as work. The question today is how that unwaged work should be organized and controlled, including masses of ex-proletarians, – without conjuring up the 'danger of socialism'. The historical examples of such organization of unwaged·

work on a mass scale can be seen as in housework, in agriculture and in the Third World in general.

The production of human beings in present-day society is, however, not only the most important, constant, essential and most difficult task, it is also particularly frustrating, because human beings are consistently humiliated, robbed and exploited. That is why women have developed a specifically feminine capacity for work, they *had* to develop it. It gets its orientation from the fertility of their bodies. Creating new life (through childbirth) is the principle that women also apply to all other activities, once for the common benefit of all, but today for the benefit of the system. Everything that women do must bear fruit and be gratis, like the air we breathe. This applies not only to producing and rearing children, but also to the sundry housework and wage labour, the emotional care bestowed on colleagues, the friendliness, submissiveness, being-always-at-others'-disposal, healing-all-wounds, being-sexually-usable; the putting-everything-again-in-order, the sense of respon-sibility and self-sacrifice, frugality and unpretentiousness, the renunciation in favour of others, the putting-up-with and helping-out-in-all-matters, with-drawing-oneself and being-invisible and always-there, the passive being-available and the active 'pulling-the-cart-out-of-the-mud' – the endurance and the discipline of a soldier. All this makes up the feminine work capacity. It is the most general and comprehensive work capacity imaginable, because it draws in and mobilizes the whole person. And its production 'costs nothing', no formal training is necessary or conceivable for its practice. Women's 'unqualifiedness' is in reality a super-qualification; on its free-of-cost production and appropriation rests not only wage labour, but the whole system of capitalist accumulation.

Not the generalization of wage labour, but the generalization of housework is, therefore, the dream of all capitalists. There is no cheaper, more productive and more fruitful human labour, and it can also be enforced without the whip. I believe that the restructuring of our economy will involve the effort to re-educate the men and force upon them, as far as possible, the feminine work capacity. For the wage labourer does too little and knows too little. He can do only what he is paid for and what has been agreed upon by contract. He does no more than that and has absolutely no idea of how human beings are reproduced. He functions like a robot, as an appendage of the machine, de-emotionalized, he avoids and sabotages every effort to extract still more life out of him. He works for too short a time and is exhausted too quickly. He has no reason to take initiative and no motivation for work, he cannot be mobilized for all purposes, as a person, as a whole human being. The masculine work capacity is much too inflexible and 'unfruitful', it is short of blood. That is why it is so rarely used.

Perspectives: 'femalization' of the proletarian and new forms of the socio-sexual division of labour

The import of fresh 'guest-workers' – who, because of their use-value-orientation and peasant background, approximate more closely to the female's work capacity – has its reason in these facts, similar to the reverse: the utilization of cheap, young, female labour power through the transfer of industries to the Third World. That – and not wage labour as we know it – provides the model of the future: the world-housewife or the world-wide 'industrial reserve army', 'marginal mass' or the 'relative surplus population'. The more and more frequently formulated threats against this 'surplus population' are, therefore, directed not only against the Third World, but equally against the West. Those who cannot be used as wage labourers are everywhere considered to be the cause of the crisis, while they are in reality nothing but the necessary result and also the necessary condition of Western modes of production. The most urgent question today is what to do with the increasing number of 'redundant people'? All forms of work that non-wage labourers had to develop, and which nowadays are being induced from above, are of concern for us in the West, because soon we shall also experience them. The Alternative Scene has already begun: whether on the farm, in the workshop, or at home as houseman. The state has also begun it: in West Germany, for example, through the 'women are able to do more' campaign, by propagating the idea of honorary social work and the participation of the citizens in community work in general, through the back-to-the-family and 'mothers save the nation' programme of the Christian Democratic Party, and so on.

Enterprises too, are involved, through the dismissal of free wage labourers, and more and more frequent use of unfree, 'housewifized', 'naturized' wage labourers, of illegal, 'black', 'borrowed', imported and part-time workers, among them many women, until the men are also prepared to sink from their position of proletarian, the equal and the free, and to accept conditions of work similar to those of the women and the Third World, and to agree, in principle and now also in reality to be no more than 'land', a natural resource, an object of capital. But they will do this only if they acquire and retain guaranteed control over women. So there is a danger that men will let themselves be corrupted, just as they once let themselves be compensated with the housewife for the introduction of – by no means popular – wage labour, at the cost of the women. Will they repeat the mistake? They can see what it has led to; in any case it has not led to men's happiness.

That is the beginning of 'the change' (according to Franz Josef Strauss). It does not proclaim a new, different capitalism, nor even socialism, it proclaims the perfectly logical continuation of the existing system, the no longer embellished emergence of its latent nature. Equality and freedom are luxuries that a war economy cannot even pretend to afford.

The so-called world-market factories and production by contract (Bennholdt-Thomsen) in the cities and villages of the Third World, provide a foretaste of the future in the Western world: part-time and unfree wage labour in the factories, organized like army barracks, plus collective forced labour in the countryside, regulated not through wages but through credits, and all that on the foundation of the individual prison of the patriarchal nuclear family: the sexual division of labour survives the abolition of free wage labour and may even be reinforced.

An alternative is possible only if we all, men and women, succeed in recapturing, once and for all, not simply the wage, but more than that – the means of production: our bodies and children, our houses and land, our knowledge and creativity, and the results of our labour. We want all this without continuing, like puppets, to depend on 'central powers', so that we can work for our own, autonomous existence. For that, however, not only do we need no proletarians, but also no housewives.

Notes/References

1. The system under which producer companies hire labourers for particular work monthly/weekly/daily from another company, whose only business is to hire out labourers.
2. Those who work at home for a company. The various parts thus produced are assembled later in a factory or sold directly in the market by middlemen.

Sources

Bennholdt-Thomsen, V. (1980), 'Investition in die Armen. Zur Entwicklungspolitik der Weltbank', *Lateinamerika, Analysen und Berichte*, 4, Berlin, pp. 74–96.
Bock, G. and Duden, B. (1977), 'Arbeit aus Liebe – Liebe als Arbeit. Zur Entstehung der Hausarbeit im Kapitalismus', in: Dokumentationsgruppe der Berliner Sommeruniversität für Frauen 1976: *Frauen und Wissenschaft*, Berlin, pp. 118–199.
Fröbel, F: Heinrichs, J. and O. Kreye (1977), *Die neue internationale Arbeitsteilung*, Reinbek/Hamburg.
Gorz, A. (1980) *Abschied vom Proletariat*, Frankfurt.
Illich, I. (1980) 'Shadow-Work', *Man*. Cuernavaca.
James, S. (1975), 'Sex, Race and Working Class Power', in *Sex, Race and Class*, London, pp. 9–19.
Kittler, G. (1980) *Hausarbeit. Zur Geschichte einer 'Naturressource'*, München.
Werlhof, C. v. (1978) 'Frauenarbeit: der blinde Fleck in der Kritik der Politishchen Ökonomie', in *Beiträge zur feministischen Theorie und Praxis*, 1, München, pp. 18–32.
———— 1981 'Frauen und Dritte Welt als "Natur" des Kapitals. Oder Ökonomie auf die Füsse gestellt', in: Dauber/Simpfendörfer (ed.): Eigener Haushalt und bewohnter Erdkreis, Wuppertal, pp. 207–14.

Index

Zed Books Ltd

is a publisher whose international and Third World lists span:

- **Women's Studies**
- **Development**
- **Environment**
- **Current Affairs**
- **International Relations**
- **Children's Studies**
- **Labour Studies**
- **Cultural Studies**
- **Human Rights**
- **Indigenous Peoples**
- **Health**

We also specialize in Area Studies where we have extensive lists in African Studies, Asian Studies, Caribbean and Latin American Studies, Middle East Studies, and Pacific Studies.

For further information about books available from Zed Books, please write to: Catalogue Enquiries, Zed Books Ltd, 57 Caledonian Road, London N1 9BU. Our books are available from distributors in many countries (for full details, see our catalogues), including:

In the USA
Humanities Press International, Inc., 165 First Avenue, Atlantic Highlands, New Jersey 07716.
Tel: (201) 872 1441;
Fax: (201) 872 0717.

In Canada
DEC, 229 College Street, Toronto, Ontario M5T 1R4.
Tel: (416) 971 7051.

In Australia
Wild and Woolley Ltd, 16 Darghan Street, Glebe, NSW 2037.

In India
Bibliomania, C-236 Defence Colony, New Delhi 110 024.

In Southern Africa
David Philip Publisher (Pty) Ltd, PO Box 408, Claremont 7735, South Africa.